VISUAL QUICKSTART GUIDE

MICROSOFT OFFICE EXCEL 2007 FOR WINDOWS

Maria Langer

 Peachpit Press

Visual QuickStart Guide
Microsoft Office Excel 2007 for Windows
Maria Langer

Peachpit Press
1249 Eighth Street
Berkeley, CA 94710
510-524-2178 • 800-283-9444
510-524-2221 (fax)

Find us on the Web at: www.peachpit.com

Peachpit Press is a division of Pearson Education

Editors: Nancy Davis, Tracy O'Connell
Indexer: Julie Bess
Cover Design: Peachpit Press
Production: Maria Langer, David Van Ness

Colophon

This book was produced with Adobe InDesign CS and Adobe Photoshop 7 on a dual-processor Power Macintosh G5. The fonts used were Utopia, Meta Plus, and PIXymbols Command.

Notice of Rights

Notice of Liability

Trademarks

ISBN-13 978-0-321-46152-0
ISBN-10 0-321-46152-5

9 8 7 6 5 4 3 2 1

Printed and bound in the United States of America.

Dedication

To Aunt Rose and Uncle Jerry

Thanks!

To Nancy Davis and Tracy O'Connell, for their excellent tag-team editing.

To David Van Ness, for his usual great job fine-tuning my layout and preparing the book for the printer.

To Julie Bess, for yet another spur-of-the-moment index.

To Microsoft Corporation, for continuing to revise and improve the best spreadsheet program on earth.

And to Mike, for the usual reasons.

www.marialanger.com

Table of Contents

Introduction

Introduction

Microsoft Excel 2007, a component of Microsoft Office 2007, is a powerful spreadsheet software package. With it, you can create picture-perfect worksheets, charts, and tables based on just about any data you can enter.

This *Visual QuickStart Guide* will help you take control of Excel by providing step-by-step instructions, plenty of illustrations, and a generous helping of tips. On these pages, you'll find what you need to know to get up and running quickly with Excel 2007—and more!

This book was designed for page flipping. Use the thumb tabs, index, or table of contents to find the topics for which you need help. If you're brand new to Excel or spreadsheets, however, I recommend that you begin by reading at least the first two chapters. **Chapter 1** provides basic information about Excel's interface. **Chapter 2** introduces spreadsheet concepts and explains exactly how they work in Excel.

If you've used other versions of Excel and are interested in information about new Excel 2007 features, be sure to browse through this **Introduction**. It'll give you a good idea of the new things Excel has in store for you.

One word of advice: don't let Excel intimidate you! Sure, it's big, and yes, it has lots of commands. But as you work with Excel, you'll learn the techniques you need to get your work done. That's when you'll be on your way to harnessing the real power of Excel.

New & Improved Features in Excel 2007

Excel 2007 is a complete reworking of Microsoft's spreadsheet program. It includes a wide range of revised features and a bunch of brand new ones. Here's a summary of the changes you'll find discussed in detail in this book.

Major changes

◆ Excel's brand new user interface replaces the old menu bar with a task-oriented Ribbon (**Figure 1**). You click tabs to display various groups of commands and menus for completing tasks.

◆ Excel's new XML-based file format makes it easier to integrate Excel workbook contents with external data sources, reduces file sizes, and improves data recovery.

Worksheet structure

◆ The new Page Layout View (**Figure 1**) makes it easy to see how a worksheet will look when printed.

◆ Excel now supports up to 1 million rows and 16 thousand columns per worksheet.

Entering formulas

◆ The formula bar now automatically resizes to accommodate long formulas without overwriting other data in your worksheet.

◆ The new Function AutoComplete feature helps you use functions with correct formula syntax (**Figure 2**).

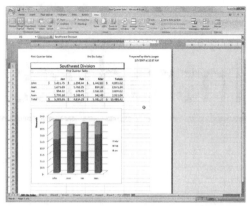

Figure 1 Here's a worksheet in Page Layout View. You can see the Ribbon at the top of the screen.

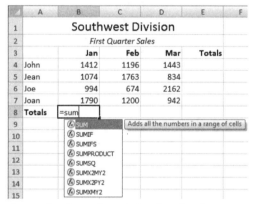

	A	B	C	D	E	F
1		Southwest Division				
2		First Quarter Sales				
3		Jan	Feb	Mar	Totals	
4	John	1412	1196	1443		
5	Jean	1074	1763	834		
6	Joe	994	674	2162		
7	Joan	1790	1200	942		
8	Totals	=sum				
9		SUM	Adds all the numbers in a range of cells			
10		SUMIF				
11		SUMIFS				
12		SUMPRODUCT				
13		SUMSQ				
14		SUMX2MY2				
15		SUMX2PY2				
		SUMXMY2				

Figure 2 Excel's new Formula AutoComplete feature helps you use functions correctly.

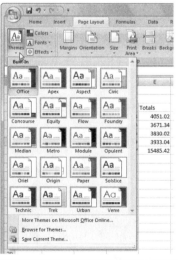

Figure 3 You can now format worksheets by applying themes.

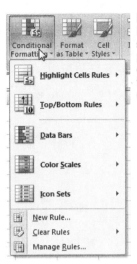

Figure 4
Excel includes several predefined conditional formatting options.

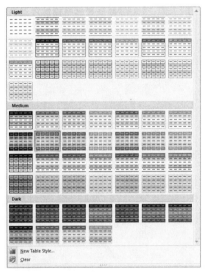

Figure 5 Table styles make it easy to format tables.

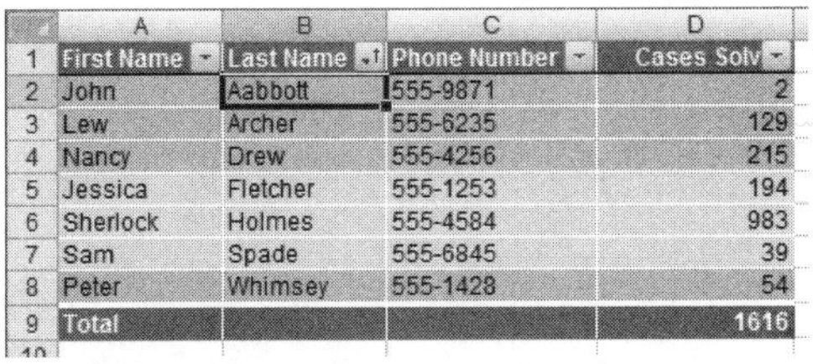

	A	B	C	D
1	First Name	Last Name	Phone Number	Cases Solv
2	John	Aabbott	555-9871	2
3	Lew	Archer	555-6235	129
4	Nancy	Drew	555-4256	215
5	Jessica	Fletcher	555-1253	194
6	Sherlock	Holmes	555-4584	983
7	Sam	Spade	555-6845	39
8	Peter	Whimsey	555-1428	54
9	Total			1616

Figure 6 Sorting and filtering data has never been easier.

Formatting worksheets

- ◆ Excel's new themes (**Figure 3**) and styles features make it easy to apply color-coordinated, consistent formatting througout worksheets and charts.

- ◆ Excel's conditional formatting feature (**Figure 4**) has been improved to make it more flexible and easier to apply.

Creating & formatting charts

- ◆ New charting tools make it quicker and easier to create and format charts based on worksheet data.

- ◆ Excel's charting feature now makes it possible to use custom graphic elements within charts.

Managing data

- ◆ Excel's data management feature—renamed as the table feature—is now more intelligent and easier to use.

- ◆ Excel now offers table styles (**Figure 5**) that you can use to quickly apply formatting to tables of data.

- ◆ Excel's sorting (**Figure 6**) and filtering features have been modified to make them more flexible and easier to use.

Working with names

- ◆ The new Name Manager feature makes it easier to manage multiple named ranges wihin a workbook file.

Performance

- ◆ Excel now supports multiple processors, making Excel's performance signficantly faster for large worksheets edited on multi-processor computers.

NEW & IMPROVED FEATURES IN EXCEL 2007

The Excel Workplace

Meet Microsoft Excel

Microsoft Excel is a full-featured spreadsheet program that you can use to create worksheets, charts, lists, and even Web pages.

Excel 2007 introduces a whole new interface that combines standard Windows elements with buttons, commands, and controls that are specific to Excel. To use Excel effectively, you must have at least a basic understanding of these elements.

This chapter introduces the Excel workplace by illustrating and describing the following elements:

- ◆ The Excel screen, including window elements.

- ◆ The Ribbon, command buttons and menus, shortcut keys, and dialogs.

- ◆ Document scrolling techniques.

- ◆ Excel's Help feature.

✔ Tips

- ■ If you're brand new to Windows, don't skip this chapter. Many of the interface elements discussed in this chapter apply to all Windows programs, not just Excel.

- ■ If you've used previous versions of Excel, you should browse through this chapter to learn about the interface elements that are new to this version of Excel.

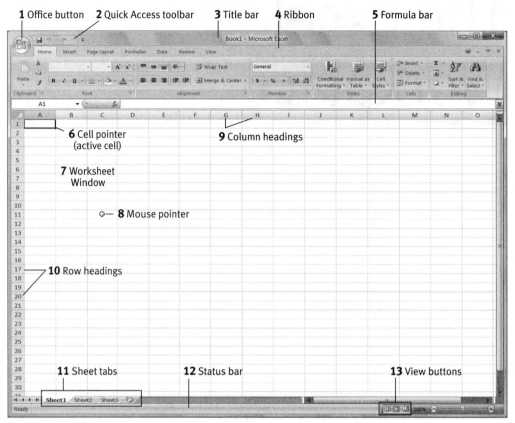

Figure 1 The Excel screen.

Key to the Excel screen

1 Office button

The Microsoft Office button offers access to File-related commands, including commands for working with other Office programs.

2 Quick Access toolbar

The Quick Access toolbar is a customizable row of buttons for accessing commonly used Excel commands.

3 Title bar

The title bar displays the document's title. You can drag the title bar to move the window.

4 Ribbon

The Ribbon organizes all Excel commands and options by group, using buttons and menus to access commands.

5 Formula bar

The formula bar displays the contents of the active cell, as well as that cell's address or reference.

THE EXCEL SCREEN

6 Cell pointer (active cell)

The cell pointer is a heavy or colored border surrounding the active cell. The active cell is the cell in which text and numbers appear when you type.

7 Worksheet window

The worksheet window is where you'll do most of your work with Excel. This window has columns and rows which intersect at cells. You enter data and formulas in the cells to build your spreadsheet.

8 Mouse pointer

When positioned within the worksheet window, the mouse pointer appears as a hollow plus sign. You can use the mouse pointer to select cells, enter data, choose menu commands, and click buttons.

9 Column headings

Column headings are the alphabetical labels that appear at the top of each column.

10 Row headings

Row headings are the numbered labels that appear on the left side of each row.

11 Sheet tabs

Each Excel document has one or more sheets combined together in a workbook. The sheet tabs let you move from one sheet to another within the workbook. To use the sheet tabs, just click on the tab for the sheet that you want to view.

12 Status bar

The status bar displays information about the document.

13 View buttons

The View buttons enable you to switch between Excel's three views: Normal, Page Layout, and Page Break.

✔ Tips

- Standard Windows window elements are not discussed in detail in this book. For more information about how to use standard window elements such as the Close button, Minimize button, Maximize button, Restore button, and scroll bars, consult the documentation that came with your computer or Windows online help.

- The figures throughout this book were created with Microsoft Vista installed. Although Excel may look different if you're using Windows XP on your computer, it works the same way.

THE EXCEL SCREEN

The Mouse

As with most Windows programs, you use the mouse to select text, activate buttons, and choose menu commands.

Mouse pointer appearance

The appearance of the mouse pointer varies depending on its location and the item to which it is pointing. Here are some examples:

◆ In the worksheet window, the mouse pointer usually looks like a hollow plus sign (**Figure 1**).

◆ On a button (**Figure 2**) or menu, the mouse pointer appears as an arrow pointing up and to the left.

◆ In the formula bar (**Figure 3**) or when positioned over a cell being edited (**Figure 4**), the mouse pointer appears as an I-beam pointer.

◆ On a selection border, the mouse pointer looks like a standard pointer with a four-headed arrow (**Figure 5**).

To use the mouse

There are four basic mouse techniques:

◆ **Pointing** means to position the mouse pointer so that its tip is on the item to which you are pointing (**Figure 2**).

◆ **Clicking** means to press the mouse button once and release it. You click to make a cell active, position the insertion point, or choose a button.

◆ **Double-clicking** means to press the mouse button twice in rapid succession. You double-click to open an item or to select a word for editing.

◆ **Dragging** means to press the mouse button down and hold it while moving the mouse. You drag to resize a window, select multiple cells, or draw shapes.

Figure 2 The mouse pointer looks like an arrow when pointing to a button or menu.

Figure 3 The mouse pointer looks like an I-beam pointer when positioned over the formula bar ...

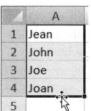

Figure 4 ... or over the contents of a cell being edited.

Figure 5
The mouse pointer looks like a standard pointer with a four-headed arrow when positioned over a selection border.

✔ Tip

■ Throughout this book, when I instruct you to simply *click*, press the left mouse button. When I instruct you to *right-click*, press the right mouse button.

THE MOUSE

The Ribbon & Commands

All of Excel's commands are accessible through the Ribbon, which is brand new in Excel 2007. The Ribbon organizes Excel's commands by category or task (**Figure 6**):

◆ *Tabs* at the top of the Ribbon organize commands by major category or task.

◆ *Groups* on the displayed tab organize commands into related tasks.

◆ *Buttons* and *menus* within a group offer access to specific commands.

✔ Tips

■ The Ribbon replaces the menu bar and toolbars, which appeared in previous versions of Excel.

■ The appearance of the Ribbon varies depending on the resolution of your computer screen and the width of Excel's application window. The wider the window, the larger the buttons and menus appear. Compare **Figures 6** and **7** for an example.

To activate a command

1. Click the Ribbon tab on which the command appears.

2. If the command is a button, click the button.

   or

   If the command is a menu, choose the command from the menu on which it appears.

✔ Tip

■ I explain how to use menus and buttons on the next pages.

Tab   Group   Button   Menu

Figure 6 Excel's Ribbon, displaying the Home tab's groups, buttons, and menus.

Figure 7 When the application window is not wide enough to display the full view of each button of menu, they are resized so they fit.

Menus

Excel includes three kinds of menus:

◆ The Office Button displays a menu that offers access to file management commands (**Figure 8**). Its options are basically the same in all Microsoft Office programs.

◆ Ribbon menus are pop-up menus (**Figure 9**) or drop-down lists (**Figure 10**) that appear on the Ribbon. Some of these menus are coupled with buttons (**Figure 9**); click the button to access the default setting of a menu or use the menu to choose and apply a different setting.

◆ Shortcut menus appear at the mouse pointer when you right-click on an item. When you display a contextual menu for a worksheet cell, a formatting toolbar may also appear (**Figure 11**).

Here are some rules to keep in mind when working with menus:

◆ A menu command that appears in gray cannot be selected (**Figure 9**).

◆ A menu command followed by an ellipsis (…) displays a dialog (**Figure 11**).

◆ A menu command followed by a triangle has a submenu (**Figure 12**). The submenu displays additional commands when the main command is selected.

✔ Tips

■ These menu rules apply to the menus of most Windows programs, not just Excel.

■ Menus that display text boxes (**Figure 10**) can be changed by typing a new value into the box. Just click the contents of the box to select it, type in the new value and press Enter.

■ Dialogs are discussed later in this chapter.

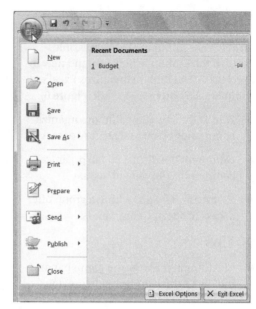

Figure 8 Clicking the Office button displays a menu of file management commands.

Figure 9 A pop-up menu may be coupled with a button.

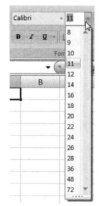

Figure 10 A drop-down list is always coupled with a text box.

Figure 11 In this example, a shortcut menu and formatting toolbar appear at the mouse pointer.

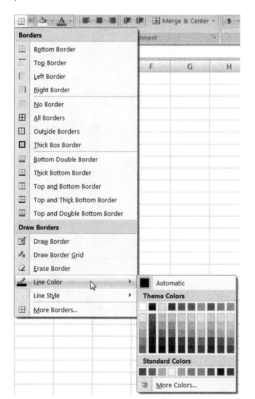

Figure 12 Selecting a command with a triangle beside it displays a submenu like this one.

To choose a menu command

1. Point to the menu from which you want to choose the command.

2. Click on the menu name to display the menu (**Figures 9** though **11**).

3. Click the command you want.

   or

   If the command is on a submenu, click on the name of the submenu to display it (**Figure 12**) and then click on the command you want.

✔ Tip

■ Throughout this book, I use the following shorthand to refer to menu choices: *Ribbon Tab Name* > *Group Name* > *Menu Name* > *Submenu name* (if applicable) > *Command Name*. For example, to instruct you to choose the Paste Values command from the Paste menu on the Clipboard group of the Home tab, I'll write "Choose Home > Clipboard > Paste > Paste Values."

To use a shortcut menu

1. Right-click on the item for which you want to display the shortcut menu. The shortcut menu appears (**Figure 11**).

2. Click to choose the command you want.

✔ Tips

■ A shortcut menu only displays the commands that can be applied to the item to which you are pointing.

■ Shortcut menus are often referred to as *contextual menus*.

Buttons

Word's Quick Access toolbar and Ribbon display many commands as buttons. Clicking a button activates its command on the entire worksheet or on selected cells.

Here are some things to remember when working with buttons:

◆ Buttons with faint icon images (for example, Paste in **Figures 6** and **7**) cannot be selected.

◆ Buttons that appear in a different color (orange, by default) are "turned on."

◆ A toolbar button that includes a triangle (for example, Paste in **Figures 6** and **7**), displays a menu (**Figure 9**).

◆ You can identify a button by its ScreenTip (**Figure 13**).

To view ScreenTips

Point to a button. A box containing the name of the button and a shortcut key (if one is available) appears beneath the Ribbon (**Figure 13**).

To use a toolbar button

1. Point to the button for the command or option that you want (**Figure 13**).

2. Click once.

To use a button's menu

1. Click on the triangle beside or beneath the button to display the menu and its commands (**Figure 9**).

2. Click a command to select it.

Figure 13
When you point to a button on the Ribbon, a ScreenTip with information about the button appears.

Shortcut Keys

Shortcut keys are combinations of keyboard keys that, when pressed, choose a menu command without using the mouse to click a button or menu command. For example, the shortcut key for the Bold command on the Ribbon's Home tab (**Figure 13**) is Ctrl B. Pressing this key combination chooses the command.

✔ Tips

- All shortcut keys use at least one of the following modifier keys:

Key Name	Keyboard Key
Control	Ctrl
Shift	Shift
Alt	Alt

- A command's shortcut key is displayed in its ScreenTip (**Figure 13**).

- Many shortcut keys are standardized from one program to another. The Save and Print commands are two good examples; they're usually Ctrl S and Ctrl P.

- The shortcut keys that worked with previous versions of Excel will continue to work with Excel 2007.

- **Appendix A** includes a list of shortcut keys.

To use a shortcut key

1. Hold down the modifier key for the shortcut (normally Ctrl).

2. Press the letter or number key for the shortcut.

For example, to choose the Bold command, hold down Ctrl and press B.

Dialogs

Excel, like most other Windows programs, uses *dialogs* to get additional information from you about tasks you want to perform.

Excel can display many different dialogs, each with its own purpose. There are two basic types of dialogs:

◆ Dialogs that simply provide information (**Figure 14**).

◆ Dialogs that offer options to select (**Figure 15**) before Excel completes the execution of a command.

Although the interface changes in Excel 2007 have placed most of Excel's commands and features where they are easily accessible on the Ribbon's tabs, you can still display many of the dialogs that appeared automatically in previous versions of Excel.

✔ Tip

■ Often, when a dialog is onscreen, you must dismiss it by clicking OK or Cancel before you can continue working.

To display a dialog

Choose a menu command that displays an ellipsis (**Figure 11**).

or

Click the Dialog Box Launcher button in the corner of a Ribbon tab's group (**Figure 16**).

Figure 14 The dialog that appears at the end of a spelling check just displays information.

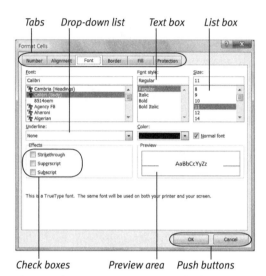

Figure 15 The Font tab of the Format Cells dialog.

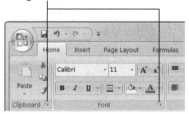

Figure 16 Most groups on the Ribbon include a Dialog Box Launcher button. Clicking the button displays the appropriate dialog box.

Option buttons

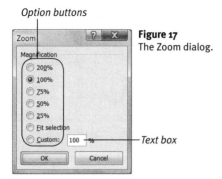

Figure 17
The Zoom dialog.

Text box

Anatomy of an Excel dialog

Here are the components of many Excel dialogs, along with information about how they work.

◆ **Tabs** (**Figure 15**), which appear at the top of some dialogs, let you move from one group of dialog options to another. To switch to another group of options, click its tab.

◆ **Text boxes** or **entry fields** (**Figures 15 and 17**) let you enter information from the keyboard. You can press ⌷Tab⌷ to move from one box to the next or click in a box to position the insertion point within it. Then enter a new value.

◆ **List boxes** (**Figure 15**) offer a number of options to choose from. Use the scroll bar to view options that don't fit in the list window. Click an option to select it; it becomes highlighted and appears in the text box.

◆ **Check boxes** (**Figure 15**) let you turn options on or off. Click in a check box to toggle it. When a check mark or X appears in the check box, its option is turned on.

◆ **Option buttons** (**Figure 17**) let you select only one option from a group. Click on an option to select it; the option that was selected before you clicked is deselected.

◆ **Drop-down lists** (**Figure 15**) also let you select one option from a group. Display a list as you would a menu (**Figure 10**), then choose the option that you want.

◆ **Preview areas** (**Figure 15**), when available, illustrate the effects of your changes before you finalize them by clicking the OK button.

Continued on next page...

DIALOGS

Continued from previous page.

◆ **Push buttons** (**Figures 14**, **15**, and **17**) let you access other dialogs, accept the changes and close the dialog (OK), or close the dialog without making changes (Cancel). To choose a button, click it once.

✔ Tips

■ When the contents of a text box are selected, whatever you type will replace the selection.

■ Excel often uses text boxes and list boxes together (**Figure 15**). You can use either one to make a selection.

■ In some list boxes, double-clicking an option selects it and dismisses the dialog.

■ You can turn on any number of check boxes in a group, but you can select only one option button in a group.

■ Pressing Enter while a push button is active—that is, when it has a dotted border inside it like the OK button in **Figure 17**—"clicks" that button.

■ You can usually "click" the Cancel button by pressing Esc.

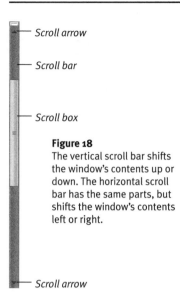

— *Scroll arrow*

— *Scroll bar*

— *Scroll box*

Figure 18
The vertical scroll bar shifts the window's contents up or down. The horizontal scroll bar has the same parts, but shifts the window's contents left or right.

— *Scroll arrow*

Scrolling Window Contents

You can use Excel's scroll bars to shift the contents of a document window so you can see items that don't fit in the window.

✔ Tip

- I tell you more about working with document windows in **Chapter 4**.

To scroll the contents of the document window

Click the scroll arrow (**Figure 18**) for the direction that you want to view. For example, to scroll down to view the end of a document, click the down arrow.

Or

Drag the scroll box (**Figure 18**) in the direction that you want to view. The contents of the window shift accordingly.

Or

Click in the scroll bar above or below the scroll box (**Figure 18**). This shifts the window contents one screenful at a time.

✔ Tips

- Having trouble remembering which scroll arrow to click? Just remember this: click up to see up, click down to see down, click left to see left, and click right to see right.

- Although some keyboard keys change the portion of the document being viewed, they also move the cell pointer. I tell you about these keys in **Chapter 2**.

Excel Help

Excel has an extensive onscreen help feature that draws from help files automatically installed with Excel as well as help information available on Microsoft's Web site. This makes it possible to get accurate, up-to-date information for getting assistance and solving problems with Excel.

Excel offers two kinds of help:

◆ **Excel Help and How-to** (**Figure 19**) is a window full of links for browsing Excel Help topics.

◆ **Context-sensitive Help** (**Figure 20**) displays help topics and information about a specific topic.

Both types of help include clickable links for accessing related items, as well as a search box near the top of the window. You can also view a Table of Contents (**Figure 21**) and use that to browse through Help topics.

This part of the chapter explains how to access Excel Help to get assistance using Excel features.

To display Excel Help and How-to

Click the Help button, which looks like a question mark in a blue circle, at the top-right end of the Ribbon or press F1.

To display context-sensitive help

Click the Help button, which looks like a question mark, at the top-right corner of a dialog in which it appears or press F1 while the dialog is displayed.

Figure 19
Excel Help and How-to lists topics you can browse to learn more about Excel.

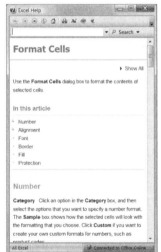

Figure 20
Context-sensitive help provides information about a specific Excel feature.

Show/Hide Table of Contents

Figure 21 You can browse Excel help by displaying its Table of Contents and clicking links for the topics that interest you.

To browse Excel help

1. Display the Excel Help window (**Figure 19** and **20**).

2. If necessary, click the Show Table of Contents button in the window's toolbar. It will look like an open or closed book, depending on whether the Table of Contents is displayed.

   The window expands to display the Table of Contents on the left side (**Figure 21**).

3. Click a topic in the Table of Contents to display subtopics or information about a topic (**Figure 21**).

4. Repeat step 3 as necessary to view the information you are interested in.

To search Excel Help

1. In the Search box at the top of the Excel Help window, type a word or phrase to describe what you want to find help for (**Figure 22**).

Figure 22 Enter a word or phrase to describe what you need help with.

2. Click Search

   Excel begins searching and displays the search results with topics that may provide the help you need. If you have an active Internet connection, the search results will be from Microsoft's Web site (**Figure 23**). If you don't have an Internet connection, the search results will be from offline help installed with Microsoft Excel.

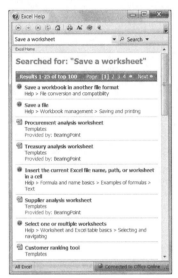

Figure 23 Excel displays a list of help topics that might interest you.

3. Click a topic name in the search results. Information about the topic appears in the Excel Help window (**Figure 24**).

4. Read the information in the Excel Help window to learn about the topic.

   or

   Click links in the Excel Help window to display additional information or other topics in the window.

✔ Tips

- In step 1, if you have already used Excel's help feature, you can use the drop-down list to display a search word or phrase you have used in the past.

- In step 2, to instruct Excel to display only results from offline help, choose Excel Help from the bottom of the Search pop-up menu beside the Search box.

Figure 24 Clicking a topic name displays information and other links in the window.

Worksheet Basics

Numeric values

Text values

Formula: =B1–B2

	A	B
1	Sales	$1,000.00
2	Cost	400.00
3	Profit	$ 600.00

Figure 1 This very simple worksheet illustrates how a spreadsheet program like Excel works with values and formulas.

	A	B
1	Sales	$1,150.00
2	Cost	400.00
3	Profit	$ 750.00

Figure 2 When the value for Sales changes from $1,000 to $1,150, the Profit result changes automatically.

How Worksheets Work

Microsoft Excel is most commonly used to create *worksheets*. A worksheet is a collection of information laid out in columns and rows. As illustrated in **Figure 1**, each worksheet cell can contain one of two kinds of input:

◆ A *value* is a piece of information that does not change. Values can be text, numbers, dates, or times. A cell containing a value usually displays the value.

◆ A *formula* is a collection of values, cell references, operators, and predefined functions that, when evaluated by Excel, produces a result. A cell containing a formula displays the results of the formula.

Although any information can be presented in a worksheet, spreadsheet programs like Excel are usually used to organize and calculate numerical or financial information. Why? Well, when properly prepared, a worksheet acts like a super calculator. You enter values and formulas and it calculates and displays the results. If you change one of the values, Excel automatically recalculates the results (**Figure 2**).

How does this work? By using cell *references* rather than actual numbers in formulas, Excel knows that it should use the contents of those cells in its calculations. Thus, changing one or more values affects the results of calculations that include references to the changed cells. As you can imagine, this makes worksheets powerful business planning and analysis tools!

Starting Excel

To use Excel, you must start the Excel program. This loads Excel into RAM (**random access memory**), so your computer can work with it.

To run Excel from the Taskbar

Click Start > All Programs > Microsoft Office > Microsoft Office Excel 2007 (**Figure 3**).

The Excel splash screen appears briefly, then an empty document window named *Book1* appears (**Figure 4**).

To run Excel by opening an Excel document

1. In Windows, locate the icon for the document that you want to open.

2. Double-click the icon.

   The Excel splash screen appears briefly, then a document window containing the document that you opened appears.

✔ Tip

- In Excel 2007, a document icon displays a preview of the worksheet or chart on the first sheet. Documents created with previous versions of Excel display standard Excel document icons (**Figure 5**).

Figure 3
You can start Excel from the Start button on the Taskbar.

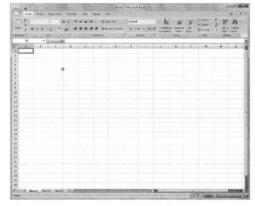

Figure 4 When you start Excel from the Windows Taskbar, it displays an empty document window.

Figure 5
A document created with a previous version of Excel has an icon like this one.

Expenses

Figure 6 Excel's Office button menu.

Figure 7 A dialog like this appears if a document with unsaved changes is open when you exit Excel.

Exiting Excel

When you're finished using Excel, you should use the Exit command to close the program. This completely clears Excel out of RAM, freeing up RAM for other programs.

✔ Tip

- Exiting Excel also instructs Excel to save preference settings.

To exit Excel

Choose Office button > Exit Excel (**Figure 6**). Here's what happens:

- If any documents are open, they close.

- If an open document contains unsaved changes, a dialog appears (**Figure 7**) so you can save the changes. I explain how to save documents in **Chapter 4**.

- The Excel program closes.

✔ Tips

- As you've probably guessed, Excel automatically exits when you restart or shut down your computer.

- Another way to Exit Excel is to click the Close button in the upper-right corner of Excel's application window.

Creating a New Workbook

The documents you create and save using Excel are *workbook* files. A workbook is an Excel document.

In Excel, all workbooks are based on *templates*. A template is a file with built-in settings that control appearance and functionality. Some templates can include predefined contents such as values, formulas, formatting, and macros. Even a blank workbook file is based on a template—in this case, the Blank Workbook template.

Excel's New Workbook dialog (**Figure 8**) offers several ways to create a workbook file:

◆ **Blank and recent** (**Figure 8**) makes it possible to create a workbook file based on the Blank Workbook template or any other recently used template.

◆ **Installed Templates** (**Figure 9**) lets you create a workbook file based on templates installed with Excel.

◆ **My templates** lets you create a workbook file based on templates you may have created or saved while working with Excel. You can also use this option to create a workbook based on a template created by someone else and accessible from your computer—such as a template designed by a co-worker for a specific company task.

◆ **New from existing** (**Figure 14**) enables you to create a workbook file based on an existing workbook. This makes it possible to duplicate a workbook without accidentally overwriting it with new information.

◆ **Microsoft Office Online** (**Figure 11**) lets you go online to the Microsoft Web site to choose a template from a wide variety of categories.

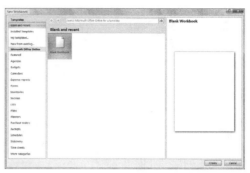

Figure 8 Creating a Blank Workbook with the New Workbook dialog.

✔ Tips

■ Basing a workbook on a template or existing workbook can save a lot of time if you need to create a standard document—such as a monthly report or invoice—repeatedly. Creating templates is covered in **Chapter 4**.

■ Throughout this book, I often use the term *document* to refer to an Excel workbook file. For the purpose of this book, these terms are interchangeable.

■ You can find more information about Excel workbook files in **Chapter 4**.

Figure 9 The New Workbook dialog enables you to select from several installed templates.

Figure 10 Here's an example of a workbook based on one of the installed templates.

To create a blank workbook

1. Choose Office button > New to display the New Workbook dialog (**Figure 8**).

2. In the left panel, select Blank and recent.

3. In the center panel, select Blank Workbook.

4. Click Create.

A blank workbook window appears (**Figure 4**).

To create a workbook based on an installed template

1. Choose Office button > New to display the New Workbook dialog (**Figure 8**).

2. In the left panel, select Installed Templates.

3. In the Center Panel, select the icon for one of the installed templates. A preview of that template appears in the right panel (**Figure 9**).

4. Click Create.

A workbook with the name of the template followed by a number appears (**Figure 10**). Make changes to the workbook as desired.

To create a workbook based on an online template

1. Choose Office button > New to display the New Workbook dialog (**Figure 8**).

2. In the left panel, select one of the categories under Microsoft Office Online.

3 If a list of links appears in the center panel, click the link for the subcategory you want.

4. In the center panel, select the icon for one of the templates. A preview of that template appears in the right panel (**Figure 11**).

5. Click Download.

A workbook with the name of the template followed by a number appears (**Figure 12**). Make changes to the workbook as desired.

✔ Tips

■ You must have an Internet connection to create a workbook based on a template on the Microsoft Office Online Web site.

■ After step 4, a dialog may appear, informing you that templates are only available to customers running Genuine Microsoft Office (**Figure 13**). To never see this dialog again, turn on the Do not show this message again check box and click Continue.

Figure 11 You can also access templates from Microsoft Office Online.

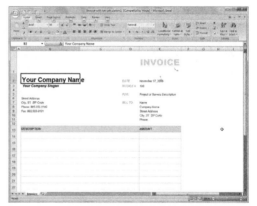

Figure 12 Here's an example of a workbook created from an online template.

Figure 13 Excel may display this dialog to let you know that you must have a "genuine" copy of Office to download templates.

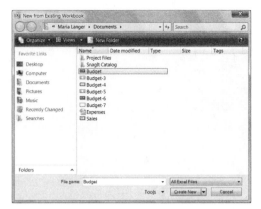

Figure 14 The New from Existing Workbook dialog enables you to choose an existing workbook on which to base a new one.

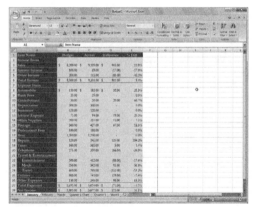

Figure 15 The existing workbook appears with a new name so you can change it and save it as a new file.

To create a workbook based on an existing workbook

1. Choose Office button > New to display the New Workbook dialog (**Figure 8**).

2. In the left panel, select New from existing.

3. The New from Existing Workbook dialog appears (**Figure 14**). Use it to locate and select the workbook you want to base a new workbook on.

4. Click Create New.

A workbook with the name of the existing document followed by a number appears (**Figure 15**). Make changes to the workbook as desired.

✔ Tips

■ The New from Existing Workbook dialog (**Figure 14**) is very similar to the Open dialog, which I cover in **Chapter 4**.

■ This is the best way to create a new workbook from an existing workbook. If you simply open an existing workbook and make changes to it, you might accidentally overwrite the original workbook when you save the new one.

Activating & Selecting Cells

Worksheet information is entered into cells. A *cell* is the intersection of a column and a row. Each little "box" in the worksheet window is a cell.

Each cell has a unique *address* or *reference*. The reference uses the letter(s) of the column and the number of the row. Thus, cell *B6* would be at the intersection of column *B* and row *6*. The reference for the active cell appears in the name box at the left end of the formula bar (**Figure 16**).

To enter information in a cell, you must make that cell *active*. When a cell is active, anything you type is entered into it.

To use Excel commands on a cell or its contents, you must *select* the cell. The active cell is also a selected cell. If desired, however, you can select multiple cells or a *range* of cells. This enables you to use commands on all selected cells at once. A range (**Figure 17**) is a rectangular selection of cells defined by the top-left and bottom-right cell references.

✔ Tips

- Although the active cell is always part of a selection of multiple cells, it is never highlighted like the rest of the selection (**Figure 17**).

- Although you can select multiple cells, only one cell—the one referenced in the name box (**Figure 17**)—is active.

- The column and row headings for selected cells appear colored (**Figures 16** and **17**).

- Using the scroll bars does not change the active or selected cell(s). It merely changes your view of the worksheet's contents.

Cell reference in name box of formula bar

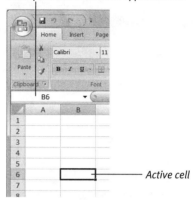

Figure 16 The reference for an active cell appears in the formula bar.

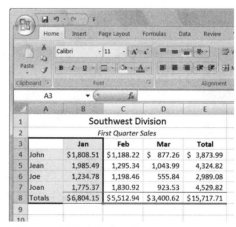

Figure 17 In this illustration, the range *A3:B8* is selected, and cell *A3* is the active cell.

Table 1

Keys for Moving the Cell Pointer	
Key	Movement
↑	Up one cell
↓	Down one cell
→	Right one cell
←	Left one cell
Tab	Right one cell
Shift Tab	Left one cell
Home	First cell in row
Page Up	Up one window
Page Down	Down one window
Ctrl Home	Cell A1
Ctrl End	Cell at intersection of last column and last row containing data

	A	B	C	D	E
1		Southwest Division			
2		First Quarter Sales			
3	⬦	Jan	Feb	Mar	Total
4	John	$1,808.51	$1,188.22	$ 877.26	$ 3,873.99
5	Jean	1,985.49	1,295.34	1,043.99	4,324.82
6	Joe	1,234.78	1,198.46	555.84	2,989.08
7	Joan	1,775.37	1,830.92	923.53	4,529.82
8	Totals	$6,804.15	$5,512.94	$3,400.62	$15,717.71

Figure 18 To select cells, begin in one corner of the range ...

	A	B	C	D	E
1		Southwest Division			
2		First Quarter Sales			
3		Jan	Feb	Mar	Total
4	John	$1,808.51	$1,188.22	$ 877.26	$ 3,873.99
5	Jean	1,985.49	1,295.34	1,043.99	4,324.82
6	Joe	1,234.78	1,198.46	555.84	2,989.08
7	Joan	1,775.37	1,830.92	923.53	4,529.82
8	Totals	$6,804.15	$5,512.94	$3,400.62	$15,717.71

Figure 19 ... hold the mouse button down, and drag to the opposite corner of the range.

To activate a cell

Use the mouse pointer to click in the cell.

Or

Press the appropriate keystroke (**Table 1**) to move the cell pointer.

To select a range of cells with the mouse

1. Position the mouse pointer in the first cell you want to select (**Figure 18**).

2. Hold the mouse button down and drag to highlight all the cells in the selection (**Figure 19**).

Or

1. Click in the first cell of the range you want to select.

2. Hold down Shift and click in the last cell of the range. Everything between the first and second clicks is selected. (This technique is known as *shift-click*.)

To go to a cell or range of cells

1. Choose Home > Editing > Find & Select > Go To (**Figure 20**) or press $\boxed{\text{Ctrl}}\,\boxed{\text{G}}$ to display the Go To dialog (**Figure 21**).

2. Enter the reference for the cell you want to activate or the range that you want to select in the Reference text box.

3. Click OK. If you entered a single cell reference, the cell is activated. If you entered a range reference, the range is selected.

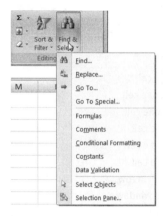

Figure 20
Choose Go To from the Find & Select menu.

✔ Tip

■ To specify a reference for a range, enter the addresses of the first and last cells of the range, separated with a colon (:). For example, **Figure 17** shows *A3:B8* selected and **Figure 19** shows *A3:E8* selected.

To select an entire column

1. Position the mouse pointer on the heading for the column you want to select. The mouse pointer turns into an arrow pointing down (**Figure 22**).

2. Click once. The column is selected.

To select an entire row

1. Position the mouse pointer on the heading for the row you want to select. The mouse pointer turns into an arrow pointing to the right (**Figure 23**).

2. Click once. The row is selected.

Figure 21 The Go To dialog lets you move to any cell quickly.

Figure 22
Click a column heading to select the column.

Figure 23
Click a row heading to select the row.

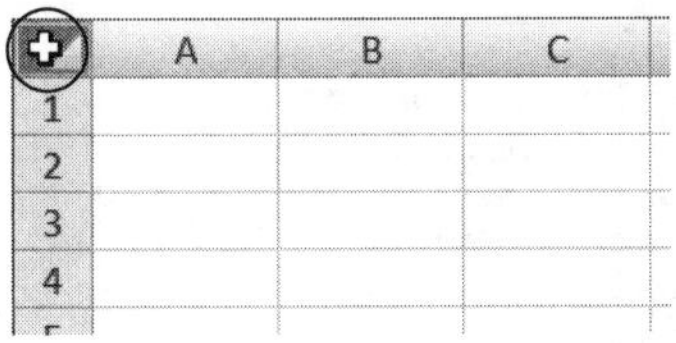

Figure 24
Click the Select All button to select all cells in the worksheet.

To select multiple columns or rows

1. Position the mouse pointer on the first column or row heading.

2. Press the mouse button down, and drag along the headings until all the desired columns or rows are selected.

✔ Tip

■ When selecting multiple columns or rows, be careful to position the mouse pointer on the heading and not between two headings! If you drag the border of two columns, you will change a column's width rather than make a selection.

To select the entire worksheet

1. Position the mouse pointer on the Select All button in the upper-left corner of the worksheet window. The mouse pointer appears as a hollow plus sign (**Figure 24**).

2. Click once.

Or

Press Ctrl A.

The worksheet is selected.

SELECTING MULTIPLE CELLS

To select multiple ranges

1. Use any selection technique to select the first cell or range of cells (**Figure 25**).

2. Hold down $\boxed{\text{Ctrl}}$ and drag to select the second cell or range of cells (**Figure 26**).

3. Repeat step 2 until all desired ranges are selected.

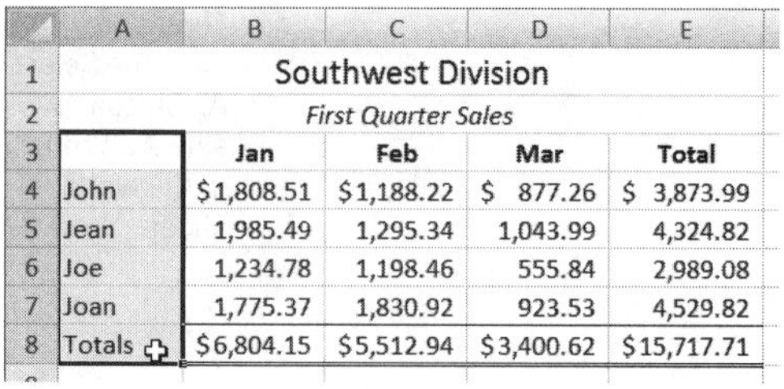

✔ Tips

■ Selecting multiple ranges can be tricky. It takes practice. Don't be frustrated if you can't do it on the first few tries!

■ To add ranges that are not visible in the worksheet window, be sure to use the scroll bars to view them. Using the keyboard to move to other cells while selecting multiple ranges will remove the selections you've made so far or add undesired selections.

■ Do not click in the worksheet window or use the movement keys while multiple ranges are selected unless you are finished working with them. Doing so will deselect all the cells.

To deselect cells

Click anywhere in the worksheet.

Or

Press any of the keys in **Table 1**.

✔ Tip

■ Remember, at least one cell must be selected at all times—that's the active cell.

	A	B	C	D	E
1		Southwest Division			
2		First Quarter Sales			
3		Jan	Feb	Mar	Total
4	John	$1,808.51	$1,188.22	$ 877.26	$ 3,873.99
5	Jean	1,985.49	1,295.34	1,043.99	4,324.82
6	Joe	1,234.78	1,198.46	555.84	2,989.08
7	Joan	1,775.37	1,830.92	923.53	4,529.82
8	Totals	$6,804.15	$5,512.94	$3,400.62	$15,717.71

Figure 25 To select two ranges of cells, start by selecting the first range, ...

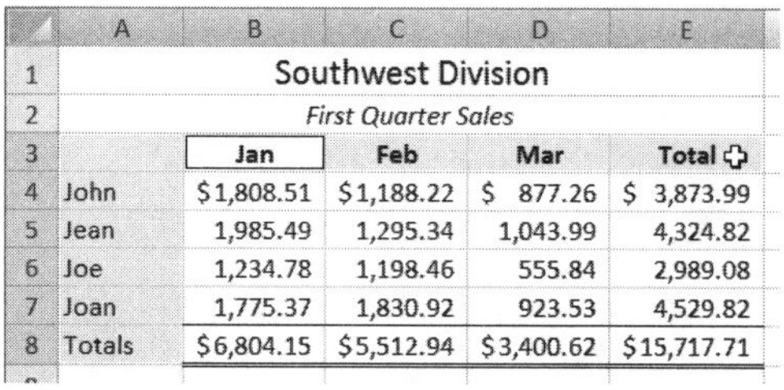

	A	B	C	D	E
1		Southwest Division			
2		First Quarter Sales			
3		Jan	Feb	Mar	Total
4	John	$1,808.51	$1,188.22	$ 877.26	$ 3,873.99
5	Jean	1,985.49	1,295.34	1,043.99	4,324.82
6	Joe	1,234.78	1,198.46	555.84	2,989.08
7	Joan	1,775.37	1,830.92	923.53	4,529.82
8	Totals	$6,804.15	$5,512.94	$3,400.62	$15,717.71

Figure 26 ... then hold down $\boxed{\text{Ctrl}}$ and select the second range.

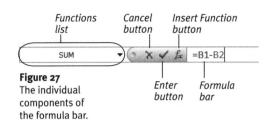

Functions list   *Cancel button*   *Insert Function button*

SUM ▼   ✗ ✓ *fx*   =B1-B2

Enter button   *Formula bar*

Figure 27
The individual components of the formula bar.

Entering Values & Formulas

To enter a value or formula into a cell, begin by making the cell active. As you type or click to enter information, the information appears in both the cell and in the formula bar just above the window's title bar. You complete the entry by pressing ⌷Enter⌷ or clicking the Enter button on the formula bar.

While you are entering information into a cell, the formula bar is *active*. You can tell that it's active because the name box on the left end of the formula bar turns into a Functions list and two additional buttons appear between it and the cell contents area (**Figure 27**).

There are two important things to remember when the formula bar is active:

◆ Anything you type or click on may be included in the active cell.

◆ Some Excel options and menu commands are unavailable.

You deactivate the formula bar by accepting or cancelling the current entry.

✔ Tips

■ Pressing ⌷Enter⌷ to complete a formula entry accepts the entry and moves the cell pointer one cell down. Clicking the Enter button accepts the entry without moving the cell pointer.

■ To cancel an entry before it has been completed, press ⌷Esc⌷ or click the Cancel button on the formula bar. This restores the cell to the way it was before you began.

■ If you include formatting notation such as dollar signs, commas, and percent symbols when you enter numbers, Excel may apply formatting styles. Formatting the contents of cells is discussed in **Chapter 6**.

Values

As discussed at the beginning of this chapter, a value is any text, number, date, or time you enter into a cell. Values are constant—they don't change unless you change them.

Figure 28 As data is entered into a cell, it appears in the cell and in the formula bar.

To enter a value

1. Activate the cell in which you want to enter the value.

2. Type in the value. As you type, the information appears in two places: the active cell and the formula bar, which becomes active (**Figure 28**).

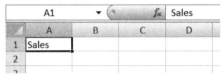

Figure 29 A completed entry. The insertion point is gone.

3. To complete and accept the entry (**Figure 29**), press [Enter], or click the Enter button on the formula bar.

✔ Tips

- Although you can often use the arrow keys or other movement keys in **Table 1** to complete an entry by moving to another cell, it's a bad habit because it won't always work.

- Pressing [Enter] to complete an entry automatically advances the cell pointer to the next cell.

- By default, Excel aligns text against the left side of the cell and aligns numbers against the right side of the cell. I explain how to change alignment in **Chapter 6**.

- Don't worry if the data you put into a cell doesn't seem to fit. You can always change the column width or use the AutoFit Text feature to make it fit. I explain how in **Chapter 6**.

Table 2

Basic Mathematical Operators Understood by Excel

Operator	Use	Example
+	Addition	=A1+B10
−	Subtraction	=A1−B10
−	Negation	=−A1
*	Multiplication	=A1*B10
/	Division	=A1/B10
^	Exponential	=A1^3
%	Percentage	=20%

Table 3

How Excel Evaluates Expressions

Assumptions

A1=5

B10=7

C3=4

Formula	Evaluation	Result
=A1+B10*C3	=5+7*4	33
=C3*B10+A1	=4*7+5	33
=(A1+B10)*C3	=(5+7)*4	48
=A1+10%	=5+10%	5.1
=(A1+10)%	=(5+10)%	0.15
=A1^2−B10/C3	=5^2−7/4	23.25
=(A1^2−B10)/C3	=(5^2−7)/4	4.5
=A1^(2−B10)/C3	=5^(2−7)/4	0.00008

Formula Basics

Excel makes calculations based on formulas you enter into cells. When you complete the entry of a formula, Excel displays the results of the formula rather than the formula.

Here are some important things to keep in mind when writing formulas:

◆ If a formula uses cell references to refer to other cells and the contents of one or more of those cells changes, the result of the formula changes, too.

◆ All formulas begin with an equal (=) sign. This is how Excel knows that a cell entry is a formula and not a value.

◆ Formulas can contain any combination of values, references, operators (**Table 2**), and functions. I tell you about using operators in formulas in this chapter and about using functions in **Chapter 5**.

◆ Formulas are not case sensitive. This means that =*A1+B10* is the same as =*a1+b10*. Excel automatically converts characters in cell references and functions to uppercase.

When calculating the results of expressions with a variety of operators, Excel makes calculations in the following order:

1. Negation

2. Expressions in parentheses

3. Percentages

4. Exponentials

5. Multiplication or division

6. Addition or subtraction

Table 3 shows some examples of formulas and their results to illustrate this. As you can see, the inclusion of parentheses can really make a difference when you write a formula!

Continued on next page...

FORMULA BASICS

Continued from previous page.

✔ Tips

- Do not use the arrow keys or other movement keys to complete an entry by moving to another cell. Doing so may add cells to the formula!

- Whenever possible, use references rather than values in formulas. This way, you won't have to rewrite formulas when values change. **Figures** 30 and 31 illustrate this.

- A reference can be a cell reference, a range reference, or a cell or range name. I tell you about name references in **Chapter 13**.

- To add a range of cells to a formula, type the first cell in the range followed by a colon (:) and then the last cell in the range. For example, *B1:B10* references the cells from *B1* straight down through *B10*.

- If you make a syntax error in a formula, Excel tells you (**Figures 32**, **33**, and **34**). If the error is one of the common errors programmed into Excel's Formula Auto-Correct feature, Excel offers to correct the formula for you (**Figure 34**). Otherwise, you will have to troubleshoot the formula and correct it yourself.

- I explain how to edit formulas in **Chapter 3** and how to include functions in formulas in **Chapter 5**.

	A	B	
1	Sales	1000	
2	Cost	400	
3	Profit	600	—— =1000–400
4			
5	Commission	90	—— =600*15%

Figure 30 If any of the values change, the formulas will need to be rewritten!

	A	B	
1	Sales	1000	
2	Cost	400	
3	Profit	600	—— =B1–B2
4			
5	Rate	15%	
6			
7	Commission	90	—— =B3*B5

Figure 31 But if the formulas reference cells containing the values, when the values change, the formulas will not need to be rewritten to show correct results.

Figure 32 Excel tells you when a formula has an error and provides information on where you can get help.

Figure 33 This dialog appears when a formula contains a *circular reference*—a reference to its own cell.

Figure 34 If the error is one of the common formula errors Excel knows about, Excel offers to fix it for you.

FORMULA BASICS

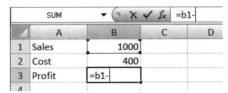

Figure 35 To enter a formula, type it into a cell.

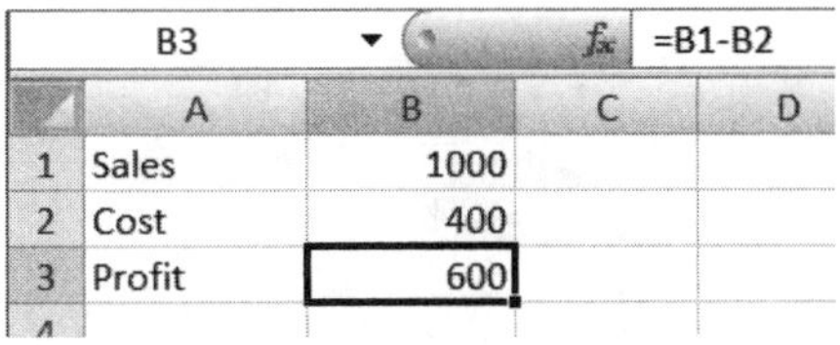

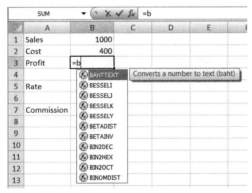

Figure 36 A completed formula entry.

To enter a formula by typing

1. Activate the cell in which you want to enter the formula.

2. Type in the formula. As you type, the formula appears in two places: the active cell and the formula bar (**Figure 35**).

3. To complete the entry (**Figure 36**), press (Enter) or click the Enter button on the formula bar.

✔ Tip

- As you type cell references, Excel may attempt to suggest functions you might be trying to type. These functions will appear in a drop-down list, as shown in **Figure 37**. You can ignore this list; it will disappear as you type. I tell you how to use functions in **Chapter 5**.

Figure 37 If you type a cell reference in a formula, Excel assumes you're trying to type in a function and suggests a few.

To enter a formula by clicking

1. Activate the cell in which you want to enter the formula.

2. Type an equal (=) sign to begin the formula (**Figure 38**).

3. To enter a cell reference, click on the cell you want to reference (**Figures 39** and **41**).

   or

   To enter a constant value or operator, type it in (**Figure 40**).

4. Repeat step 3 until the entire formula appears in the formula bar.

5. To complete the entry (**Figure 42**), press (Enter) or click the Enter button on the formula bar.

✔ Tips

■ If you click a cell reference without typing an operator, Excel assumes you want to add that reference to the formula.

■ Be careful where you click when writing a formula! Each click adds a reference to the formula. If you add an incorrect reference, press (Backspace) until it has been deleted or click the Cancel button on the formula bar to start the entry from scratch. I explain how to edit a cell's contents in **Chapter 3**.

■ You can add a range of cells to a formula by dragging over the cells.

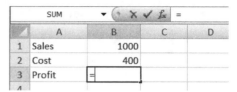

Figure 38 To enter the formula =B1–B2, type = to begin the formula, ...

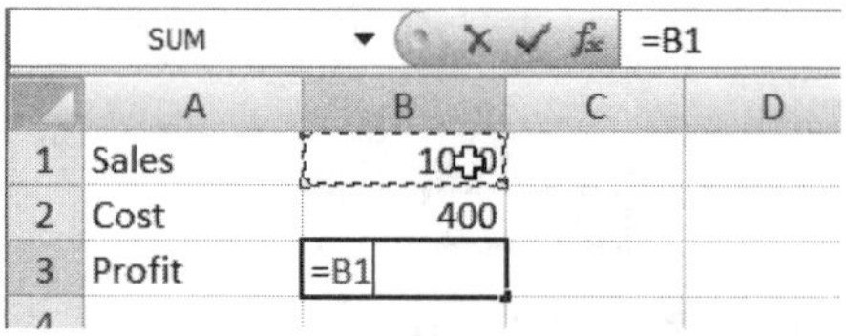

SUM		▼	X ✔ ƒx	=B1
	A	B	C	D
1	Sales	10⊕0		
2	Cost	400		
3	Profit	=B1		

Figure 39 ... click cell B1 to add its reference to the formula, ...

SUM		▼	X ✔ ƒx	=B1-
	A	B	C	D
1	Sales	1000		
2	Cost	400		
3	Profit	=B1-		

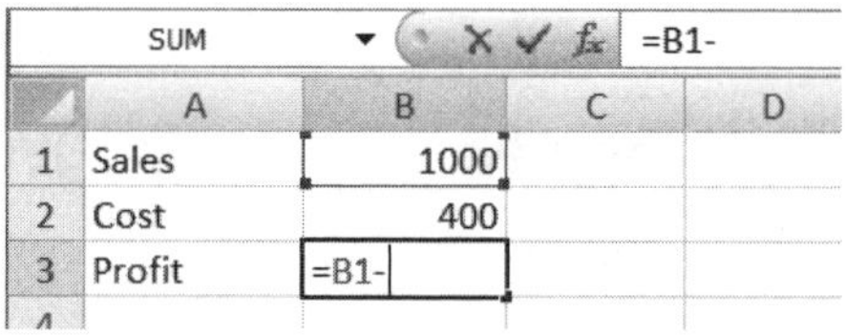

Figure 40 ... type – to tell Excel to subtract, ...

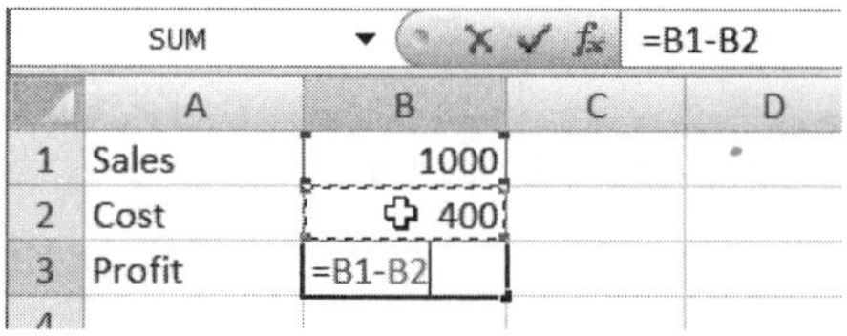

SUM		▼	X ✔ ƒx	=B1-B2
	A	B	C	D
1	Sales	1000		·
2	Cost	⊕ 400		
3	Profit	=B1-B2		

Figure 41 ... click cell B2 to add its reference to the formula, ...

B3		▼	ƒx	=B1-B2
	A	B	C	D
1	Sales	1000		
2	Cost	400		
3	Profit	600		

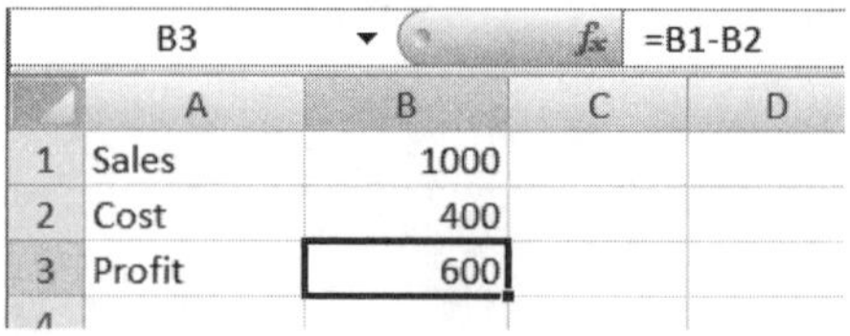

Figure 42 ... and finally, click the Enter button to complete the formula.

	A	B
1		Sout
2		Fir:
3		Jan
4	John	1,808.51
5	Jean	1,985.49
6	Joe	1,234.78
7	Joan	1,775.37
8	Totals	5,028.78

Figure 43
A tiny green error marker appears in the corner of a cell that contains a possible error.

	A	B
1		Sout
2		Fir:
3		Jan
4	John	1,808.51
5	Jean	1,985.49
6	Joe	1,234.78
7	Joan	1,775.37
8	Tota ⟡	5,028.78

Figure 44
When you activate a cell with a possible error, the Error Checking Smart Tag icon appears.

Explanation of possible problem

	A	B	C	D
1		Southwest Division		
2		*First Quarter Sales*		
3		Jan	Feb	Mar
4	John	1,808.51	1,188.22	877.:
5	Jean	1,985.49	1,295.34	1,043.!
6	Joe	1,234.78	1,198.46	555.:
7	Joan	1,775.37	1,830.92	923.!
8	Tota ⟡ ▼	5,028.78	5,512.94	3,400.(
9				
10		Formula Omits Adjacent Cells		
11		Update Formula to Include Cells		
12		Help on this error		
13		Ignore Error		
14		Edit in Formula Bar		
15		Error Checking Options...		
16				

Figure 45 Choose an option from the Smart Tag menu to resolve the possible error.

Error Checking Smart Tags

Excel's Error Checking Smart Tag feature alerts you to possible errors in cells. For example, suppose you write a formula that sums all the numbers in a column, but you leave out the last cell reference for the last cell in the column. Excel assumes this is an error and marks the cell with a small green triangle in the upper-left corner of the cell (**Figure 43**). When you select the cell, a Smart Tag icon appears beside it (**Figure 44**). Clicking the Smart Tag displays a menu of options for correcting, learning more about, or ignoring the possible error (**Figure 45**).

✔ Tip

■ The green error marker that appears in a cell (**Figure 43**) does not print.

To correct an error with a Smart Tag

1. Click the Smart Tag icon that appears beside a cell with a possible error (**Figure 44**). A menu of options appears (**Figure 45**).

2. Choose the option immediately below the description of the error.

To ignore an error & remove its Smart Tag

1. Click the Smart Tag icon that appears beside a cell with a possible error (**Figure 44**). A menu of options appears (**Figure 45**).

2. Choose Ignore Error. The Smart Tag and green triangle disappear.

Editing
Worksheets

Editing Worksheets

Microsoft Excel offers a number of features and techniques that you can use to modify your worksheets.

◆ Use standard editing techniques and the Clear command to change or clear the contents of cells.

◆ Use Cells group commands to insert or delete cells, columns, and rows.

◆ Use Clipboard group commands, the fill handle, and drag-and-drop editing to copy cells from one location to another, including cells containing formulas.

◆ Use the fill handle and Editing group commands to copy cell contents to multiple cells or create a series.

◆ Modify formulas so they are properly updated by Excel when copied.

◆ Use Clipboard group commands and drag-and-drop editing to move cells from one location to another.

◆ Undo and redo multiple actions.

This chapter covers all of these techniques.

Editing Cell Contents

You can use standard editing techniques to edit the contents of cells either as you enter values or formulas or after you have completed an entry. You can also clear a cell's contents, leaving the cell empty.

To edit as you enter

1. If necessary, click to position the blinking insertion point cursor in the cell (**Figure 1**) or formula bar (**Figure 2**).

2. Press Backspace to delete the character to the left of the insertion point.

   or

   Type the characters that you want to insert at the insertion point.

To edit a completed entry

1. Double-click the cell containing the incorrect entry to activate it for editing.

2. If the cell contains a value, follow the instructions in the previous section to insert or delete characters as desired.

   or

   If the cell contains a formula, color-coded Range Finder frames graphically identify cell references (**Figures 3 and 5**). There are three ways to edit cell references:

   ▲ Edit the reference as discussed in the previous section.

   ▲ Drag a frame border to move the frame over another cell. As shown in **Figure 4**, the mouse pointer looks like an arrow as you drag.

   ▲ Drag a frame handle to expand or contract it so the frame includes more or fewer cells. As shown in **Figure 6**, the mouse pointer turns into a two-headed arrow when you position it on a frame handle and drag.

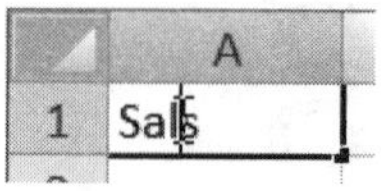

Figure 1 To edit a cell's contents while entering information, click to reposition the insertion point in the cell …

Figure 2 … or in the formula bar and make changes as desired.

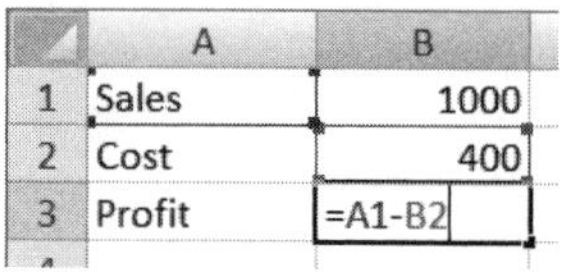

	A	B
1	Sales	1000
2	Cost	400
3	Profit	=A1-B2

Figure 3 The range Finder frames clearly indicate the problem with this formula.

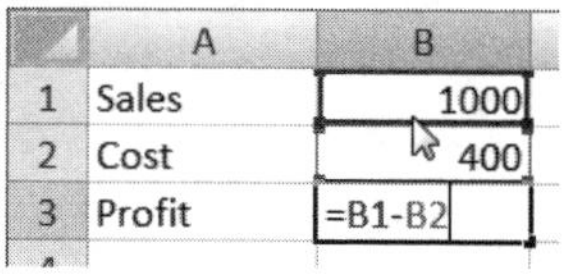

	A	B
1	Sales	1000
2	Cost	400
3	Profit	=B1-B2

Figure 4 You can drag a Range Finder frame to correct the cell reference. In this example, the Range Finder frame on cell A1 is dragged to cell B1.

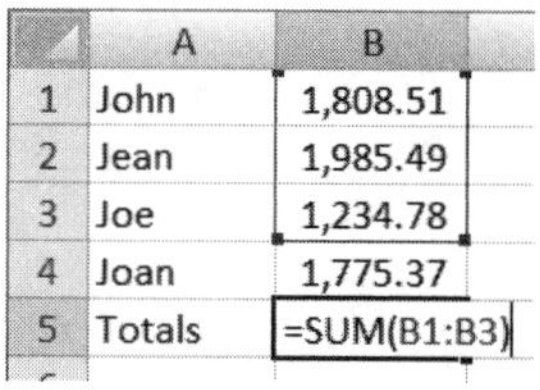

	A	B
1	John	1,808.51
2	Jean	1,985.49
3	Joe	1,234.78
4	Joan	1,775.37
5	Totals	=SUM(B1:B3)

Figure 5 In this example, the Range Finder indicates that the range of cells in the formula excludes a cell.

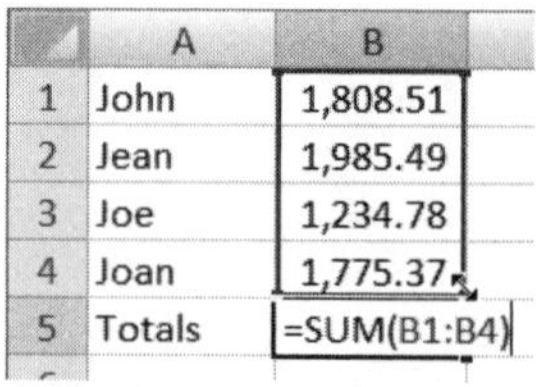

	A	B
1	John	1,808.51
2	Jean	1,985.49
3	Joe	1,234.78
4	Joan	1,775.37
5	Totals	=SUM(B1:B4)

Figure 6 You can drag a Range Finder frame handle to expand the range and correct the reference in the formula.

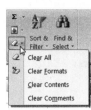

Figure 7
Use options under the Clear menu in the Editing group to remove cell contents or formatting.

To clear cell contents

1. Select the cell(s) you want to clear.

2. Choose Home > Editing > Clear > Clear Contents (**Figure 7**).

   or

   Press [Delete].

✔ Tips

■ Another way to clear the contents of just one cell is to select the cell, press [Backspace], and then press [Enter].

■ Do not press [Spacebar] to clear a cell's contents! Doing so inserts a space character into the cell. Although the contents seem to disappear, they are just replaced by an invisible character.

■ Clearing a cell is very different from deleting a cell. When you clear a cell, the cell remains in the worksheet—only its contents are removed. When you delete a cell, the entire cell is removed from the worksheet and other cells shift to fill the gap. I tell you about inserting and deleting cells next.

■ The Clear Contents command clears only the values or formulas entered into a cell. The other Clear menu commands (**Figure 7**) work as follows:

   ▲ **Clear All** clears everything, including formatting and comments.

   ▲ **Clear Formats** clears only cell formatting.

   ▲ **Clear Comments** clears only cell comments.

   I tell you about formatting cells in **Chapter 6** and about adding cell comments in **Chapter 11**.

Inserting & Deleting Cells

Commands in Excel's Insert and Delete menus enable you to insert and delete columns, rows, or cells.

◆ When you insert cells, Excel shifts cells down or to the right to make room for the new cells.

◆ When you delete cells, Excel shifts cells up or to the left to fill the gap left by the missing cells.

Figures 9, **11**, **13**, and **15** show examples of how inserting a column or deleting a row in a simple worksheet (**Figure 8**) affects the cells in a worksheet. Fortunately, Excel is smart enough to adjust cell references in formulas so the formulas you write remain correct.

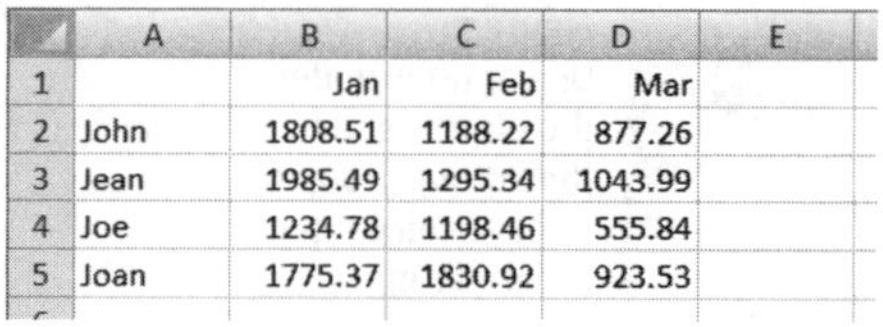

To insert a column or row

1. Select a column or row (**Figure 9**).

2. Click Home > Cells > Insert or choose an option from the Insert menu (**Figure 10**). The column or row is inserted and the Insert Options button appears (**Figure 11**).

3. If desired, choose a formatting option for the inserted column or row from the Insert Options pop-up menu (**Figure 12**).

✔ Tip

■ To insert multiple columns or rows, in step 1, select the number of columns or rows you want to insert. For example, if you want to insert three columns before column *B*, select columns *B*, *C*, and *D*.

	A	B	C	D	E
1		Jan	Feb	Mar	
2	John	1808.51	1188.22	877.26	
3	Jean	1985.49	1295.34	1043.99	
4	Joe	1234.78	1198.46	555.84	
5	Joan	1775.37	1830.92	923.53	

Figure 8 A simple worksheet.

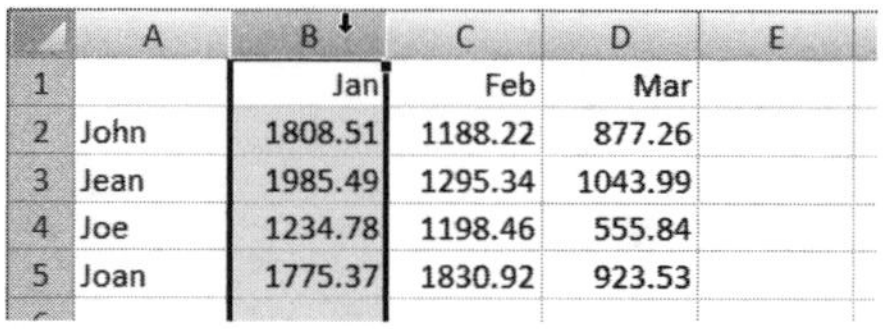

	A	B	C	D	E
1		Jan	Feb	Mar	
2	John	1808.51	1188.22	877.26	
3	Jean	1985.49	1295.34	1043.99	
4	Joe	1234.78	1198.46	555.84	
5	Joan	1775.37	1830.92	923.53	

Figure 9 Selecting a column.

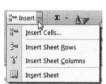

Figure 10
The Insert menu.

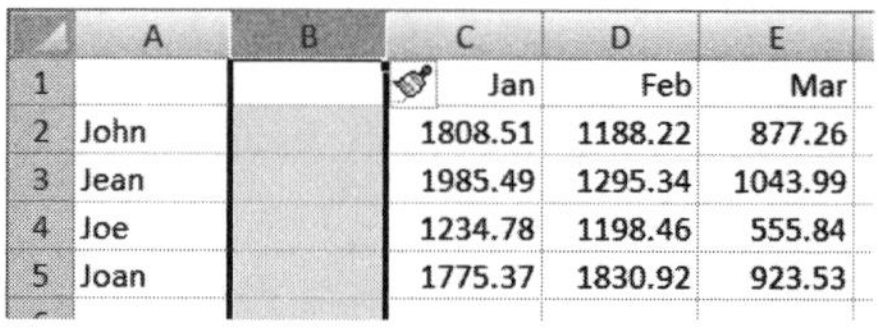

	A	B	C	D	E
1			Jan	Feb	Mar
2	John		1808.51	1188.22	877.26
3	Jean		1985.49	1295.34	1043.99
4	Joe		1234.78	1198.46	555.84
5	Joan		1775.37	1830.92	923.53

Figure 11 An inserted column.

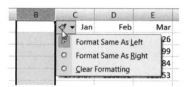

Figure 12 You can use the Insert Options pop-up menu to set formatting options for inserted cells.

	A	B	C	D
1		Jan	Feb	Mar
2	John	1808.51	1188.22	877.26
3	Jean	1985.49	1295.34	1043.99
4	Joe	1234.78	1198.46	555.84
5	Joan	1775.37	1830.92	923.53

Figure 13 Selecting a row.

Figure 14
The Delete menu.

	A	B	C	D
1		Jan	Feb	Mar
2	John	1808.51	1188.22	877.26
3	Jean	1985.49	1295.34	1043.99
4	Joan	1775.37	1830.92	923.53
5				

Figure 15 The row selected in **Figure 13** is deleted.

	A	B
1	Sales	1000
2	Cost	400
3	Profit	600
4		
5		
6	Commission	#REF!

Figure 16 In this example, I deleted a row containing a value referenced in the formula in *B6*. Because Excel can't find one of the references it needs, it displays a *#REF!* error.

To delete a column or row

1. Select a column or row (**Figure 13**).

2. Click Home > Cells > Delete or choose an option from the Delete menu (**Figure 14**).

   The column or row (**Figure 15**)—along with all of its contents—disappears.

✔ Tips

- To delete more than one column or row at a time, in step 1, select all of the columns or rows you want to delete.

- If you delete a column or row that contains referenced cells, the formulas that reference the cells may display a #REF! error message (**Figure 16**). This means that Excel can't find a referenced cell. If this happens, you'll have to rewrite any formulas in cells displaying the error.

To insert cells

1. Select a cell or range of cells (**Figure 17**).

2. Choose Home > Cells > Insert > Insert Cells (**Figure 10**).

3. In the Insert dialog that appears (**Figure 18**), select the appropriate option to tell Excel how to shift the selected cells to make room for new cells—Shift cells right or Shift cells down.

4. Click OK. The cells are inserted and the Insert Options button appears (**Figure 19**).

5. If desired, choose a formatting option for the inserted column or row from the Insert Options pop-up menu.

✔ Tip

- Excel always inserts the number of cells that is selected when you use the Insert command (**Figures 17 and 19**).

To delete cells

1. Select a cell or range of cells to delete (**Figure 17**).

2. Click Home > Cells > Delete > Delete Cells (**Figure 14**).

3. In the Delete dialog that appears (**Figure 20**), select the appropriate option to tell Excel how to shift the other cells when the selected cells are deleted—Shift cells left or Shift cells up.

4. Click OK.

   The cells are deleted (**Figure 21**).

✔ Tip

- If you delete a referenced cell, the formulas that reference the cell may display a #REF! error message (**Figure 16**). If this happens, you'll have to rewrite formulas in cells displaying the error.

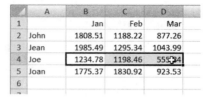

Figure 17 Selecting a range of cells.

Figure 18 The Insert dialog.

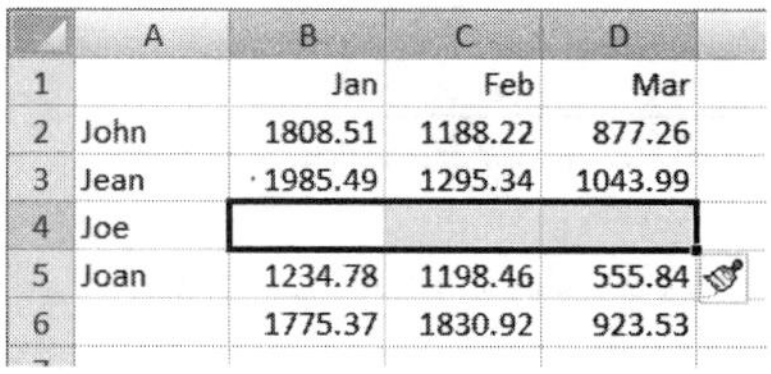

Figure 19 Here's what happens when you insert cells selected in **Figure 17,** using the Shift cells down option.

Figure 20 The Delete dialog.

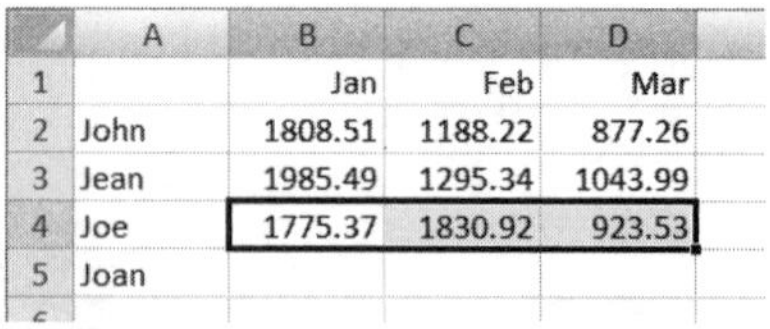

Figure 21 Here's what happens when you delete the cells selected in **Figure 17,** using the Shift cells up option.

John
John
Jean
Jean
Joe
Joe
Joan
Joan

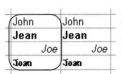

Figure 22 The Copy and Paste commands can make an exact copy.

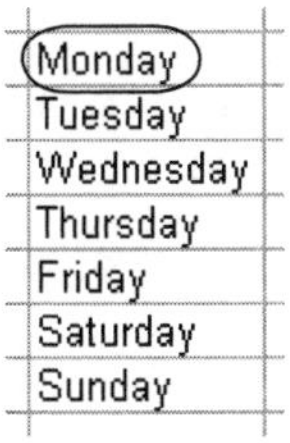

Monday
Tuesday
Wednesday
Thursday
Friday
Saturday
Sunday

Figure 23 Using the fill handle on a cell containing the word *Monday* generates a list of the days of the week.

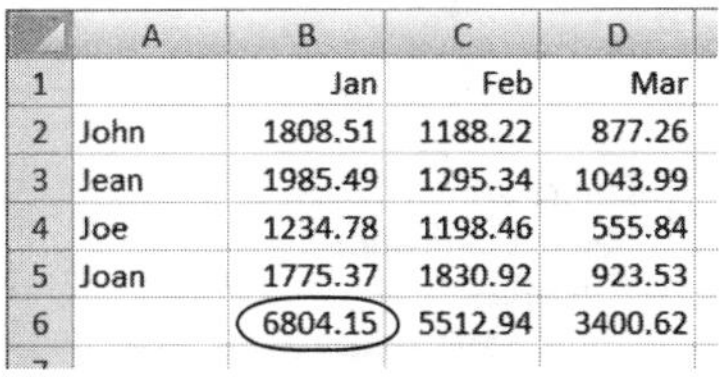

	A	B	C	D
1		Jan	Feb	Mar
2	John	1808.51	1188.22	877.26
3	Jean	1985.49	1295.34	1043.99
4	Joe	1234.78	1198.46	555.84
5	Joan	1775.37	1830.92	923.53
6		6804.15	5512.94	3400.62

Figure 24 Copying a formula that totals a column automatically writes correctly referenced formulas to total similar columns.

Copying Cells

Excel offers several ways to copy the contents of one cell to another: the Copy and Paste commands, the fill handle, and the Fill menu command.

How Excel copies depends not only on the method used, but on the contents of the cell(s) being copied.

- When you use the Copy and Paste commands to copy a cell containing a value, Excel makes an exact copy of the cell, including any formatting (**Figure 22**). I tell you about formatting cells in **Chapter 6**.
- When you use the fill handle or a Fill menu command to copy a cell containing a value, Excel either makes an exact copy of the cell, including any formatting, or creates a series based on the original cell's contents (**Figure 23**).
- When you copy a cell containing a formula, Excel copies the formula, changing any relative references in the formula so they're relative to the destination cell(s) (**Figure 24**).

✔ Tip

- Copy cells that contain formulas whenever possible to save time and ensure consistency.

Copy & Paste

The Copy and Paste commands in Excel work very much the way they do in other programs. Begin by selecting the source cells and copying them to the Clipboard. Then select the destination cells and paste the Clipboard contents in.

To copy with Copy & Paste

1. Select the cell(s) you want to copy (**Figure 25**).

2. Click Home > Clipboard > Copy (**Figure 26**) or press Ctrl C. An animated marquee appears around the selection (**Figure 27**).

3. Select the cell(s) in which you want to paste the selection (**Figure 28**). If more than one cell has been copied, you can select either the first cell of the destination range or the entire range.

4. Click Home > Clipboard > Paste (**Figure 26**) or press Ctrl V or Enter. The originally selected cells are copied to the new location and the Paste Options button appears (**Figure 29**).

5. If desired, choose an option for the pasted cell(s) from the Paste Options pop-up menu (**Figure 30**).

Figure 25
Begin by selecting the cell(s) you want to copy.

Figure 26
The Clipboard group includes the Paste button/menu and the Cut, Copy, and Format Painter buttons.

Figure 27
A marquee appears around the selection when it has been copied to the Clipboard.

Figure 28
Select the destination cell(s).

Figure 29
The contents of the copied cells appear in the destination cells.

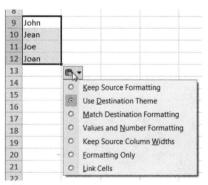

Figure 30 You can set formatting for pasted in cells by choosing an option from the Paste Options pop-up menu.

Figure 31
The Paste button includes a menu of options for pasting Clipboard contents.

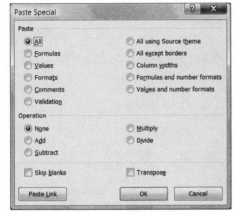

Figure 32 The Paste Special dialog offers additional options for pasting Clipboard contents.

✔ Tips

■ If the destination cells contain information, Excel may overwrite them without warning you.

■ If you click the Paste button or press Ctrl V, the marquee remains around the copied range, indicating that it is still in the Clipboard and may be pasted elsewhere. The marquee disappears automatically as you work, but if you want to remove it manually, press Esc.

■ The Paste Options button will not appear if you press Enter in step 4.

■ The Paste button's pop-up menu (**Figure 31**) offers additional options for pasting Clipboard contents. For example, you can convert formulas in the selection into values or paste a cell without border formatting. Choosing Paste Special displays a dialog with even more options (**Figure 32**).

The Fill Handle

The *fill handle* is a small black or colored box in the lower-right corner of the cell pointer (**Figure 33**) or selection (**Figure 34**). You can use the fill handle to copy the contents of one or more cells to adjacent cells.

To copy with the fill handle

1. Select the cell(s) containing the information you want to copy (**Figure 34**).

2. Position the mouse pointer on the fill handle. The mouse pointer turns into a black plus sign (**Figure 35**).

3. Press the mouse button down and drag to the adjacent cells. A gray border surrounds the source and destination cells (**Figure 36**).

4. When all the destination cells are surrounded by the gray border, release the mouse button. The cells are filled and the Fill Options button appears (**Figure 37**).

5. If desired, choose an option for the filled cell(s) from the Fill Options pop-up menu (**Figure 38**).

✔ Tips

■ You can use the fill handle to copy any number of cells. The destination cells, however, must be adjacent to the original cells.

■ When using the fill handle, you can only copy in one direction (up, down, left, or right) at a time.

■ If the destination cells contain information, Excel may overwrite them without warning you.

b	Mar
2	877.26
4	1043.99
5	555.84
2	923.53
4	3400.62

—— *Fill handle*

Figure 33 The fill handle on a single cell.

b	Mar
2	877.26
4	1043.99
5	555.84
2	923.53
4	3400.62

—— *Fill handle*

Figure 34 The fill handle on a range of cells.

b	Mar
2	877.26
4	1043.99
5	555.84
2	923.53
4	3400.62

Figure 35 When the mouse pointer is over the fill handle, it turns into a black plus sign.

⊃	Mar	
2	877.26	
4	1043.99	
5	555.84	
2	923.53	
4	3400.62	877.26

Figure 36 As you drag the fill handle, a gray border indicates the source and destination cell(s).

⊃	Mar	
2	877.26	877.26
4	1043.99	1043.99
5	555.84	555.84
2	923.53	923.53
4	3400.62	

Figure 37 The destination cells fill with the contents of the source cells.

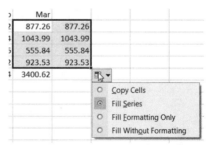

⊃	Mar	
2	877.26	877.26
1	1043.99	1043.99
5	555.84	555.84
2	923.53	923.53
1	3400.62	

- ○ Copy Cells
- ◉ Fill Series
- ○ Fill Formatting Only
- ○ Fill Without Formatting

Figure 38 Use the Fill Options pop-up menu to set options for the filled in cells.

Figure 39
The Fill menu on the Home tab's Editing group.

	Mar
2	877.26
4	1043.99
5	555.84
2	923.53
4	3400.62

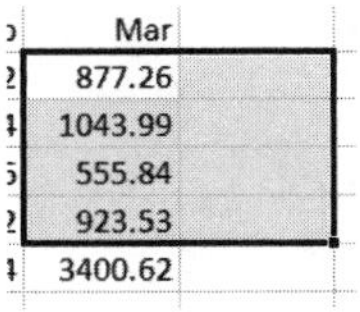

Figure 40
To use a Fill command, begin by selecting the source and destination cells.

The Fill Commands

The Fill commands work a lot like the fill handle in that they copy information to adjacent cells. But rather than dragging to copy, you select the source and destination cells at the same time and then use a Fill command to complete the copy. The Fill menu in the Home tab's Editing group (**Figure 39**) offers several options for copying to adjacent selected cells:

◆ **Down** copies the contents of the top cell(s) in the selection to the selected cells beneath it.

◆ **Right** copies the contents of the left cell(s) in the selection to the selected cells to the right of it.

◆ **Up** copies the contents of the bottom cell(s) in the selection to the selected cells above it.

◆ **Left** copies the contents of the right cell(s) in the selection to the selected cells to the left of it.

To copy with the Fill command

1. Select the cell(s) you want to copy along with the adjacent destination cell(s) (**Figure 40**).

2. Choose the appropriate command from the Fill menu in the Editing group (**Figure 39**): Down, Right, Up, Left. The cells are filled as specified (**Figure 37**).

   or

   To fill down, press Ctrl D or to fill right, press Ctrl R.

✔ Tip

■ You must select both the source and destination cells when using a Fill command. If you select just the destination cells, Excel won't copy the correct cells.

COPYING WITH THE FILL COMMAND

Series & AutoFill

A *series* is a sequence of cells that forms a logical progression. Excel's AutoFill feature can generate a series of numbers, months, days, dates, and quarters.

To create a series with the fill handle

1. Enter the first item of the series in a cell (**Figure 41**). Be sure to complete the entry by pressing Enter or clicking the Enter button on the formula bar.

2. Position your mouse pointer on the fill handle and drag. All the cells that will be part of the series are surrounded by a gray border and a yellow box indicates the value that will be in the last cell in the range (**Figure 42**).

3. Release the mouse button to complete the series (**Figure 43**).

To create a series with the Series command

1. Enter the first item of the series in a cell (**Figure 41**).

2. Select all cells that will be part of the series, including the first cell (**Figure 44**).

3. Choose Home > Editing > Fill > Series (**Figure 39**).

4. In the Series dialog that appears (**Figure 45**), select the AutoFill option.

5. Click OK to complete the series (**Figure 43**).

✔ Tip

■ To generate a series that skips values, enter the first two values of the series in adjoining cells, then use the fill handle or Series command to create the series, including both cells as part of the source (**Figures 46 and 47**).

Figure 41 To create an AutoFill series, start by entering the first value in a cell.

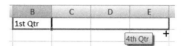

Figure 42 Drag the fill handle to include all cells that will be part of the series.

Figure 43 Excel creates the series automatically.

Figure 44 To use the Series command, select the source and destination cells.

Figure 45 Select the AutoFill option in the Series dialog.

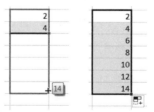

Figures 46 & 47 Enter the first two values in the series, then select both cells and drag the fill handle (left) to complete the series (right).

CREATING AN AUTOFILL SERIES

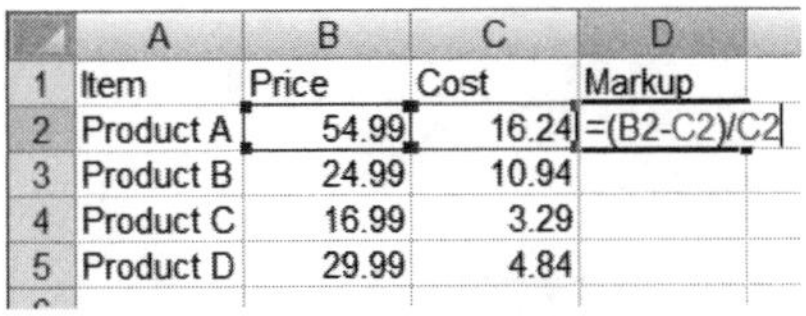

	A	B	C	D
1	Item	Price	Cost	Markup
2	Product A	54.99	16.24	=(B2-C2)/C2
3	Product B	24.99	10.94	
4	Product C	16.99	3.29	
5	Product D	29.99	4.84	

Figure 48 Here's a formula to calculate markup percentage. If the company has 763 products, would you want to write the same basic formula 762 more times? Of course not!

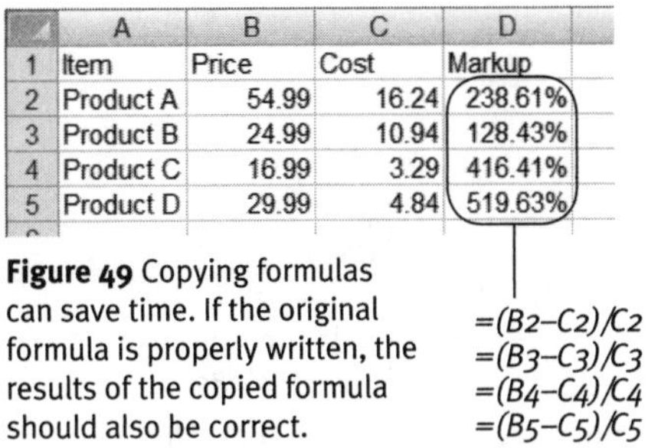

	A	B	C	D
1	Item	Price	Cost	Markup
2	Product A	54.99	16.24	238.61%
3	Product B	24.99	10.94	128.43%
4	Product C	16.99	3.29	416.41%
5	Product D	29.99	4.84	519.63%

Figure 49 Copying formulas can save time. If the original formula is properly written, the results of the copied formula should also be correct.

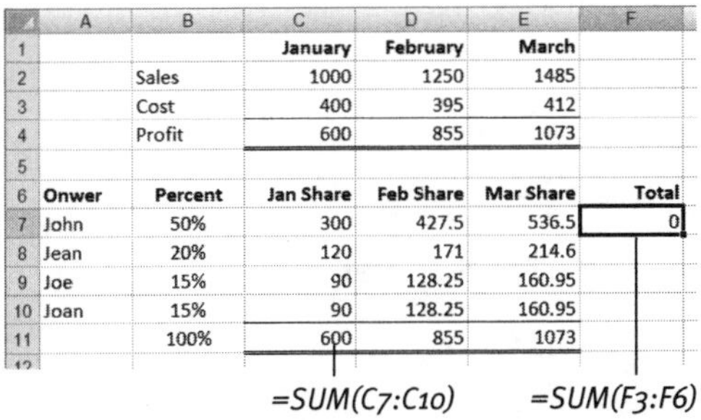

$=(B2–C2)/C2$
$=(B3–C3)/C3$
$=(B4–C4)/C4$
$=(B5–C5)/C5$

	A	B	C	D	E	F
1			January	February	March	
2		Sales	1000	1250	1485	
3		Cost	400	395	412	
4		Profit	600	855	1073	
5						
6	Onwer	Percent	Jan Share	Feb Share	Mar Share	Total
7	John	50%	300	427.5	536.5	0
8	Jean	20%	120	171	214.6	
9	Joe	15%	90	128.25	160.95	
10	Joan	15%	90	128.25	160.95	
11		100%	600	855	1073	

$=SUM(C7:C10)$ $=SUM(F3:F6)$

Figure 50 In this illustration, the formula in cell *C11* was copied to cell *F7*. This doesn't work because the two cells don't add up similar ranges. The formula in cell *F7* would have to be rewritten from scratch. It could then be copied to *F8* through *F10*. (I tell you about the SUM function in **Chapter 5**.)

Copying Formulas

You copy a cell containing a formula the same way you copy any other cell in Excel: with the Copy and Paste commands, with the fill handle, or with a Fill command. These methods are discussed earlier in this chapter.

Generally speaking, Excel does not make an exact copy of a formula. Instead, it copies the formula based on the kinds of references used within it. If relative references are used, Excel changes them based on the location of the destination cell in relation to the source cell. You can see an example of this in **Figures 48** and **49**.

✔ Tips

■ You'll find it much quicker to copy formulas rather than to write each and every formula from scratch.

■ Not all formulas can be copied with accurate results. For example, you can't copy a formula that sums up a column of numbers to a cell that should represent a sum of cells in a row (**Figure 50**).

■ I explain the various types of cell references—relative, absolute, and mixed—beginning on the next page.

Relative vs. Absolute Cell References

There are two primary types of cell references:

- A *relative cell reference* is the address of a cell relative to the cell the reference is in. For example, a reference to cell *B1* in cell *B3*, tells Excel to look at the cell two cells above *B3*. Most of the references you use in Excel are relative references.
- An *absolute cell reference* is the exact location of a cell. To indicate an absolute reference, enter a dollar sign ($) in front of the column letter(s) and row number(s) of the reference. An absolute reference to cell *B1*, for example, would be written *$B$1*.

As **Figures 51** and **52** illustrate, relative cell references change when you copy them to other cells. Although in many cases, you might want the references to change, sometimes you don't. That's when you use absolute references **(Figures 53** and **54)**.

✔ Tips

- Here's a trick for remembering the meaning of the notation for absolute cell references: in your mind, replace the dollar sign with the word *always*. Then you'll read *$B$1* as *always B always 1—always B1*!
- If you're having trouble understanding how these two kinds of references work and differ, don't worry. This is one of the most difficult spreadsheet concepts you'll encounter. Try creating a worksheet like the one illustrated on this page and working your way through the figures one at a time. Pay close attention to how Excel copies the formulas you write!

	A	B	C
1	Sales	1000	
2	Cost	400	
3	Profit	600	
4			
5	**Owner**	**Percent**	**Share**
6	John	50%	=B3*B6
7	Jean	20%	
8	Joe	15%	
9	Joan	15%	

Figure 51 This formula correctly calculates a partner's share of profit.

	A	B	C
1	Sales	1000	
2	Cost	400	
3	Profit	600	
4			
5	**Owner**	**Percent**	**Share**
6	John	50%	300
7	Jean	20%	0
8	Joe	15%	#VALUE!
9	Joan	15%	0.075

*=B3*B6*
*=B4*B7*
*=B5*B8*
*=B6*B9*

Figure 52 But when the formula is copied for the other partners, the relative reference to cell *B3* is changed, causing incorrect results and an error message!

	A	B	C
1	Sales	1000	
2	Cost	400	
3	Profit	600	
4			
5	**Owner**	**Percent**	**Share**
6	John	50%	=$B$3*B6
7	Jean	20%	0
8	Joe	15%	#VALUE!
9	Joan	15%	0.075

Figure 53 Rewrite the original formula so it includes an absolute reference to cell *B3*, which all of the formulas must reference.

	A	B	C
1	Sales	1000	
2	Cost	400	
3	Profit	600	
4			
5	**Owner**	**Percent**	**Share**
6	John	50%	300
7	Jean	20%	120
8	Joe	15%	90
9	Joan	15%	90

*=$B$3*B6*
*=$B$3*B7*
*=$B$3*B8*
*=$B$3*B9*

Figure 54 When the formula is copied for the other partners, only the relative reference (to the percentages) changes. The results are correct.

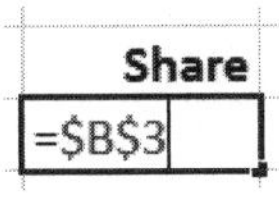

Share

=$B$3

Figure 55
Type in the dollar signs as needed when you enter an absolute cell reference.

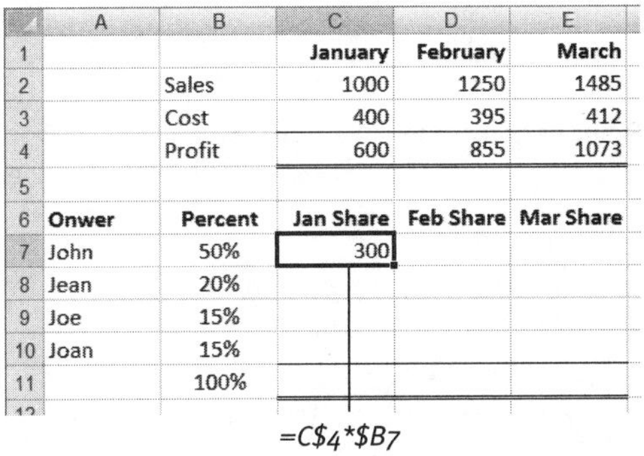

	A	B	C	D	E
1			January	February	March
2		Sales	1000	1250	1485
3		Cost	400	395	412
4		Profit	600	855	1073
5					
6	Onwer	Percent	Jan Share	Feb Share	Mar Share
7	John	50%	300		
8	Jean	20%			
9	Joe	15%			
10	Joan	15%			
11		100%			
12					

=C$4*$B7

Figure 56 The formula in cell *C7* includes two different kinds of mixed references. It can be copied to cells *C8* through *C10* and *C7* through *E10* for correct results in all cells. Try it and see for yourself!

To include an absolute cell reference in a formula

1. Enter the formula by typing or clicking as discussed in **Chapter 2**.

2. Insert a dollar sign before the column and row references for the cell reference you want to make absolute (**Figure 55**).

3. Complete the entry by pressing (Enter) or clicking the Enter button on the formula bar.

✔ Tips

■ You can edit an existing formula to include absolute references by inserting dollar signs where needed. I tell you how to edit cell contents earlier in this chapter.

■ Do not use a dollar sign in a formula to indicate currency formatting. I tell you how to apply formatting to cell contents, including currency format, in **Chapter 6**.

Mixed References

Once you've mastered the concept of relative vs. absolute cell references, consider another type of reference: a *mixed cell reference*.

In a mixed cell reference, either the column or row reference is absolute while the other reference remains relative. Thus, you can use cell references like *A$1* or *$A1*. Use this when a column reference must remain constant but a row reference changes or vice versa. **Figure 56** shows a good example.

USING ABSOLUTE CELL REFERENCES

Moving Cells

Excel offers two ways to move the contents of one cell to another: the Cut and Paste commands and dragging the border of a selection. Either way, Excel moves the contents of the cell.

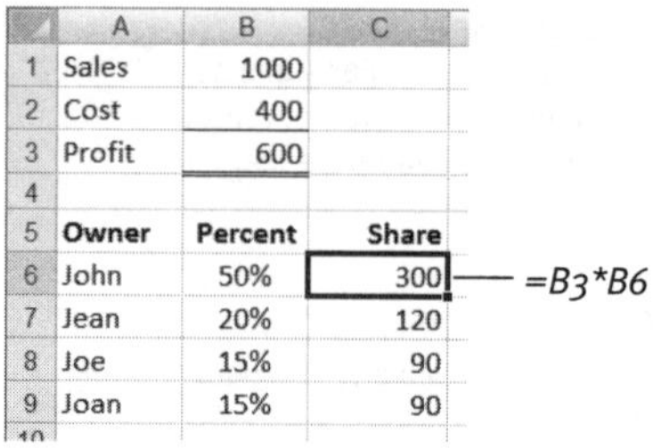
A B C
1 Sales 1000
2 Cost 400
3 Profit 600
4
5 Owner Percent Share
6 John 50% 300
7 Jean 20% 120
8 Joe 15% 90
9 Joan 15% 90
=B3*B6

Figure 57 Note the formula in cell *C6*.

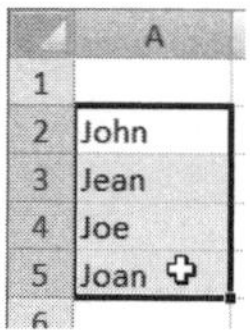

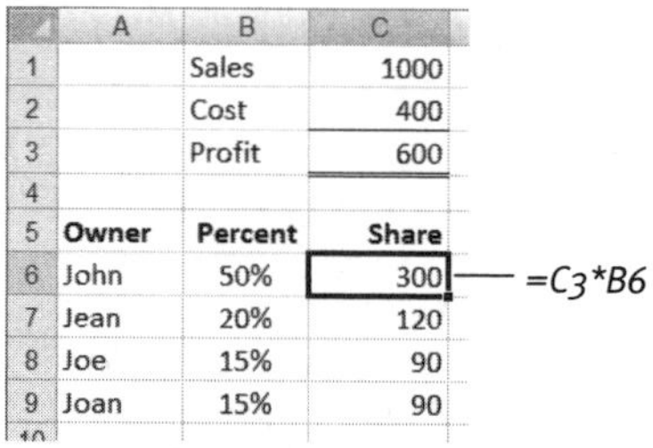
A B C
1 Sales 1000
2 Cost 400
3 Profit 600
4
5 Owner Percent Share
6 John 50% 300
7 Jean 20% 120
8 Joe 15% 90
9 Joan 15% 90
=C3*B6

Figure 58 See how it changes when one of the cells it references moves?

✔ Tip

- When you move a cell, Excel searches the worksheet for any cells that contain references to it and changes the references to reflect the cell's new location (**Figures 57** and **58**).

To move with Cut & Paste

1. Select the cell(s) you want to move (**Figure 59**).
2. Click Home > Clipboard > Cut (**Figure 26**) or press Ctrl X. An animated marquee appears around the selection (**Figure 60**).
3. Select the cell(s) in which you want to paste the selection (**Figure 61**).
4. Click Home > Clipboard > Paste (**Figure 26**) or press Ctrl V or Enter. The cell contents are moved to the new location (**Figure 62**).

✔ Tip

- Consult the tips beneath the section titled "To copy with Copy & Paste" for Paste command warnings and tips.

A
1
2 John
3 Jean
4 Joe
5 Joan

Figure 59
Select the cell(s).

A
1
2 John
3 Jean
4 Joe
5 Joan

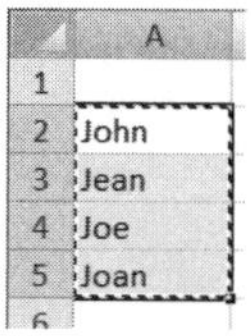

Figure 60
When you use the Cut command, a marquee appears around the selection but the selected cells do not disappear.

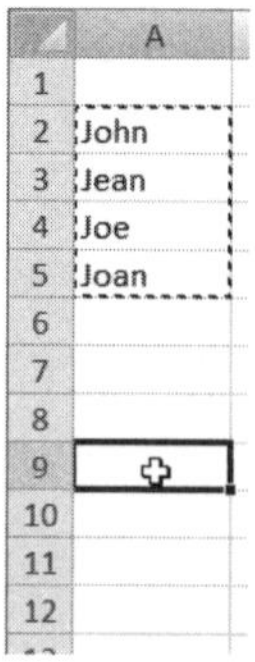
A
1
2 John
3 Jean
4 Joe
5 Joan
6
7
8
9
10
11
12

Figure 61
Select the destination cell(s).

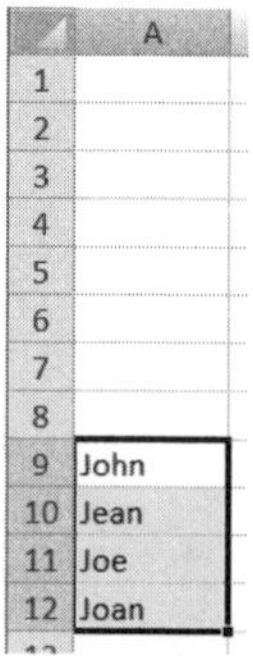
A
1
2
3
4
5
6
7
8
9 John
10 Jean
11 Joe
12 Joan

Figure 62
When you use the Paste command, the selection moves.

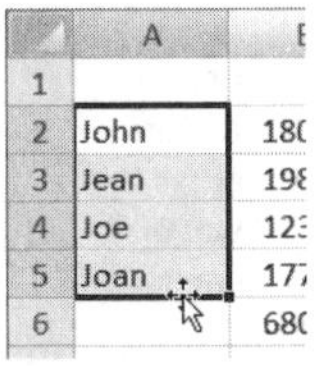

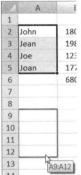

Figure 63
When you move the mouse pointer onto the border of a selection, a four-headed arrow appears beneath it.

Figure 64
As you drag, a gray border moves along with the mouse pointer.

Figure 65 Excel warns you when you will overwrite cells with a selection you drag.

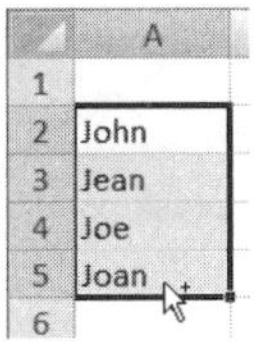

Figure 66
Hold down ⌈Ctrl⌉ to copy a selection by dragging it. A plus sign appears beside the mouse pointer.

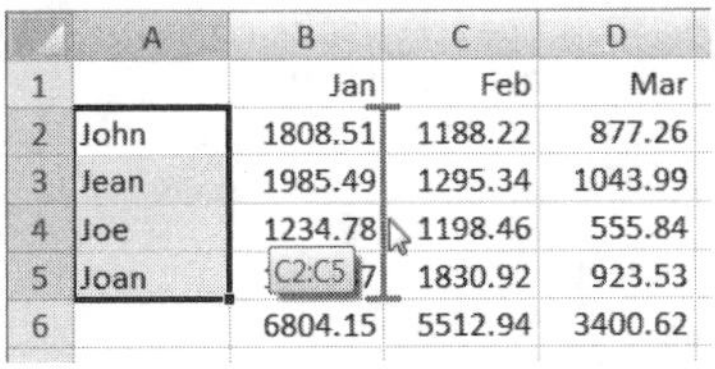

Figure 67 Hold down ⌈Shift⌉ while dragging to insert a selection between other cells. A bar indicates where the cells will be inserted.

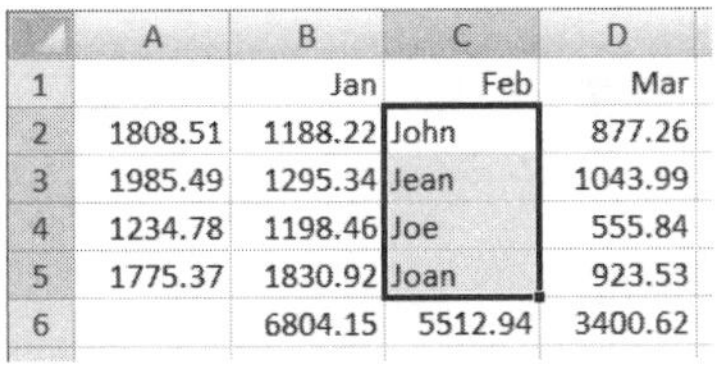

Figure 68
This makes it possible to rearrange the cells in a worksheet.

To move with drag & drop

1. Select the cell(s) you want to move (**Figure 59**).

2. Position the mouse pointer on the border of the selection. A four-headed arrow appears beneath the mouse pointer (**Figure 63**).

3. Press the mouse button down and drag toward the new location. As you move the mouse, a gray border the same shape as the selection moves along with it and a box indicates the range where the cells will move (**Figure 64**).

4. Release the mouse button. The selection moves to its new location (**Figure 62**).

✔ Tips

- If you try to drag a selection to cells already containing information, Excel warns you with a dialog like the one in **Figure 65**. If you click OK to complete the move, the destination cells will be overwritten with the contents of the cells you are moving.

- To copy using drag and drop, hold down ⌈Ctrl⌉ as you press the mouse button down. The mouse pointer turns into an arrow with a tiny plus sign (+) beside it (**Figure 66**). When you release the mouse button, the selection is copied.

- To move and insert cells using drag and drop, hold down ⌈Shift⌉ as you press the mouse button down. As you drag, a gray bar moves along with the mouse pointer and a yellow box indicates where the cells will be inserted (**Figure 67**). When you release the mouse button, the cells are inserted (**Figure 68**).

The Office Clipboard

The Office Clipboard enables you to "collect and paste" multiple items. You simply display the Office Clipboard task pane, then copy text or objects as usual. But instead of the Clipboard contents being replaced each time you use the Copy or Cut command, all items are stored on the Office Clipboard (**Figure 69**). You can then paste any of the items on the Office Clipboard into your Excel document.

✔ Tips

- The Office Clipboard works with all Microsoft Office applications—not just Excel—so you can store items from different types of Office documents.

- This feature was referred to as *Collect and Paste* in previous versions of Microsoft Office for Windows.

To display the Office Clipboard

Click the Dialog Box Launcher button in the bottom-right corner of the Home tab's Clipboard group (**Figure 26**). The Office Clipboard appears as a task pane beside the document window (**Figure 70**).

To add an item to the Office Clipboard

1. If necessary, display the Office Clipboard (**Figure 70**).

2. Select the cells or object you want to copy (**Figure 59**).

3. Click Home > Clipboard > Copy (**Figure 26**) or press (Ctrl)(C). The selection appears on the Office Clipboard (**Figure 71**).

Figure 69
The Clipboard task pane with four items: a picture from Word, an Excel chart, some Excel worksheet cells, and some text from Word.

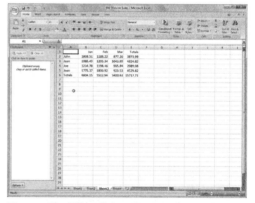

Figure 70 The Office Clipboard appears as a task pane.

Figure 71
The cells you selected are added to the Clipboard.

Figure 72
Select the top-left cell where you want to paste the item.

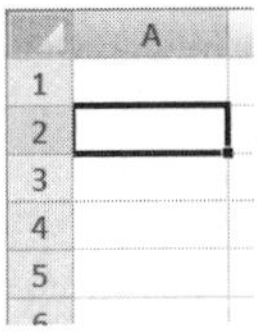

Figure 73
When you point to or click an item, a border appears around it.

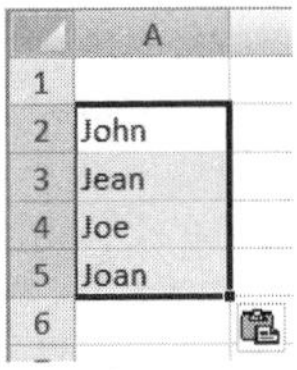

Figure 74
The item you pasted appears in the document.

Figure 75
You can access a pop-up menu like this one for each item on the Office Clipboard.

Figure 76
Choosing Delete for an item removes it from the Office Clipboard.

To use Office Clipboard items

1. If necessary, display the Office Clipboard.

2. In the document window, select the top-left cell where you want to paste the Office Clipboard item (**Figure 72**).

3. In the Office Clipboard task pane, click the item you want to paste into the document (**Figure 73**).

Or

1. If necessary, display the Office Clipboard.

2. Drag the item you want to use from the Office Clipboard into the document window.

The item you pasted or dragged appears in the document window (**Figure 74**).

✔ Tip

■ Not all items can be pasted into worksheet cells. Graphics, for example, are pasted on top of the worksheet layer. Graphic objects are covered in **Chapter 7**.

To remove Office Clipboard items

1. In the Office Clipboard window, point to the item you want to remove (**Figure 73**). A blue border appears around it and a pop-up menu button appears beside it.

2. Click the pop-up menu button to display a menu of two options (**Figure 75**).

3. Choose Delete. The item is removed from the Office Clipboard (**Figure 76**).

Or

Click the Clear All button at the top of the Office Clipboard (**Figure 69**) to remove all items.

Undoing & Redoing Actions

Excel's Quick Access toolbar (**Figure 77**) offers buttons and menus that enable you to undo or redo the last things you did.

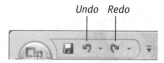

Undo Redo

Figure 77 The Undo and Redo buttons on the Quick Access toolbar.

◆ **Undo** reverses your last action. Excel supports multiple levels of undo, enabling you to reverse more than just the very last action.

◆ **Redo** reverses the Undo command. This command is only available if the last thing you did was use the Undo command.

✔ Tip

■ Think of the Undo command as the Oops command—anytime you say "Oops," you'll probably want to use it.

To undo the last action

Click the Undo button (**Figure 77**) or press [Ctrl][Z].

To undo multiple actions

Click the Undo button (**Figure 77**) or press [Ctrl][Z] repeatedly.

Or

1. Click the triangle beside the Undo button to display a pop-up menu of recent actions.

2. Drag down to select all the actions that you want to undo (**Figure 78**).

3. Release the mouse button to undo all selected actions.

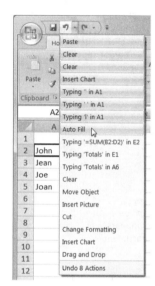

Figure 78
Use the Undo button's menu to select multiple actions to undo.

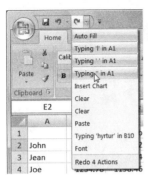

Figure 79
You can also use the Redo button's menu to select multiple actions to redo.

To reverse the last undo

Click the Redo button (**Figure 77**) or press Ctrl Y.

To reverse multiple undos

Click the Redo button (**Figure 77**) or press Ctrl Y repeatedly.

Or

1. Click the triangle beside the Redo button on the Standard toolbar to display a drop-down list of recently undone actions.

2. Drag down to select all the actions that you want to redo (**Figure 79**).

3. Release the mouse button to reverse all selected undos.

Working with Files

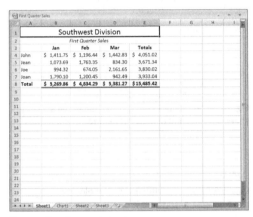

Figure 1 Here's a worksheet.

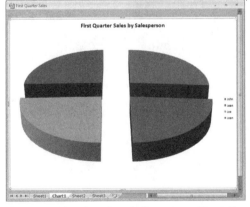

Figure 2 Here's a chart sheet in the same workbook file.

Excel Files

Microsoft Excel document files are called *workbooks*:

◆ Each workbook file includes multiple sheets.

◆ Workbook files appear in document windows.

◆ Workbook files can be saved on disk and reopened for editing and printing.

This chapter, explains how to perform a variety of tasks with workbook sheets, windows, and files.

Workbook Sheets

Excel workbook files can include many individual *sheets*, which are like pages in the workbook. Each workbook, by default, includes three sheets named *Sheet1* through *Sheet3*.

There are two kinds of sheets:

◆ A *worksheet* (**Figure 1**) is for entering information and performing calculations. You can also embed charts in a worksheet.

◆ A *chart sheet* (**Figure 2**) is for creating charts that aren't embedded in a worksheet.

✔ Tips

■ Use the multiple sheet capabilities of workbook files to keep sheets for the same project together. This is an excellent way to organize related work.

■ I tell you about worksheets throughout this book and about charts and chart sheets in **Chapter 8**.

To switch from one sheet to another

Click the sheet tab at the bottom of the workbook window (**Figure 3**) for the sheet you want.

Or

Press [Ctrl] [Page Up] or [Ctrl] [Page Down] to scroll through all of the sheets in a workbook, one at a time.

✔ Tips

- If the sheet tab for the sheet you want is not displayed, use the tab scrolling buttons (**Figure 4**) to scroll through the sheet tabs.

- To display more or fewer sheet tabs, drag the tab split box (**Figure 5**) to increase or decrease the size of the sheet tab area. As you change the size of the sheet tab area, you'll also change the size of the horizontal scroll bar at the bottom of the workbook window.

To select multiple sheets

1. Click the sheet tab for the first sheet you want to select.

2. Hold down [Ctrl] and click the sheet tab(s) for the other sheet(s) you want to select. The sheet tabs for each sheet you include in the selection turn white (**Figure 6**).

✔ Tips

- To select multiple adjacent sheets, click the sheet tab for the first sheet, then hold down [Shift] and click on the sheet tab for the last sheet you want to select. All sheet tabs in between also become selected.

- Selecting multiple sheets makes it quick and easy to print, delete, edit, format, or perform other tasks with more than one sheet at a time.

Figure 3 Use sheet tabs to move from sheet to sheet in a workbook. *New sheet button*

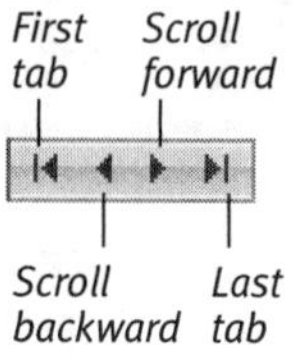

First tab *Scroll forward*

Figure 4
Use the sheet tab scrolling buttons to view sheet tabs that are not displayed.

Scroll backward *Last tab*

Figure 5 Drag the tab split box to change the size of the sheet tab area and display more or fewer sheet tabs.

Figure 6 To select multiple sheets, hold down [Ctrl] while clicking each sheet tab.

Figure 7 Begin by selecting the sheet you want the new sheet to be inserted before.

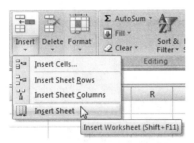

Figure 8 Choose Insert Sheet from the Insert menu.

Figure 9 An inserted worksheet.

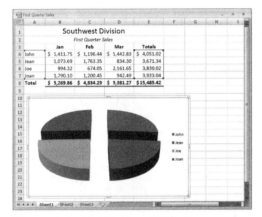

Figure 10 A chart inserted in a worksheet.

Figure 11 The Move Chart dialog lets you insert the chart as a new sheet.

Figure 12 An inserted chart sheet.

To insert a worksheet

1. Click the tab for the sheet you want to insert a new sheet before (**Figure 7**).

2. Click the New sheet button on the right end of the row of sheet tabs (**Figure 3**), choose Home > Cells > Insert > Insert Sheet (**Figure 8**), or press Shift F11.

   A new worksheet is inserted before the one you originally selected (**Figure 9**).

✔ Tip

- By default, the new worksheet is named with the word *Sheet* followed by a number. I tell you how to rename sheets on the next page.

To insert a chart sheet

1. Follow the instructions in Chapter 8 to insert a chart in a worksheet (**Figure 10**).

2. Click the chart to select it.

3. Click Chart Tools > Design > Location > Move Chart to display the Move Chart dialog (**Figure 11**).

4. Select the New sheet option and enter a name for the chart sheet.

5. Click OK.

   A new chart sheet with the name you provided is inserted in the workbook file (**Figure 12**).

To delete a sheet

1. Click the sheet tab for the sheet you want to delete to select it.

2. Choose Home > Cells > Delete > Delete Sheet (**Figure 13**).

3. A warning dialog (**Figure 14**) appears. Click Delete to confirm that you want to delete the sheet.

✔ Tips

- As the dialog in **Figure 14** warns, sheets are permanently deleted. That means even the Undo command won't get a deleted sheet back.

- If another cell in the workbook contains a reference to a cell on the sheet you've deleted, that cell will display a #REF! error message. The formula in that cell will need to be rewritten.

To rename a sheet

1. Click the sheet tab for the sheet you want to rename to select it.

2. Choose Home > Cells > Format > Rename Sheet (**Figure 15**) or double-click the sheet tab.

3. The sheet tab becomes highlighted (**Figure 16**). Enter a new name for the sheet (**Figure 17**) and press [Enter] to save it.

   The sheet tab displays the new name (**Figure 18**).

✔ Tip

- The appearance of the Format menu (**Figure 15**) varies depending on the type of sheet.

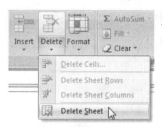

Figure 13 The Delete menu.

Figure 14 When you delete a sheet, Excel warns you that the sheet may contain data.

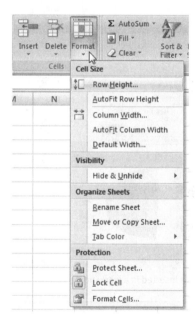

Figure 15 The Format menu.

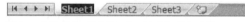

Figure 16 Double-click the sheet tab to select its name.

Figure 17 Enter a new name for the sheet.

Figure 18 Press [Enter] to save the new name.

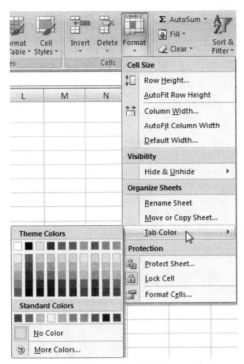

Figure 19 Use the Tab Color palette to specify a color for a sheet tab.

Figure 20 When the tab is selected, it is white but shaded at the bottom with the tab color you specified.

Figure 21 When a tab is not selected, its name appears in the color you specified.

To change a tab's color

1. Click the sheet tab for which you want to change the color.

2. Choose Home > Cells > Format > Tab Color to display a palette of theme and standard colors (**Figure 19**).

3. Select the desired color.

   The tab color changes as follows:

   ▲ When the tab is selected, it is white but shaded at the bottom with the tab color you specified (**Figure 20**).

   ▲ When the tab is not selected, it appears in the color you specified (**Figure 21**).

✔ Tips

- You can use this feature to "color code" workbook sheets. This can make sheets easier to find.

- You can change the color of more than one tab at a time. Simply follow the instructions earlier in this chapter to select all the tabs you want to change, then follow steps 2 and 3 above.

- To remove a color from a tab sheet, follow the instructions above, but select No Color in step 3.

CHANGING TAB COLORS

To hide a sheet

1. Select the sheet(s) you want to hide (**Figure 18**).

2. Choose Home > Cells > Format > Hide & Unhide > Hide Sheet (**Figure 22**).

   The sheet and its sheet tab disappear (**Figure 23**), just as if it had been deleted. But don't worry, the sheet still exists in the workbook file.

✔ Tips

- You cannot hide a sheet if it is the only sheet in a workbook.

- Don't confuse the Hide Sheet command with the Hide command on the View tab's Window group. These commands do two different things! I tell you about the View tab's Hide command later in this chapter.

To unhide a sheet

1. Choose Home > Cells > Format > Hide & Unhide > Unhide Sheet (**Figure 22**).

2. In the Unhide dialog that appears (**Figure 24**), select the sheet you want to unhide.

3. Click OK. The sheet and its sheet tab reappear.

✔ Tips

- You can only unhide one sheet at a time.

- If the Unhide command is gray, no sheets are hidden.

- Don't confuse the Unhide Sheet command with the Unhide command on the View tab's Window group. I tell you about the View tab's Unhide command later in this chapter.

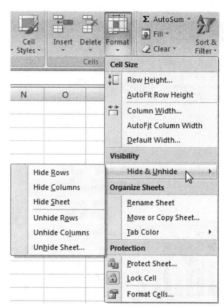

Figure 22 The Hide & Unhide submenu on the Format menu.

Figure 23 When you hide a sheet, its tab disappears.

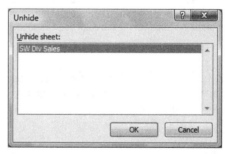

Figure 24 The Unhide dialog lists all hidden sheets.

Figure 25 Use the Move or Copy dialog to pick a destination for the selected sheet(s) and tell Excel to copy them rather than move

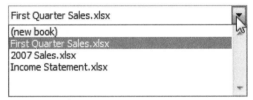

Figure 26 The To book drop-down list includes all of the currently open workbook files.

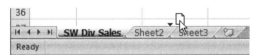

Figure 27 You can also drag a sheet tab to move it ...

Figure 28 ... or hold down Ctrl while dragging a sheet tab to copy it.

To move or copy a sheet

1. Select the tab(s) for the sheet(s) you want to move or copy.

2. Choose Home > Cells > Format > Move or Copy Sheet (**Figure 15**). The Move or Copy dialog appears (**Figure 25**).

3. Use the To book drop-down list (**Figure 26**) to choose the workbook you want to move or copy the sheet(s) to.

4. Use the Before sheet list to choose the sheet you want the sheet(s) to be copied before.

5. If you want to copy or duplicate the sheet rather than move it, turn on the Create a copy check box.

6. Click OK.

✔ Tips

- To move or copy sheets to another workbook, make sure that workbook is open (but not active) before you choose the Move or Copy Sheet command. Otherwise, it will not be listed in the To book drop-down list (**Figure 26**).

- If you choose (new book) from the To book drop-down list (**Figure 26**), Excel creates an empty workbook file and places the selected sheet(s) into it.

- You can use the Move or Copy Sheet command to change the order of sheets in a workbook. Just make sure the current workbook is selected in the To book drop-down list (**Figure 26**). Then select the appropriate sheet from the Before sheet scrolling list or select (move to end).

- You can also move or copy a sheet by dragging. To move the sheet, drag the sheet tab to the new position (**Figure 27**). To copy the sheet, hold down Ctrl while dragging the sheet tab (**Figure 28**).

MOVING & COPYING SHEETS

Workbook Windows

Like most Windows programs, Excel allows you to have more than one document window open at a time. You can manipulate Excel's workbook windows a number of ways:

◆ Activate a window so you can work with its contents.

◆ Create a new window for a workbook so you can see two sheets from the same workbook at once.

◆ Arrange windows so you can see and work with more than one at a time.

◆ Close and hide windows to get them out of the way.

◆ Change a window's magnification so you can see more of its contents or see its contents more clearly.

◆ Split a window so you can see and work with two or more parts of a sheet at a time.

✔ Tip

■ I explain how to create a new workbook in **Chapter 2** and how to open an existing workbook later in this chapter.

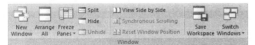

Figure 29 The View tab's Window group offers commands for working with—you guessed it—windows.

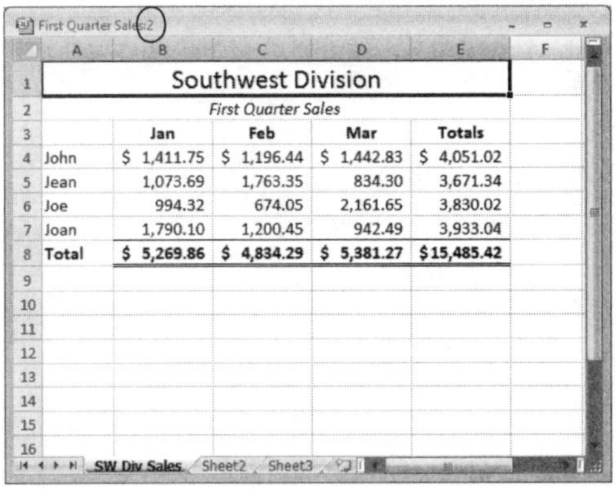

	A	B	C	D	E	F
1			Southwest Division			
2			First Quarter Sales			
3			Jan	Feb	Mar	Totals
4	John	$ 1,411.75	$ 1,196.44	$ 1,442.83	$ 4,051.02	
5	Jean	1,073.69	1,763.35	834.30	3,671.34	
6	Joe	994.32	674.05	2,161.65	3,830.02	
7	Joan	1,790.10	1,200.45	942.49	3,933.04	
8	Total	$ 5,269.86	$ 4,834.29	$ 5,381.27	$15,485.42	

Figure 30 When you open more than one window for a workbook file, the window number appears in the title bar ...

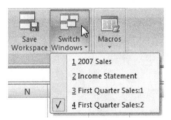

Figure 31 ... and both windows are listed on the Switch Windows menu.

To create a new window

1. Activate the workbook for which you want to create another window.

2. Click View > Window > New Window (**Figure 29**).

   A new window for that workbook appears (**Figure 30**) and the new window's name appears at the bottom of the Switch Windows menu (**Figure 31**).

✔ Tip

■ If more than one window is open for a workbook and you close one of them, the workbook does not close—just that window. I tell you about closing windows later in this section.

To activate another window

Choose the name of the window you want to make active from the list of open windows at the bottom of the Switch Windows menu on the View tab (**Figure 31**).

To arrange windows

1. Click View > Window > Arrange All (**Figure 29**).

2. In the Arrange Windows dialog that appears (**Figure 32**), select an Arrange option. **Figures 33** through **36** illustrate all of them.

3. To arrange only the windows of the active workbook, turn on the Windows of active workbook check box.

4. Click OK.

✔ Tips

■ To work with one of the arranged windows, click in it to make it active.

■ The window with the Excel document icon to the left of the document name is the active window.

■ To make one of the arranged windows full size again, click on it to make it active and then click the window's Maximize button. The window fills the screen while the other windows remain arranged behind it. Click the Restore window button to shrink it back down to its arranged size.

Figure 32
The Arrange Windows dialog.

Figure 33 Tiled windows.

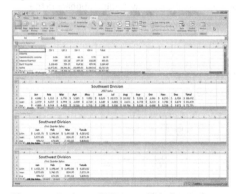

Figure 34 Horizontally arranged windows.

Figure 35 Vertically arranged windows.

Figure 36 Cascading windows.

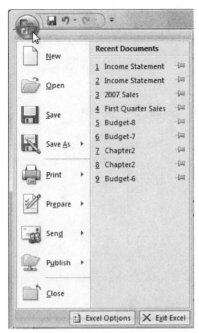

Figure 37 The Microsoft Office menu.

Figure 38 When you close a document with unsaved changes, Excel gives you a chance to save it.

Figure 39 Use the Unhide dialog to select the window you want to unhide.

To close a window

Click the window's close button or choose Microsoft Office > Close (**Figure 37**).

✔ Tip

- If the file you are closing has unsaved changes, Excel warns you (**Figure 38**). Click Yes to save changes. I tell you about saving files later in this chapter.

To hide a window

1. Activate the window you want to hide.

2. Click View > Window > Hide (**Figure 29**). The window disappears from your screen and from the Switch Windows menu.

✔ Tips

- Hiding a window is not the same as closing it. A hidden window remains open, even though it is not listed at the bottom of the Switch Windows menu.

- Hiding a window is not the same as hiding a sheet in a workbook. I tell you about hiding sheets earlier in this chapter.

To unhide a window

1. Click View > Window > Unhide (**Figure 29**).

2. In the Unhide dialog that appears (**Figure 39**), choose the window you want to unhide.

3. Click OK. The window appears.

✔ Tip

- If the Unhide button is gray (**Figures 29**), no windows are hidden.

To change a window's magnification

1. Choose View > Zoom > Zoom (**Figure 40**).

2. In the Zoom dialog that appears (**Figure 41**), select the option button for the magnification you want.

3. Click OK.

Or

Drag the slider in the Zoom control on the bottom-right corner of the application window (**Figure 42**).

✔ Tips

■ To zoom selected cells so they fill the window, select the Fit selection option button in the Zoom dialog (**Figure 41**) or click View > Zoom > Zoom to Selection (**Figure 40**).

■ You can enter a custom magnification in the Zoom dialog (**Figure 41**) by selecting the Custom option button and entering a value of your choice.

■ To return a window's zoom percentage back to 100%, click View > Zoom > 100% (**Figure 40**).

■ Zooming the window using techniques discussed here does not affect the way a worksheet will print.

■ A "zoomed" window's sheet works just like any other worksheet.

■ When you save a workbook, the magnification settings of its sheets are saved. When you reopen the workbook, the sheets appear with the last used zoom magnification.

Figure 40
The View tab's
Zoom group.

Figure 41
Use the Zoom
dialog to set
the window's
magnification.

Figure 42 You can also change the magnification by dragging the slider on the Zoom control.

CHANGING WINDOW MAGNIFICATION

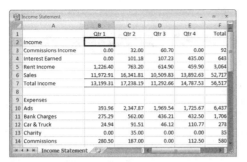

Figure 43 Select the cell below and to the right of where you want the split to occur.

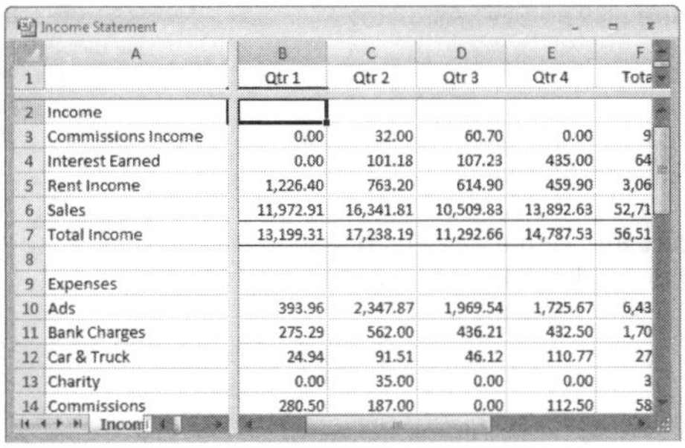

Figure 44 When you choose the Split command, the window splits.

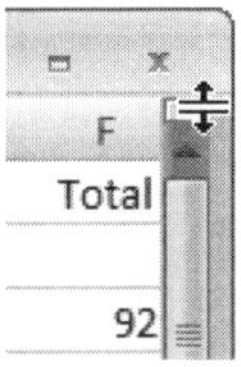

Figure 45
Position the mouse pointer on the split bar at the end of the scroll bar.

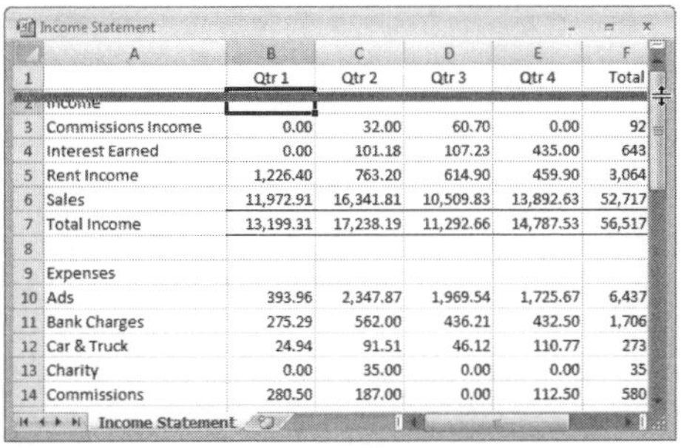

Figure 46 Drag the split bar into the window.

To split a window

1. Select the cell immediately below and to the right of where you want the split(s) to occur (**Figure 43**).

2. Click View > Window > Split (**Figure 29**). The window splits at the location you specified (**Figure 44**).

Or

1. Position the mouse pointer on the split bar at the top of the vertical scroll bar or right end of the horizontal scroll bar. The mouse pointer turns into a double line with arrows coming out of it (**Figure 45**).

2. Press the mouse button down and drag. A split bar moves along with the mouse pointer (**Figure 46**).

3. Release the mouse button. The window splits at the bar (**Figure 47**).

To adjust the size of panes

1. Position the mouse pointer on a split bar.

2. Press the mouse button down and drag until the split bar is in the desired position.

3. Release the mouse button. The window split moves.

To remove a window split

Click View > Window > Split or double-click a split bar.

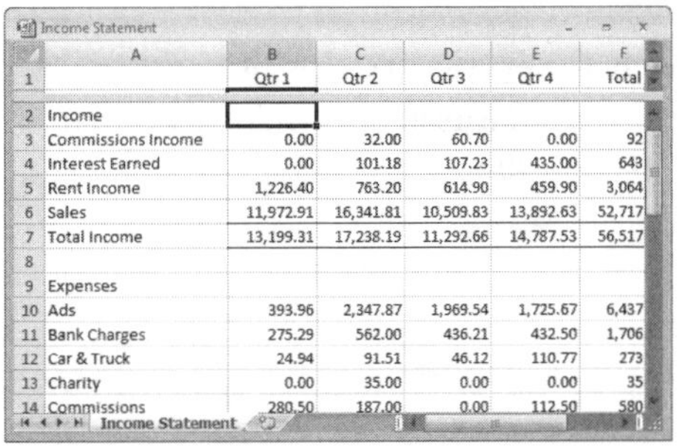

Figure 47 When you release the mouse button, the window splits.

Saving Files

As you work with a file, everything you do is stored in only one place: *random access memory* or *RAM*. The contents of RAM are a lot like the light in a lightbulb—as soon as you turn it off or pull the plug, it's gone. Your hard disk or a networked disk provide a much more permanent type of storage area.

You use the Save command to copy the workbook file in RAM to disk. This part of the chapter explains how.

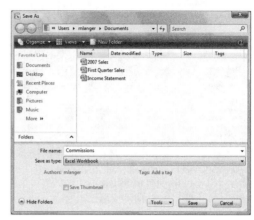

Figure 48 The Save As dialog.

✔ Tip

■ It's a very good idea to save documents frequently as you work to prevent data loss in the event of a computer problem.

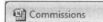

Figure 49 The file's name appears in the title bar, along with a tiny Excel workbook file icon.

To save a workbook file for the first time

1. Choose Office > Save (**Figure 37**), press Ctrl S, or click the Save button on the Quick Access Toolbar.

2. The Save As dialog appears. If necessary, click the Browse Folders button at the bottom of the dialog to expand it so it looks like **Figure 48**.

3. Use the Save As dialog to navigate to the folder (and disk, if necessary) in which you want to save the file.

4. Enter a name for the file in the File name box.

5. Click Save. The file is saved to disk. Its name appears in the window's title bar (**Figure 49**).

Figure 50 Use the Save as type drop-down list to save the document as a template or another type of file.

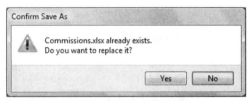

Figure 51 Excel checks to make sure you want to overwrite a file with the same name.

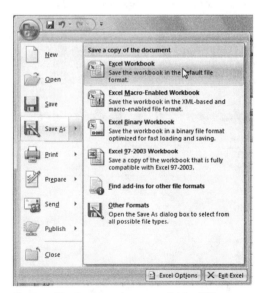

Figure 52 The Save As submenu under the Office menu.

✔ Tips

- You can use the Save as type drop-down list at the bottom of the Save As dialog (**Figure 50**) to specify a format for the file. This enables you to save the document as a template or in a format that can be opened and read by other versions of Excel or other programs.

- If you turn on the Save Thumbnail check box, Excel creates a thumbnail image of the document, which may help you identify it in folders or when opening it from within Excel. I explain how to open documents on the next page.

- If you save a file with the same name and same disk location as another file, a dialog appears, asking if you want to replace the file (**Figure 51**).

  ▲ Click Yes to replace the file already on disk with the file you are saving.

  ▲ Click No to return to the Save As dialog where you can enter a new name or specify a new disk location.

- For more information about using the Save As dialog, consult Windows Help.

To save changes to a file

Choose Office > Save (**Figure 37**), press Ctrl S, or click the Save button on the Quick Access Toolbar.

The file is saved with the same name in the same location on disk.

To save a file with a different name or in a different location

1. Choose Office > Save As > Excel Workbook (**Figure 52**).

2. Follow steps 2 through 5 on the previous page.

Opening Existing Files

Once a file has been saved on disk, you can reopen it to read, modify, or print it.

To open an existing file

1. Choose Office > Open (**Figure 37**) or press Ctrl O.

2. Use the Open dialog that appears (**Figure 53**) to locate the file that you want to open.

3. Select the file that you want to open and click the Open button.

   or

   Double-click the file that you want to open.

✔ Tips

- To view only specific types of files in the Open dialog, select a format from the file type drop-down list to the right of the File name box (**Figure 54**).

- If you select All Files from the file type drop-down list (**Figure 54**), you can open just about any kind of file. Be aware, however, that a file in an incompatible format may not appear the way you expect when opened.

- You can open a recent file by selecting it from the list of recently opened files on the right side of the Office menu (**Figure 37**).

- You can use the Views menu to change the appearance of items in the Open dialog's file list. The icon views show thumbnail images of saved Excel 2007 files (**Figure 55**).

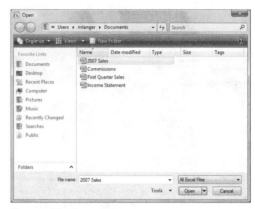

Figure 53 The Open dialog.

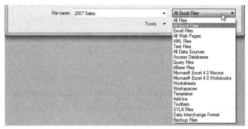

Figure 54 You can narrow down or expand the list of files shown by choosing an option from the file type drop-down list.

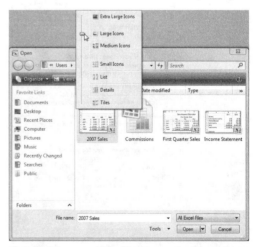

Figure 55 You can use the Views menu to change the appearance of the file list. If you choose one of the icon views, you can see the thumbnail images for the Excel 2007 files on disk.

Using Functions in Formulas

	A	B	C
1	Product Inventory		
2			
3	**Item Name**	**Item No.**	**Qty**
4	Dreamboys	D-783	382
5	Happy Ankles	H-390	473
6	Night at the Gallery	N-302	293
7	Shelly's Web	S-492	582
8	Stoney Balboa	S-973	229
9	Miss Panner	M-301	371
10	Slow Track	S-730	399
11	Pirates of the Pacific	P-888	471
12	Total		

Figure 1 Using the SUM function makes it easier to add up a column of numbers.

Function name   *Arguments*

SUM(**number1**,number2,...)

Figure 2 The parts of a function. Bold components are required.

✔ Tips

- If a function comes at the beginning of a formula, it must begin with an equal sign (=).

- Some arguments are optional. In the SUM function, for example, you can have only one argument, such as a reference to a single range of cells.

Functions

A function is a predefined formula for making a specific kind of calculation. Functions make it quicker and easier to write formulas.

For example, say you need to add up a column of numbers like the one in **Figure 1**. It's perfectly acceptable to write a formula using cell references separated by the addition operator (+) like this:

$$=C4+C5+C6+C7+C8+C9+C10+C11$$

But rather than enter a lengthy formula, you can use the SUM function to add up the same numbers like this:

$$=SUM(C4:C11)$$

The SUM function is only one of over 300 functions built into Excel.

Anatomy of a Function

As shown in **Figure 2**, each function has two main parts.

- ◆ The *function name* determines what the function does.

- ◆ The *arguments* determine what values or cell references the function should use in its calculation. Arguments are enclosed in parentheses and, if there's more than one, separated by commas.

Arguments

The argument component of a function can consist of any of the following:

◆ **Numbers** (**Figure 3**). Like any other formula, the result of a function that uses values for arguments will not change unless the formula is changed.

◆ **Text** (**Figure 4**). Excel includes a number of functions just for text. I tell you about them later in this chapter.

◆ **Cell references** (**Figures 4** through **8**). This is a practical way to write functions, since when you change cell contents, the results of functions that reference them change automatically.

◆ **Formulas** (**Figures 6** and **7**). This lets you create complex formulas that perform a series of calculations at once.

◆ **Functions** (**Figures 7** and **8**). When a function includes another function as one of its arguments, it's called *nesting functions*.

◆ **Error values** (**Figure 8**). You may find this useful to "flag" errors or missing information in a worksheet.

◆ **Logical values**. Some function arguments require TRUE or FALSE values.

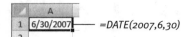

Figure 3 This example uses numbers as arguments for the DATE function.

=IF(B8>400, "Good Work!", "Try harder.")

Figure 4 This example uses cell references, numbers, and text as arguments for the IF function.

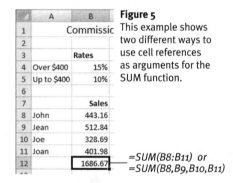

Figure 5 This example shows two different ways to use cell references as arguments for the SUM function.

=SUM(B8:B11) or
=SUM(B8,B9,B10,B11)

Figure 6 This example uses a formula as an argument for the ROUND function.

=ROUND(B4*.15,2)

	A	B	C	
1		Commissions Repo		
2				
3		Rates		
4	Over $400	15%		
5	Up to $400	10%		
6				
7			Sales	Amt. Due
8	John		443.16	66.47

Figure 7 This example uses the ROUND and IF functions to calculate commissions based on a rate that changes according to sales.

=ROUND(IF(B8>400,B8*B4,B8*B5),2)

	A	B	
1		Commissio	
2			
3		Sales	
4	John	443.16	
5	Jean	512.84	
6	Joe		
7	Joan	401.98	
8	⚠	#N/A	

Figure 8 This example uses three functions (IF, COUNTBLANK, and SUM), cell references, and error values to either indicate missing information or add a column of numbers.

=IF(COUNTBLANK(B4:B7)>0,#N/A,SUM(B4:B7))

Figure 9 If you make a mistake when entering a formula, Excel will tell you.

Figure 10 The Formula AutoCorrect feature can fix common formula errors for you.

Entering Functions

Excel offers several ways to enter a function:

◆ By typing

◆ By typing and clicking

◆ By using the Insert Function and Function Arguments dialogs

There is no "best" way—use the methods that you like most.

✔ Tips

■ Function names are not case sensitive. *Sum* or *sum* is the same as *SUM*. Excel converts all function names to uppercase characters.

■ Do not include spaces when writing formulas.

■ When writing formulas with nested functions, it's important to properly match parentheses. If parentheses don't match, Excel either displays an error message (**Figure 9**) or offers to correct the error for you (**Figure 10**).

■ Excel's Function Argument Tooltips feature (**Figures 11** and **12** on the next page) helps you enter functions correctly by providing information about arguments as you enter a formula.

ENTERING FUNCTIONS

To enter a function by typing

1. Begin the formula by typing an equal sign (=).

2. Type in the function name. As you type, a menu of functions that match what you're typing appears, along with a brief description of the selected function (**Figure 11**).

3. Type an open parenthesis character. Function Argument Tooltips appear to help you enter appropriate arguments (**Figure 12**).

4. Type in the value or cell reference for the first argument (**Figure 13**).

5. If entering more than one argument, type in each with commas between them.

6. Type a closed parenthesis character.

7. Press Enter or click the Enter button on the formula bar. The result of the function is displayed in the cell (**Figure 14**).

✔ Tip

■ In step 2, you can double-click a function on the menu to insert it in the formula and complete step 4.

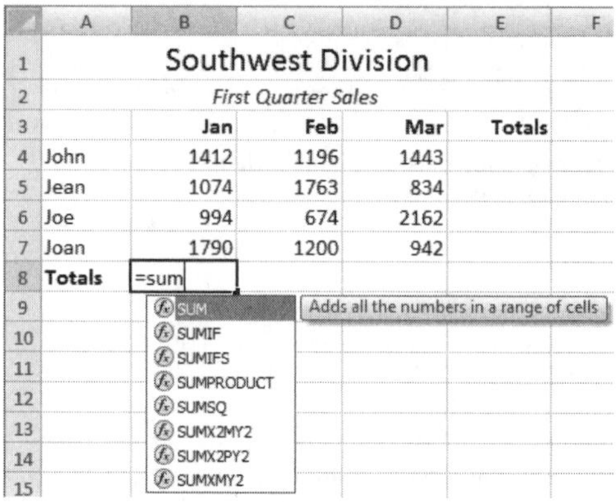

Figure 11 As you type the name of a function, Excel displays a menu of possible matches.

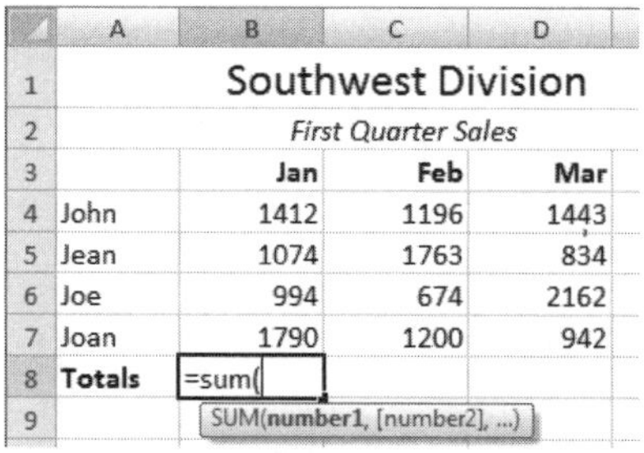

Figure 12 When you begin to enter the formula, Function Argument ToolTips appear to guide you.

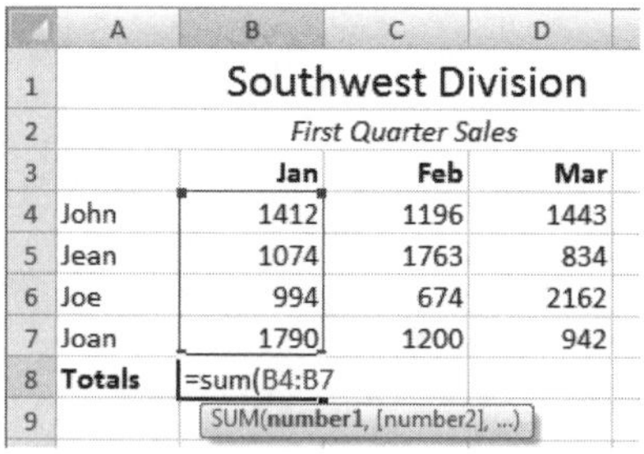

Figure 13 Continue typing to enter the formula.

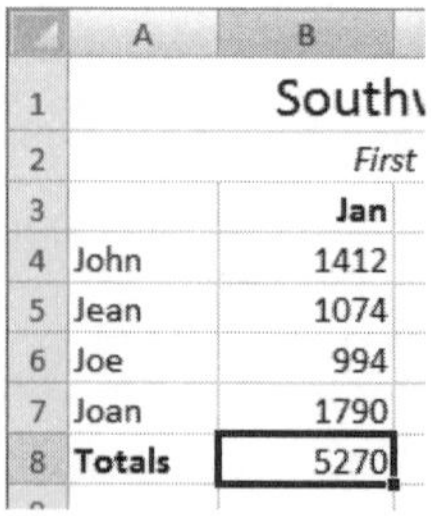

Figure 14 When you complete the entry, the cell containing the function displays the result of the formula.

ENTERING FUNCTIONS BY TYPING

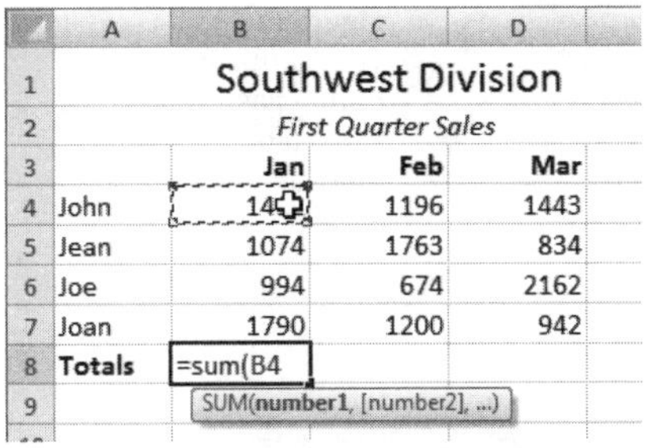

Figure 15 After typing the beginning of the function, you can click on cell references for arguments.

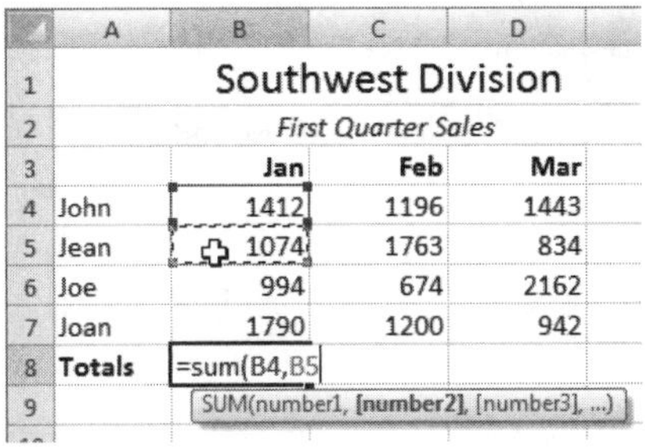

Figure 16 Type a comma before clicking to enter additional cell references for arguments.

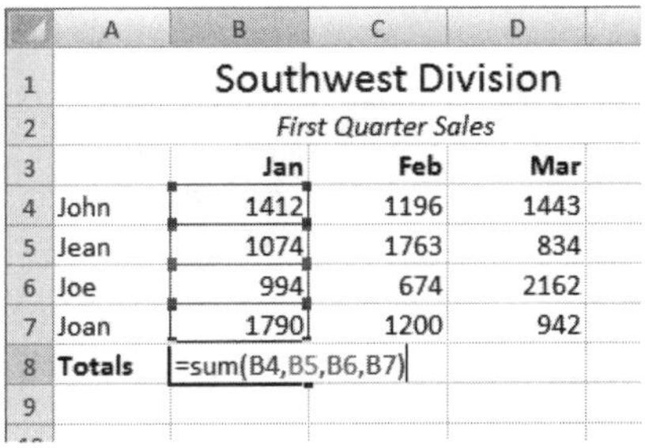

Figure 17 Be sure to type a closed parenthesis character at the end of a function.

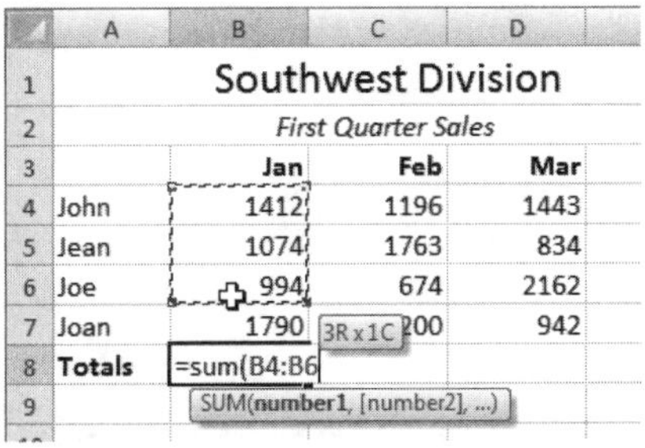

Figure 18 You can always enter a range in a formula by dragging, even when the range is an argument for a function.

To enter a function by typing & clicking

1. Begin the formula by typing an equal sign (=).

2. Type in the function name. As you type, a menu of functions that match what you're typing appears, along with a brief description of the selected function (**Figure 11**).

3. Type an open parenthesis character. Function Argument Tooltips appear to help you enter appropriate arguments (**Figure 12**).

4. Type in a value or click on the cell whose reference you want to include as the first argument (**Figure 15**).

5. If entering more than one argument, type a comma, then type in a value or click on the cell for the next reference (**Figure 16**). Repeat this step for each argument in the function.

6. Type a closed parenthesis character (**Figure 17**).

7. Press ⏎Enter or click the Enter button on the formula bar.

   The result of the function is displayed in the cell (**Figure 14**).

✔ Tips

- To include a range by clicking, in step 4 or 5 above, drag the mouse pointer over the cells you want to include (**Figure 18**).

- Be careful where you click or drag when entering a function or any formula—each click or drag may add references to the formula! If you click on a cell by mistake, you can press ⏀Backspace to delete each character of the incorrectly added reference or click the Cancel button on the formula bar to start over.

ENTERING FUNCTIONS BY TYPING & CLICKING

To enter a function with the Insert Function dialog

1. Choose Home > Editing > AutoSum > More Functions (**Figure 19**) or click the Insert Function button on the formula bar to display the Insert Function dialog (**Figure 20**).

2. Choose a category from the drop-down list (**Figure 21**).

3. Click to select a function in the list box. You may have to use the scroll bar to locate the function you want.

4. Click OK.

   The Function Arguments dialog appears (**Figure 22**). It provides information about the function you selected and may include one or more entries for the argument(s).

5. Enter a value or cell reference in the appropriate text box for each required argument.

6. When you are finished entering function arguments, click OK.

   The Function Arguments dialog closes and the result of the function is displayed in the cell (**Figure 14**).

Figure 19
The AutoSum button has a menu of functions.

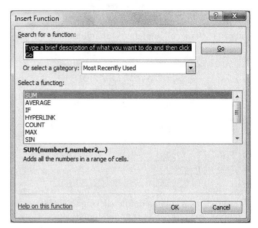

Figure 20 The Insert Function dialog.

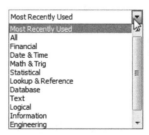

Figure 21
Functions are organized by category.

Figure 22 Use the Function Arguments dialog to enter arguments for the function.

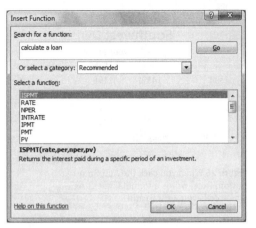

Figure 23 The Insert Function dialog can recommend functions based on what you tell it you want to do.

Figure 24
The Functions drop-down list at the far-left end of the formula bar.

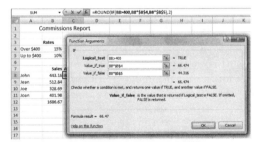

Figure 25 Only one function's options appear in the Function Arguments dialog at a time, but you can view and edit the entire formula in the formula bar.

✔ Tips

■ If you don't know which function you want, you can search for the correct function. Enter a description of what you want to do in the large text box near the top of the Insert Function dialog and click Go. A list of possible functions appears in the list (**Figure 23**).

■ In step 2, if you're not sure which category a function is in, select All. The Select a function list displays all of the functions Excel has to offer.

■ In step 5, you can click or drag in the worksheet window to enter a cell reference or range. To see obstructed worksheet cells, you can drag the Function Arguments dialog aside.

■ In step 5, you can enter a function as an argument by clicking in the argument's text box and choosing a specific function or More Functions from the Functions drop-down list at the far-left end of the formula bar (**Figure 24**). Although the Function Arguments dialog only shows function options for one function at a time, you can view and edit the entire formula in the formula bar (**Figure 25**).

■ As you enter arguments in the Function Arguments dialog, the calculated value of your entries appears at the bottom of the dialog (**Figures 22** and **25**).

Math & Trig Functions

Excel's math and trig functions perform standard mathematical and trigonometric calculations. The next few pages discuss the most commonly used ones, starting with one so popular it even has its own button: SUM.

The SUM function

The SUM function (**Figure 5**) adds up numbers. It uses the following syntax:

SUM(number1,number2,...)

Although the SUM function can accept up to 30 arguments separated by commas, only one is required.

To use the AutoSum button

1. Select the cell below the column or to the right of the row of numbers you want to add.

2. Click Home > Editing > AutoSum.

Excel examines the worksheet and makes a "guess" about which cells you want to add. It writes the corresponding formula and puts a marquee around the range of cells it used (**Figure 26**).

3. If the range in the formula is incorrect, type or select the correct range. Since the reference for the range of cells is selected in the formula, anything you type or select will automatically replace it.

4. When the formula is correct, press (Enter), click the Enter button on the formula bar, or click the AutoSum button a second time.

The formula is entered and its results appear in the cell.

	A	B	C	D
1		Southwest Divisi		
2		First Quarter Sales		
3		Jan	Feb	
4	John	1412	1196	
5	Jean	1074	1763	
6	Joe	994	674	
7	Joan	1790	1200	
8	**Totals**	=SUM(B4:B7)		
9		SUM(**number1**, [number2], ...)		

Figure 26 When you click the AutoSum button, Excel writes a formula, guessing which cells you want to add.

	A	B	C	D
1	Southwest Division			
2	First Quarter Sales			
3		Jan	Feb	Mar
4	John	1412	1196	1443
5	Jean	1074	1763	834
6	Joe	994	674	2162
7	Joan	1790	1200	942
8	Totals			

Figure 27 Select the cells adjacent to the columns (or rows) of cells that you want to add.

	A	B	C	D
1	Southwest Division			
2	First Quarter Sales			
3		Jan	Feb	Mar
4	John	1412	1196	1443
5	Jean	1074	1763	834
6	Joe	994	674	2162
7	Joan	1790	1200	942
8	Totals	5270	4833	5381

Figure 28 When you click the AutoSum button, Excel enters the appropriate formulas in the cells.

	A	B	C	D	E
1	Southwest Division				
2	First Quarter Sales				
3		Jan	Feb	Mar	Totals
4	John	1412	1196	1443	
5	Jean	1074	1763	834	
6	Joe	994	674	2162	
7	Joan	1790	1200	942	
8	Totals				

Figure 29 Select the cells containing the columns that you want to add.

	A	B	C	D	E
1	Southwest Division				
2	First Quarter Sales				
3		Jan	Feb	Mar	Totals
4	John	1412	1196	1443	
5	Jean	1074	1763	834	
6	Joe	994	674	2162	
7	Joan	1790	1200	942	
8	Totals	5270	4833	5381	

Figure 30 When you click the AutoSum button, Excel enters the appropriate formulas in the cells beneath the selected cells.

	A	B	C	D	E
1	Southwest Division				
2	First Quarter Sales				
3		Jan	Feb	Mar	Totals
4	John	1412	1196	1443	
5	Jean	1074	1763	834	
6	Joe	994	674	2162	
7	Joan	1790	1200	942	
8	Totals				

Figure 31 Select the cells you want to add, along with the cells in which you want the totals to appear.

To use the AutoSum button on multiple cells

1. Select a range of cells adjacent to the columns or rows you want to add (**Figure 27**).

2. Click the AutoSum button once. Excel writes the formulas in the cells you selected (**Figure 28**).

Or

1. Select the cells containing the columns you want to add (**Figure 29**).

2. Click the AutoSum button once. Excel writes all the formulas in the row of cells immediately below the ones you selected (**Figure 30**).

Or

1. Select the cells containing the columns and rows you want to add, along with the empty row beneath them and the empty column to the right of them (**Figure 31**).

2. Click the AutoSum button once. Excel writes formulas in the bottom and rightmost cells (**Figure 32**).

✔ Tip

- Be sure to check the formulas Excel writes when you use the AutoSum button. Excel is smart, but it's no mind-reader. The cells it includes may not be the ones you had in mind!

	A	B	C	D	E
1	Southwest Division				
2	First Quarter Sales				
3		Jan	Feb	Mar	Totals
4	John	1412	1196	1443	4051
5	Jean	1074	1763	834	3671
6	Joe	994	674	2162	3830
7	Joan	1790	1200	942	3932
8	Totals	5270	4833	5381	15484

Figure 32 When you click the AutoSum button, Excel enters the appropriate formulas in the empty cells of the selection.

USING THE AUTOSUM BUTTON

The PRODUCT function

The PRODUCT function (**Figure 33**) multiplies its arguments much like the SUM function adds them. It uses the following syntax:

PRODUCT(number1,number2,...**)**

Although the PRODUCT function can accept up to 30 arguments separated by commas, only one is required.

	A	B	C	D	E	F
1	Item	Cost	Markup	Qty	Value	
2	Product A	1.54	115%	152	269.192	=PRODUCT(B2:D2)
3	Product B	3.58	250%	142	1270.9	=PRODUCT(B3,C3,D3)
4						

Figure 33 Two ways to use the PRODUCT function. The formulas in column *E* are shown in column *F*.

The ROUND function

The ROUND function (**Figure 34**) rounds a number to the number of decimal places you specify. It uses the following syntax:

ROUND(number,num_digits)

Both arguments are required. The num_digits argument specifies how many decimal places the number should be rounded to. If 0, the number is rounded to a whole number. If less than 0, the number is rounded on the left side of the decimal point (**Figure 35**).

	A	B	C	D	E	F
1		Sales	Rate	Amount Due	Rounded	
2	John	14528.16	15%	2179.224	2179.22	=ROUND(D2,2)
3	Jean	45284.48	20%	9056.896	9056.9	=ROUND(D3,2)
4	Joe	36547.19	15%	5482.0785	5482.08	=ROUND(D4,2)
5	Joan	27582.43	15%	4137.3645	4137.36	=ROUND(D5,2)
6						

Figure 34 Use the ROUND function to round numbers to the number of decimal places you specify. The formulas in column *E* are shown in column *F*.

	A	E	F	G
1		Total	Rounded	
2	Sales	154258.65	154300	=ROUND(E2,-2)
3	Cost	58842.87		

Figure 35 You can also use the ROUND function to round numbers to the left of the decimal point. The formula in cell *F2* is shown in cell *G2*.

✔ Tips

- Rather than make a calculation in one cell and round it in another as shown in **Figures 34** and **35**, combine the two formulas in one cell (**Figure 36**).
- The ROUNDUP function works like the ROUND function, but it always rounds up to the next higher number. The num_digits argument is not required; if omitted, the number is rounded to the next highest whole number.
- The ROUNDDOWN function works just like the ROUNDUP function, but it always rounds down.

	A	B	C	D	E
1		Sales	Rate	Amount Due	
2	John	14528.16	15%	2179.22	=ROUND(B2*C2,2)
3	Jean	45284.48	20%	9056.9	=ROUND(B3*C3,2)
4	Joe	36547.19	15%	5482.08	=ROUND(B4*C4,2)
5	Joan	27582.43	15%	4137.36	=ROUND(B5*C5,2)
6					

Figure 36 You can also use the ROUND function to round the results of another formula or function. The formulas in column *D* are shown in column *E*.

	A	B	C	D	E
1	**Number**	**Even**		**Odd**	
2	159.487	160	=EVEN(A2)	161	=ODD(A2)
3	1647.1	1648	=EVEN(A3)	1649	=ODD(A3)
4	-14.48	-16	=EVEN(A4)	-15	=ODD(A4)

Figure 37 Use the EVEN and ODD functions to round a number up to the next even or odd number. The formulas in columns *B* and *D* are shown in columns *C* and *E*.

	A	B	C
1	**Number**	**Integer**	
2	159.487	159	=INT(A2)
3	1647.1	1647	=INT(A3)
4	-14.48	-15	=INT(A4)

Figure 38 Use the INT function to round a number down to the next whole number. The formulas in column *B* are shown in column *C*.

	A	B	C
1	**Number**	**Absolute Value**	
2	159.487	159.487	=ABS(A2)
3	1647.1	1647.1	=ABS(A3)
4	-14.48	14.48	=ABS(A4)

Figure 39 Use the ABS function to get the absolute value of a number. The formulas in column *B* are shown in column *C*.

The EVEN & ODD functions

The EVEN function (**Figure 37**) rounds a number up to the next even number. It uses the following syntax:

EVEN(number)

The number argument, which is required, is the number you want to round.

The ODD function works exactly the same way, but rounds a number up to the next odd number.

The INT function

The INT function (**Figure 38**) rounds a number down to the nearest whole number or integer. It uses the following syntax:

INT(number)

The number argument, which is required, is the number you want to convert to an integer.

The ABS function

The ABS function (**Figure 39**) returns the absolute value of a number—it leaves positive numbers alone but turns negative numbers into positive numbers. (Is that high school math coming back to you yet?) It uses the following syntax:

ABS(number)

The number argument, which is required, is the number you want to convert to an absolute value.

EVEN, ODD, INT, & ABS FUNCTIONS

The SQRT function

The SQRT function (**Figure 40**) calculates the square root of a number. It uses the following syntax:

SQRT(number)

The number argument, which is required, is the number you want to find the square root of.

✔ Tip

- You'll get a #NUM! error message if you try to use the SQRT function to calculate the square root of a negative number (**Figure 40**). Prevent the error by using the ABS function in the formula (**Figure 41**).

The PI function

The PI function (**Figure 42**) returns the value of pi, accurate up to 14 decimal places. It uses the following syntax:

PI( )

The RAND function

The RAND (**Figure 43**) function generates a random number greater than or equal to 0 and less than 1 each time the worksheet is calculated. It uses the following syntax:

RAND( )

✔ Tips

- Although neither the PI nor RAND function have arguments, if you fail to include the parentheses, you'll get a #NAME? error.

- The results of a formula using the RAND function changes each time the worksheet is recalculated.

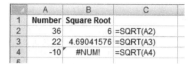

	A	B	C
1	Number	Square Root	
2	36	6	=SQRT(A2)
3	22	4.69041576	=SQRT(A3)
4	-10	#NUM!	=SQRT(A4)

Figure 40 Use the SQRT function to find the square root of a number.

	A	B	C
1	Number	Square Root	
2	36	6	=SQRT(ABS(A2))
3	22	4.69041576	=SQRT(ABS(A3))
4	-10	3.16227766	=SQRT(ABS(A4))

Figure 41 By combining the SQRT and ABS functions, you can prevent #NUM! errors when calculating the square root of a negative number. The formulas in column *B* are shown in column *C*.

Figure 42 The PI function calculates pi to 14 decimal places, although only 9 decimal places appear by default.

	A	B	C	D
1	Low	High	Random	
2	0	1	0.22075129	=RAND()
3	0	1000	774.323547	=RAND()*(B3-A3)+A3
4	36	42	36.7460726	=RAND()*(B4-A4)+A4
5	3458	4835	4812.69338	=RAND()*(B5-A5)+A5

Figure 43 The RAND function can be used alone or as part of a formula to generate a random number within a range. The formulas in column *C* are shown in column *D*.

- To generate a random number between two numbers (low and high), write a formula like this:

    $=RAND()*(high–low)+low$

See **Figure 43** for some examples.

	A	B	C	D	E
1		Radians		Degrees	
2	Entry	1		45	
3					
4	Convert to Radians			0.78539816	=RADIANS(D2)
5	Convert to Degrees	57.2957795	=DEGREES(B2)		
6					
7	Sine	0.84147098	=SIN(B2)	0.70710678	=SIN(RADIANS(D2))
8	Arcsine	1.57079633	=ASIN(B2)	0.90333911	=ASIN(RADIANS(D2))
9	Cosine	0.54030231	=COS(B2)	0.70710678	=COS(RADIANS(D2))
10	Arccosine	0	=ACOS(B2)	0.66745722	=ACOS(RADIANS(D2))
11	Tangent	1.55740772	=TAN(B2)	1	=TAN(RADIANS(D2))
12	Arctangent	0.78539816	=ATAN(B2)	0.66577375	=ATAN(RADIANS(D2))

Figure 44 This example shows several trig functions in action. The formulas for columns *B* and *D* are shown in columns *C* and *E*.

The RADIANS & DEGREES functions

The RADIANS function converts degrees to radians. The DEGREES function converts radians to degrees. They use the following syntax:

RADIANS(angle)

DEGREES(angle)

The angle argument, which is required, is the angle you want converted. Use degrees in the RADIANS function and radians in the DEGREES function. Both are illustrated in **Figure 44**.

The SIN function

The SIN function (**Figure 44**) calculates the sine of an angle. It uses the following syntax:

SIN(number)

The number argument, which is required, is the angle, in radians, for which you want the sine calculated.

The COS function

The COS function (**Figure 44**) calculates the cosine of an angle. It uses the following syntax:

COS(number)

The number argument, which is required, is the angle, in radians, for which you want the cosine calculated.

The TAN function

The TAN function (**Figure 44**) calculates the tangent of an angle. It uses the following syntax:

TAN(number)

The number argument, which is required, is the angle, in radians, for which you want the tangent calculated.

✔ Tip

■ To calculate the arcsine, arccosine, or arctangent of an angle, use the ASIN, ACOS, or ATAN function (**Figure 44**). Each works the same as its counterpart.

RADIANS, DEGREES, SIN, COS, & TAN FUNCTIONS

Statistical Functions

Excel's statistical functions make it easy to perform complex statistical analyses. Here's a handful of the functions I think you'll use most.

✔ Tips

- Excel's AVERAGE function does not include empty cells when calculating the average for a range of cells.

- Although the AVERAGE, MEDIAN, MODE, MIN, and MAX functions can each accept up to 30 arguments separated by commas, only one argument is required.

- You can use the AutoSum button's menu on the Home tab's Editing group (**Figure 19**) to enter a function using the AVERAGE, COUNT, MAX, and MIN functions.

The AVERAGE function

The AVERAGE function (**Figure 45**) calculates the average or mean of its arguments. It uses the following syntax:

AVERAGE(number1,number2,...)

The MEDIAN function

The MEDIAN function (**Figure 45**) calculates the median of its arguments. The median is the "halfway point" of the numbers—half the numbers have higher values and half have lower values. The MEDIAN function uses the following syntax:

MEDIAN(number1,number2,...)

	A	B	C
1	*Product Inventory*		
2			
3	**Item Name**	**Price**	
4	Dreamboys	14.99	
5	Happy Ankles	15.99	
6	Night at the Gallery	8.99	
7	Shelly's Web	24.99	
8	Stoney Balboa	19.99	
9	Miss Panner	19.99	
10	Slow Track	22.99	
11	Pirates of the Pacific	13.99	
12			
13	**Average**	17.74	=AVERAGE(B4:B11)
14	**Median**	17.99	=MEDIAN(B4:B11)
15	**Mode**	19.99	=MODE(B4:B11)
16	**Minimum**	8.99	=MIN(B4:B11)
17	**Maximum**	24.99	=MAX(B4:B11)

Figure 45 This example shows a few of Excel's statistical functions at work. The formulas for column *B* are shown in column *C*.

	A	B	C
1			
2		6/29/2003	
3		154.69	
4		chocolate	
5			
6		-475.69852	
7		45	
8		ice cream	
9		$ 75.00	
10			
11	Cells with Values	5	=COUNT(B2:B9)
12	Nonblank Cells	7	=COUNTA(B2:B9)

Figure 46 This example of the COUNT and COUNTA functions illustrates that while the COUNT function counts only cells containing numbers (including dates and times), the COUNTA function counts *all* non-blank cells. The formulas in column *B* are shown in column *C*.

The MODE function

The MODE function (**Figure 45**) returns the mode of its arguments. The mode is the most common value. The MODE function uses the following syntax:

MODE(number1,number2,...)

If there are no repeated values, Excel returns a #NUM! error.

The MIN & MAX functions

The MIN function (**Figure 45**) returns the minimum value of its arguments while the MAX function returns the maximum value of its arguments. They use the following syntax:

MIN(number1,number2,...)

MAX(number1,number2,...)

The COUNT & COUNTA functions

The COUNT function counts how many numbers are referenced by its arguments. The COUNTA function counts how many values are referenced by its arguments. Although this may sound like the same thing, it isn't—COUNT includes only numbers or formulas resulting in numbers while COUNTA includes any non-blank cell. **Figure 46** shows an example that clarifies the difference.

The COUNT and COUNTA functions use the following syntax:

COUNT(number1,number2,...)

COUNTA(number1,number2,...)

Although either function can accept up to 30 arguments separated by commas, only one is required.

MODE, MIN, MAX, COUNT, & COUNTA FUNCTIONS

The STDEV & STDEVP functions

Standard deviation is a statistical measurement of how much values vary from the average or mean for the group. The STDEV function calculates the standard deviation based on a random sample of the entire population. The STDEVP function calculates the standard deviation based on the entire population. **Figure 47** shows an example of each.

The STDEV and STDEVP functions use the following syntax:

STDEV(number1,number2,**...)**

STDEVP(number1,number2,**...)**

Although either function can accept up to 30 arguments separated by commas, only one is required.

✔ Tip

■ To get accurate results from the STDEVP function, the arguments must include data for the entire population.

	A	B	C
1	*Product Inventory*		
2			
3	Item Name	Price	
4	Dreamboys	14.99	
5	Happy Ankles	15.99	
6	Night at the Gallery	8.99	
7	Shelly's Web	24.99	
8	Stoney Balboa	19.99	
9	Miss Panner	19.99	
10	Slow Track	22.99	
11	Pirates of the Pacific	13.99	
12			
13	Average	17.74	=AVERAGE(B4:B11)
14	STDEV	5.230406	=STDEV(B4:B11)
15	STDVP	4.892596	=STDEVP(B4:B11)

Figure 47 In this example, the STDEV function assumes that the range is a random sample from a larger population of information. The STDEVP function assumes that the same data is the entire population. That's why the results differ. The formulas in column *B* are shown in column *C*.

	A	B	C
1	*Depreciation Comparison*		
2			
3	Cost	$ 5,000.00	
4	Salvage Value	$ 250.00	
5	Life (in years)	5	
6			
7	Year	1	
8	Straight Line	$950.00	=SLN(B3,B4,B5)
9	Declining Balance	$2,255.00	=DB(B3,B4,B5,B7)
10	Double Declining Balan	$2,000.00	=DDB(B3,B4,B5,B7)
11	Sum of the Year's Digits	$1,583.33	=SYD(B3,B4,B5,B7)

Figure 48 A simple worksheet lets you compare different methods of depreciation using the SLN, DB, DDB, and SYD functions. The formulas in column *B* are shown in column *C*.

Financial Functions

Excel's financial functions enable you to calculate depreciation, evaluate investment opportunities, or calculate the payments on a loan. On the next few pages, I tell you about a few of the functions I think you'll find useful.

The SLN function

The SLN function (**Figure 48**) calculates straight line depreciation for an asset. It uses the following syntax:

SLN(cost,salvage,life)

Cost is the acquisition cost of the asset, salvage is the salvage or scrap value, and life is the useful life expressed in years or months. All three arguments are required.

The DB function

The DB function (**Figure 48**) calculates declining balance depreciation for an asset. It uses the following syntax:

DB(cost,salvage,life,period,month)

The cost, salvage, and life arguments are the same as for the SLN function. Period, which must be expressed in the same units as life, is the period for which you want to calculate depreciation. These first four arguments are required. Month is the number of months in the first year of the asset's life. If omitted, 12 is assumed.

The SYD function

The SYD function (**Figure 48**) calculates the sum-of-years' digits depreciation for an asset. It uses the following syntax:

SYD(cost,salvage,life,period)

The cost, salvage, life, and period arguments are the same as for the DB and DDB functions. All arguments are required.

The DDB function

The DDB function (**Figure 48**) calculates the double-declining balance depreciation for an asset. It uses the following syntax:

DDB(cost,salvage,life,period,factor)

The cost, salvage, life, and period arguments are the same as for the DB function and are required. Factor is the rate at which the balance declines. If omitted, 2 is assumed.

The PMT function

The PMT function calculates the periodic payment for an annuity based on constant payments and interest rate. This function is commonly used for two purposes: to calculate the monthly payments on a loan and to calculate the monthly contribution necessary to reach a specific savings goal.

The PMT function uses the following syntax:

PMT(rate,nper,pv,fv,type**)**

Rate is the interest rate per period, nper is the total number of periods, and pv is the present value or current worth of the total payments. These three arguments are required. The fv argument is the future value or balance desired at the end of the payments. If omitted, 0 is assumed. Type indicates when payments are due: use 0 for payments at the end of the period and 1 for payments at the beginning of the period. If omitted, 0 is assumed.

	A	B
1	Loan Amount	20000
2	Annual Interest Rate	8.50%
3	Loan Term (in Months)	48
4		
5	Monthly Payment	

Figure 49 A basic structure for a worksheet that calculates loan payments.

	A	B
1	Loan Amount	20000
2	Annual Interest Rate	8.50%
3	Loan Term (in Months)	48
4		
5	Monthly Payment	($492.97)

Figure 50 The loan payment worksheet after entering a formula with the PMT function.

	A	B
1	Loan Amount	25000
2	Annual Interest Rate	8.50%
3	Loan Term (in Months)	48
4		
5	Monthly Payment	($616.21)

Figure 51 Playing "what-if." In this example, I increased the loan amount to see how much more the monthly payment would be.

To calculate loan payments

1. Enter the text and number values shown in **Figure 49** in a worksheet. If desired, use your own amounts.

2. Enter the following formula in cell *B5*:
   =*PMT(B2/12,B3,B1)*

   This formula uses only the first three arguments of the PMT function. The rate argument is divided by 12 to arrive at a monthly interest rate since the number of periods is expressed in months and payments will be made monthly (all time units must match).

3. Press (Enter) or click the Enter button on the formula bar.

   The result of the formula appears in the cell as a negative number (**Figure 50**) because it is an outgoing cash flow. (A minus sign or parentheses indicates a negative number.)

✔ Tips

■ If you prefer, you can use the Insert Function and Function Arguments dialogs to write the formula in step 2. Be sure to include the formula *B2/12* in the rate text box. Leave the fv and type text boxes blank.

■ You can calculate loan payments without creating a whole worksheet—simply enter values rather than cell references as arguments for the PMT function. But using cell references makes it easy to play "what-if"—see how payments change when the loan amount, rate, and number of periods change. **Figure 51** shows an example.

To create an amortization table

1. Create a loan payment worksheet following the steps on the previous page.

2. Enter text and number values for headings as shown in **Figure 52**. Make sure there is a row with a payment number for each month of the loan term in cell *B3*.

3. In cell *B8*, enter =*B1*.

4. In cell *C8*, enter the following formula:
   =ROUND(B8*$B$2/12,2)

   This formula calculates the interest for the period and rounds it to two decimal places.

5. In cell *D8*, enter the following formula:
   =–$B$5–C8

   This formula calculates the amount of principal paid for the current month.

6. In cell *B9*, enter the following formula:
   =ROUND(B8–D8,2)

   This formula calculates the current month's beginning balance, rounded to two decimal places.

   At this point, your worksheet should look like the one in **Figure 53**.

7. Use the fill handle to copy the formula in cell *B9* down the column for each month.

8. Use the fill handle to copy the formulas in cells *C8* and *D8* down the columns for each month.

   Your amortization table is complete. It should look like the one in **Figure 54**.

✔ Tips

- If desired, you can add column totals at the bottom of columns *C* and *D* to total interest (you may be shocked) and principal (which should match cell *B1*).

	A	B	C	D
1	Loan Amount	20000		
2	Annual Interest Rate	8.50%		
3	Loan Term (in Months)	48		
4				
5	Monthly Payment	($492.97)		
6				
7	Payment Number	Beg Balance	Interest	Principal
8	1			
9	2			
10	3			
11	4			
12	5			
13	6			

Figure 52 To create an amortization table, start with this simple worksheet.

	A	B	C	D
1	Loan Amount	20000		
2	Annual Interest Rate	8.50%		
3	Loan Term (in Months)	48		
4				
5	Monthly Payment	($492.97)		
6				
7	Payment Number	Beg Balance	Interest	Principal
8	1	20000	141.67	$351.30
9	2	$19,648.70		
10	3			
11	4			
12	5			
13	6			

Figure 53 Add formulas to calculate interest, principal, and beginning balance.

	A	B	C	D
1	Loan Amount	20000		
2	Annual Interest Rate	8.50%		
3	Loan Term (in Months)	48		
4				
5	Monthly Payment	($492.97)		
6				
7	Payment Number	Beg Balance	Interest	Principal
8	1	20000	141.67	$351.30
9	2	$19,648.70	139.18	$353.79
10	3	$19,294.92	136.67	$356.30
11	4	$18,938.62	134.15	$358.82
12	5	$18,579.81	131.61	$361.36
13	6	$18,218.45	129.05	$363.92
14	7	$17,854.53	126.47	$366.50
15	8	$17,488.04	123.87	$369.10
16	9	$17,118.94	121.26	$371.71
17	10	$16,747.24	118.63	$374.34
18	11	$16,372.90	115.97	$377.00
19	12	$15,995.90	113.3	$379.67
20	13	$15,616.24	110.62	$382.35
21	14	$15,233.89	107.91	$385.06
22	15	$14,848.84	105.18	$387.79
23	16	$14,461.05	102.43	$390.54
24	17	$14,070.51	99.67	$393.30
25	18	$13,677.22	96.88	$396.09

Figure 54 Then copy the formulas down each column for all months of the loan term.

- I tell you more about using the fill handle in **Chapter 3**.

	A	B
1	Desired Amount	30000
2	Annual Interest Rate	5.25%
3	Months	120
4		
5	Monthly Contribution	

Figure 55 A basic structure for a worksheet to calculate contributions to reach a savings goal.

	A	B
1	Desired Amount	30000
2	Annual Interest Rate	5.25%
3	Months	120
4		
5	Monthly Contribution	($190.63)

Figure 56 The PMT function calculates the monthly contribution.

	A	B
1	Desired Amount	50000
2	Annual Interest Rate	5.25%
3	Months	120
4		
5	Monthly Contribution	($317.71)

Figure 57 Change one value and the result of the formula changes.

To calculate contributions to reach a savings goal

1. Enter the text and number values shown in **Figure 55** in a worksheet. If desired, use your own amounts.
2. Enter the following formula in cell *B5*:
   =PMT(B2/12,B3,,B1)

   This formula uses the first four arguments of the PMT function, although the pv argument is left blank—that's why there are two commas after *B3*. The rate argument is divided by 12 to arrive at a monthly interest rate.
3. Press Enter or click the Enter button on the formula bar.

   The result of the formula is expressed as a negative number **(Figure 56)** because it is an outgoing cash flow. (A minus sign or parentheses indicates a negative number.)

✔ Tips

- If you prefer, you can use the Insert Function and Function Arguments dialogs to write the formula in step 2. Be sure to include the formula *B2/12* in the rate text box. Leave the pv and type text boxes blank.
- You can calculate the amount of a monthly contribution to reach a savings goal without creating a whole worksheet—simply enter values rather than cell references as arguments for the PMT function. But using cell references makes it easy to play "what-if"—see how contributions change when the desired amount, rate, and number of periods change. **Figure 57** shows an example.
- To force an outgoing cash flow to be expressed as a positive number, simply include a minus sign (–) right after the equals sign (=) at the beginning of the formula.

The FV function

The FV function (**Figure 58**) calculates the future value of an investment with constant cash flows and a constant interest rate. It uses the following syntax:

FV(rate,nper,pmt,pv,type**)**

Rate is the interest rate per period, nper is the total number of periods, and pmt is the amount of the periodic payments. These three arguments are required. The pv argument is the present value of the payments. Type indicates when payments are due: use 0 for payments at the end of the period and 1 for payments at the beginning of the period. If either optional argument is omitted, 0 is assumed.

The PV function

The PV function (**Figure 59**) calculates the total amount that a series of payments in the future is worth now. It uses the following syntax:

PV(rate,nper,pmt,fv,type**)**

The rate, nper, pmt, and type arguments are the same as in the FV function. Only the first three are required. The fv argument is the amount left after the payments have been made. If omitted, 0 is assumed.

The IRR function

The IRR function (**Figure 60**) calculates the internal rate of return for a series of periodic cash flows. It uses the following syntax:

IRR(values,guess**)**

The values argument, which is required, is a range of cells containing the cash flows. The guess argument, which is optional, is for your guess of what the result could be. Although seldom necessary, guess could help Excel come up with an answer when performing complex calculations.

	A	B
1	Monthly Payment	150
2	Annual Interest Rate	5.25%
3	Number of Months	12
4		
5	Future Value	($1,843.95)
6		=FV(B2/12,B3,B1)

Figure 58 Use the FV function to calculate the future value of constant cash flows, like those of periodic payroll savings deductions. The formula in cell *B5* is shown in cell *B6*.

	A	B
1	Initial Investment	-25000
2		
3	Monthly Cash In	200
4	Annual Interest Rate	6%
5	Number of Months	360
6		
7	Present Value	($33,358.32)
8		=PV(B4/12,B5,B3)

Figure 59 This example uses the PV function to determine whether an investment is a good one. (It is because the present value is higher than the initial investment.) The formula in cell *B7* is shown in cell *B8*.

	A	B
1	Year 1	-500
2	Year 2	150
3	Year 3	100
4	Year 4	125
5	Year 5	135
6	Year 6	200
7		
8	Internal Rate of Return:	12%
9		=IRR(B1:B6)

Figure 60 This worksheet calculates the internal rate of return of an initial $500 investment that pays out cash over the next few years. The formula in cell *B8* is shown in cell *B9*.

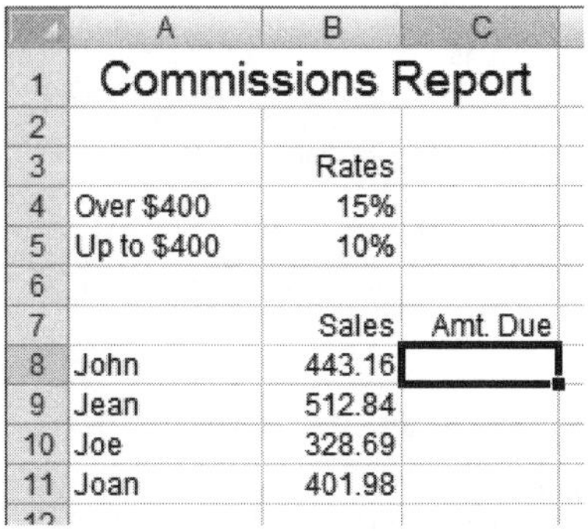

Figure 61 To try the IF function for yourself, start with a basic worksheet like this.

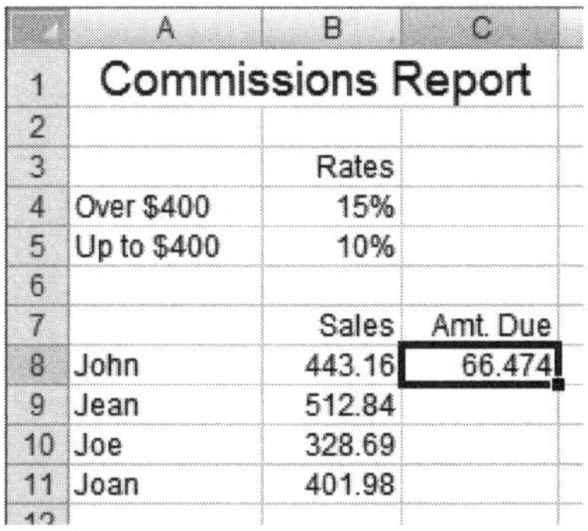

Figure 62 Enter the formula with the IF function in cell C8.

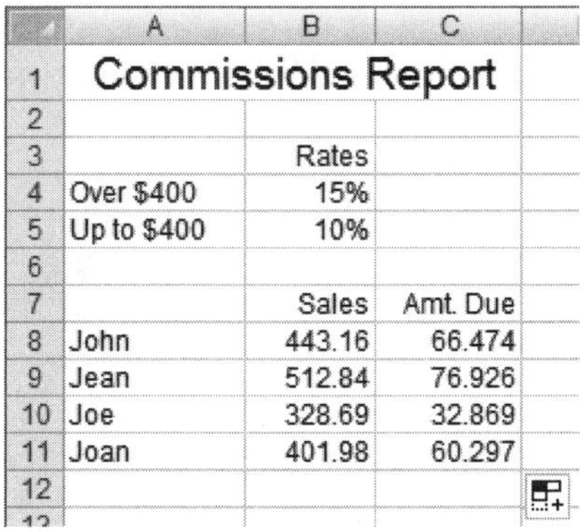

Figure 63 Then use the fill handle to copy the formula to the other cells.

Logical Functions

You can use Excel's logical functions to evaluate conditions and act accordingly. Here's the most useful one: IF.

The IF function

The IF function evaluates a condition and returns one of two different values depending on whether the condition is met (true) or not met (false). It uses the following syntax:

IF(logical_test,value_if_true,value_if_false**)**

The logical_test argument is the condition you want to meet. This argument is required. The value_if_true and value_if_false arguments are the values to return if the condition is met or not met. If value_if_false is omitted and the result is false, 0 (zero) is returned.

The following example uses the IF function to calculate commissions based on two different commission rates.

To use the IF function

1. Create a worksheet with text and number values as shown in **Figure 61**.

2. In cell *C8*, enter the following formula:
   =IF(B8>400,$B$4*B8,$B$5*B8)

   This formula begins by evaluating the sales amount to see if it's over $400. If it is, it moves to the value_if_true argument and multiplies the higher commission rate by the sales amount. If it isn't, it moves on to the value_if_false argument and multiplies the lower commission rate by the sales amount.

3. Press (Enter) or click the Enter button on the formula bar to complete the formula (**Figure 62**).

4. Use the fill handle to copy the formula down the column for the rest of the salespeople (**Figure 63**).

IF FUNCTION

97

Lookup & Reference Functions

Excel's lookup and reference functions return values based on information stored elsewhere in the workbook or in a linked worksheet.

The VLOOKUP & HLOOKUP functions

The VLOOKUP (**Figures 64 and 65**) and HLOOKUP functions return information based on data stored in a lookup table. The function attempts to match a value in one of its arguments to values in the first column (VLOOKUP) or first row (HLOOKUP) of the lookup table. If it finds a match, it returns the associated value.

The VLOOKUP and HLOOKUP functions use the following syntax:

VLOOKUP(lookup_value,table_array,
col_index_num,range_lookup**)**

HLOOKUP(lookup_value,table_array,
row_index_num,range_lookup**)**

Lookup_value is the value you want to match in the table. Table_array is the cell reference for the lookup table. Col_index_num or row_index_num is the number of the column or row, relative to the table, that contains the values you want returned. These three arguments are required. Range_lookup, which is not required, tells Excel what it should do if it can't match the lookup_value. There are two options for this argument: TRUE tells Excel to return the value associated with the next lowest value; FALSE tells Excel to return the #N/A error value. If omitted, TRUE is assumed.

✔ Tip

- The first column or row of the lookup table must be sorted in ascending order for the VLOOKUP or HLOOKUP function to work properly.

	A	B	C	D
1	Item Number:	L-108		
2	Price:	13.99	=VLOOKUP(B1,A5:D12,4,FALSE)	
3				
4	**Item Number**	**Qty**	**Item Name**	**Price**
5	D-439	159	Dreamboys	14.99
6	D-845	341	Happy Ankles	8.99
7	E-473	415	Night at the Gallery	19.99
8	G-058	167	Shelly's Web	19.99
9	L-108	684	Stoney Balboa	13.99
10	M-400	218	Miss Panner	22.99
11	M-482	189	Slow Track	24.99
12	O-571	581	Pirates of the Pacific	15.99

Figure 64 This example illustrates the VLOOKUP function. When you enter an item number in cell *B1*, the formula in *B2* attempts to match it to a value in the first column of the lookup table below it *(A5:D12)*. If it finds a match, it returns the value in the fourth column of the same row as the match. The formula in cell *B2* is shown in cell *C2*.

	A	B	C	D
1	Item Number:	L-216		
2	Price:	#N/A	=VLOOKUP(B1,A5:D12,4,FALSE)	
3				
4	**Item Number**	**Qty**	**Item Name**	**Price**
5	D-439	159	Dreamboys	14.99
6	D-845	341	Happy Ankles	8.99
7	E-473	415	Night at the Gallery	19.99
8	G-058	167	Shelly's Web	19.99
9	L-108	684	Stoney Balboa	13.99
10	M-400	218	Miss Panner	22.99
11	M-482	189	Slow Track	24.99
12	O-571	581	Pirates of the Pacific	15.99

Figure 65 If the formula in *B2* doesn't find a match, it returns the *#N/A* error value, since the optional range_lookup argument is set to *FALSE*.

	A	B	C	D	E
	Values				
1	Test	673.24	anchovy		#N/A
2	Blank Cell	FALSE	FALSE	TRUE	FALSE
3	Error other than #N/A	FALSE	FALSE	FALSE	FALSE
4	Any Error	FALSE	FALSE	FALSE	TRUE
5	Logical Value	FALSE	FALSE	FALSE	FALSE
6	#N/A Error	FALSE	FALSE	FALSE	TRUE
7	Not Text	TRUE	FALSE	TRUE	TRUE
8	Number	TRUE	FALSE	FALSE	FALSE
9	Cell Reference	TRUE	TRUE	TRUE	TRUE
10	Text	FALSE	TRUE	FALSE	FALSE

Figure 66 In this example, the IS functions were used (in the order shown to the right) to evaluate the contents of the cells in row *1* of the worksheet. The results of each function appear below the value.

	A	B	C	D
1	Enter Your Name:			
2				
3	Message:	You did not enter your name.		
4				
5	Formula in B3:	=IF(ISTEXT(B1),"Hello "&B1,"You did not enter your name.")		

	A	B	C	D
1	Enter Your Name:	Maria		
2				
3	Message:	Hello Maria		
4				
5	Formula in B3:	=IF(ISTEXT(B1),"Hello "&B1,"You did not enter your name.")		

Figures 67 & 68 In this silly example, the formula in cell *B3*, *=IF(ISTEXT(B1),"Hello "&B1,"You did not enter your name. ")*, scolds the user for not entering a name (top), then greets her by name when she does enter it (bottom).

Information Functions

Excel's information functions return information about other cells.

The IS functions

Excel's IS functions (**Figure 66**) use the following syntax:

ISBLANK(value)

ISERR(value)

ISERROR(value)

ISLOGICAL(value)

ISNA(value)

ISNONTEXT(value)

ISNUMBER(value)

ISREF(value)

ISTEXT(value)

In each case, Excel tests for a different thing. The value argument is the value or cell reference to be tested.

✔ Tip

■ Use an IS function in conjunction with the IF function to return a value based on the condition of a cell (**Figures 67** and **68**).

Date and Time Functions

Excel's date and time functions are designed specifically to work with dates and times. I tell you about the most useful ones here.

✔ Tips

- Excel treats dates and times as serial numbers. This means that although you may enter information as a date or time—like 12/29/06 or 12:20 PM—Excel converts what you type into a number for its own internal use (**see Table 1**). A date is the number of days since January 1, 1900. A time is the portion of a day since midnight. Excel's formatting makes the number look like a date or time. I tell you about cell formatting in **Chapter 6**.

- If your workbook will used by an Excel for Macintosh user, you can change Excel's date system from the Windows 1900 system to the Macintosh 1904 system. Choose Office > Excel Options, click the Advanced category, and turn on the Use 1904 date system check box under When calculating this workbook (**Figure 69**). This changes the serial numbers for dates in the current workbook file. I tell you more about Excel Options in **Chapter 15**.

- If you enter a date with a two-digit year between 00 and 29, such as *5/15/07*, Excel assumes the year is 2007, not 1907.

The DATE function

The DATE function (**Figure 3**) returns the serial number for a date. It uses the following syntax:

=DATE(year,month,day)

The year argument is the year number, the month argument is the month number, and the day argument is the day number. All arguments are required.

Table 1

Examples of How Excel Interprets Dates and Times	
You Enter	**Excel "Sees"**
12/29/2006	34986
6/29/1957	21000
2:45 PM	0.61458333
10:02:56 AM	0.4187037
1/1/1900	0
12:00 AM	0

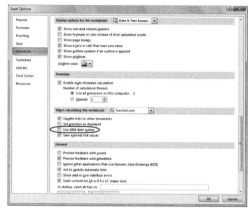

Figure 69 The Options dialog enables you to switch between the standard Windows 1900 date system and the Macintosh 1904 date system.

	A	B
1	First Date	5/7/1995
2	Second Date	12/29/2007
3	Days Between	4619
4		=B2-B1

Figure 70 Calculating the number of days between two dates is as simple as subtracting the contents of one cell from another. The formula in cell *B3* is shown in cell *B4*.

	A	B
1	12/29/2006 12:28	=NOW()
2	12/29/2006	=TODAY()

Figure 71 The NOW function returns the current date and time while the TODAY function returns just the current date.

	A	B	C
1		6/30/1961	
2	Day	30	=DAY(B1)
3	Weekday	6	=WEEKDAY(B1)
4	Month	6	=MONTH(B1)
5	Year	1961	=YEAR(B1)

Figure 72 The DAY, WEEKDAY, MONTH, and YEAR functions extract portions of a date. The formulas in column *B* are shown in column *C*.

To calculate the number of days between two dates

Enter the two dates into separate cells of a worksheet, then write a formula using the subtraction operator (–) to subtract the earlier date from the later date (**Figure 70**).

Or

In a worksheet cell, write a formula using the date function, like this:

=DATE(01,10,15)–DATE(01,5,8)

The NOW & TODAY functions

The NOW and TODAY functions (**Figure 71**) return the serial number for the current date and time (NOW) or current date (TODAY). Results are automatically formatted and will change each time the worksheet is recalculated or opened. They use the following syntax:

NOW( )

TODAY( )

Although there are no arguments, the parentheses characters must be included.

The DAY, WEEKDAY, MONTH, & YEAR functions

The DAY, WEEKDAY, MONTH, and YEAR functions (**Figure 72**) return the day of the month, the day of the week, the month number, or the year number for a serial number. They use the following syntax:

DAY(serial_number)

WEEKDAY(serial_number)

MONTH(serial_number)

YEAR(serial_number)

The serial_number argument can be a cell reference, number, or date written as text, like *10/14/02* or *15-Apr-04*.

Text Functions

Excel's text functions enable you to extract, convert, concatenate, and get information about text. I tell you about a few of the more commonly used ones here.

The LOWER, UPPER, & PROPER functions

The LOWER, UPPER, and PROPER functions (**Figure** 73) convert text to lowercase, uppercase, and title case. They use the following syntax:

LOWER(text)

UPPER(text)

PROPER(text)

The text argument, which is required, is the text you want converted.

The LEFT, RIGHT, & MID functions

The LEFT, RIGHT, and MID functions (**Figure** 74) return the leftmost, rightmost, or middle characters of a text string. They use the following syntax:

LEFT(text,num_chars)

RIGHT(text,num_chars)

MID(text,start_num,num_chars)

The text argument, which is required, is the text from which characters should be extracted. The num_chars argument is the number of characters you want extracted. If omitted from the LEFT or RIGHT function, 1 is assumed. The MID function has an additional argument, start_num, which is the number of the first character from which you want to extract text. The MID function requires all arguments.

	A	B	C
1	Original Text	This IS an eXample.	
2	Lowercase	this is an example.	=LOWER(B1)
3	Uppercase	THIS IS AN EXAMPLE.	=UPPER(B1)
4	Title Case	This Is An Example.	=PROPER(B1)

Figure 73 Use the LOWER, UPPER, and PROPER functions to change the case of text. The formulas in column *B* are shown in column *C*.

	A	B	C
1	Original Text	Mississippi	
2	First 4 characters	Miss	=LEFT(B1,4)
3	Last 4 characters	ippi	=RIGHT(B1,4)
4	4 characters starting with 3rd character	ssis	=MID(B1,3,4)

Figure 74 Use the LEFT, RIGHT, and MID functions to extract characters from text. The formulas in column *B* are shown in column *C*.

	A	B	C
1	Last Name	First Name	Full Name
2	Twain	Mark	Twain Mark
3			'=CONCATENATE(A2," ",B2)

Figure 75 Use the CONCATENATE function to join strings of text. The formula in cell *C2* is shown in cell *C3*.

	A	B	C	D	E	F
1	Amount Due	124.95				
2	Date Due	4/15/2007				
3						
4	The total amount due is $124.95. Please pay by 04/15/07.					
5						
6	="The total amount due is "&DOLLAR(B1)&". Please pay by "&TEXT(B2,"mm/dd/yy")&"."					

Figure 76 The formula in cell A4, = *"The total amount due is "&DOLLAR(B1)&". Please pay by "&TEXT(B2,"mm/dd/yy")&".",* writes a sentence using the contents of two cells, the concatenate operator, and two text functions.

The CONCATENATE Function

The CONCATENATE function (**Figure 75**) joins or concatenates two or more strings of text. It uses the following syntax:

CONCATENATE(text1,text2,...)

Each text argument can include single cell references, text, or numbers you want to join. The CONCATENATE function can accept up to 30 arguments, but only two are required.

✔ Tips

- Excel recognizes the ampersand character (&) as a concatenation operator in formulas. You can concatenate text by including an ampersand between cells or text strings in a formula, like this:
  =B2&" "&A2

- If you want spaces between the strings, be sure to include the space character, between double quote characters, as an argument (**Figure 75**).

- Creative use of the CONCATENATE function or operator makes it possible to give documents a personal touch. **Figure 76** shows an example.

CONCATENATING TEXT

Formatting Cells

Southwest Division				
First Quarter Sales				
	Jan	Feb	Mar	Totals
John	1411.75	1196.44	1442.83	4051.02
Jean	1073.69	1763.35	834.3	3671.34
Joe	994.32	674.05	2161.65	3830.02
Joan	1790.1	1200.45	942.49	3933.04
Total	5269.86	4834.29	5381.27	15485.42

Figure 1 While content should be more important than appearance, you can bet that this worksheet won't get as much attention …

Southwest Division				
First Quarter Sales				
	Jan	Feb	Mar	Totals
John	$1,411.75	$1,196.44	$1,442.83	$ 4,051.02
Jean	1,073.69	1,763.35	834.30	3,671.34
Joe	994.32	674.05	2,161.65	3,830.02
Joan	1,790.10	1,200.45	942.49	3,933.04
Total	$5,269.86	$4,834.29	$5,381.27	$15,485.42

Figure 2 … as this one.

✔ Tips

■ Excel may automatically apply formatting to cells, depending on what you enter. For example, if you use a date function, Excel formats the results of the function as a date. You can change Excel's formatting at any time to best meet your needs.

■ Most formatting is applied to cells, not cell contents. If you use the Clear Contents command to clear a cell, the formatting remains and will be applied to whatever data is next entered into it.

Formatting Basics

To paraphrase an old Excel mentor of mine, formatting a worksheet is like putting on its makeup. The worksheet's contents may be perfectly correct, but by applying formatting, you can make a better impression on the people who see it (**Figures 1** and **2**).

Excel offers a wide range of formatting options you can use to beautify your worksheets:

◆ **Number formatting** lets you change the appearance of numbers, dates, and times.

◆ **Alignment** lets you change the way cell contents are aligned within the cell.

◆ **Font formatting** lets you change the appearance of text and number characters.

◆ **Borders** let you add lines around cells.

◆ **Fill** lets you add color, shading, and patterns to cells.

◆ **Column and row formatting** let you change column width and row height.

You can apply formatting to cells using a variety of techniques: with Formatting toolbar buttons, shortcut keys, menu commands, or the Conditional Formatting or AutoFormat features.

Number Formatting

By default, Excel applies the General number format to worksheet cells. This format displays numbers just as they're entered (**Figure 3**).

Excel offers a wide variety of predefined number formatting options for different purposes:

◆ **Number** formats are used for general number display.

◆ **Currency** formats are used for monetary values.

◆ **Accounting** formats are used to line up columns of monetary values.

◆ **Date** formats are used to display dates.

◆ **Time** formats are used to display times.

◆ **Percentage** formats are used to display percentages.

◆ **Fraction** formats are used to display decimal values as fractions.

◆ **Scientific** format is used to display values in scientific notation.

◆ **Text** format is used to display cell contents as text, the way it was entered.

◆ **Special** formats include a variety of special purpose formatting options.

◆ **Custom** lets you create your own number format using formatting codes.

You can change number formatting of selected cells with options in the Number group of the Ribbon's Home tab (**Figure 5**) or in the Number tab of the Format Cells dialog (**Figures 10 through 17**).

1548.36
12458
14.2
-354.85
116.028
0.2
1.25459E+14

Figure 3 General formatting displays the numbers just as they're typed in and uses scientific notation when they're very big.

Number 1	1.5049	$ 1.50
Number 2	3.504	$ 3.50
	5.0089	$ 5.01

Figure 4 The two columns contain identical values, but the column on the right is formatted with the Accounting Number Format style. Because Excel performs calculations with the numbers underlying any formatting, the total on the right appears incorrect!

✔ Tips

■ If the integer part of a number is longer than the width of the cell or 11 digits, General number format displays it in scientific notation (**Figure 3**).

■ Number formatting changes only the appearance of a number. Although formatting may remove decimal places from displayed numbers, it does not round numbers. **Figure 4** illustrates this. Use the ROUND function, which I discuss in **Chapter 5**, to round numbers in formulas.

■ If you include characters such as dollar signs or percent symbols with a number you enter, Excel automatically assigns an appropriate built-in format to the cell.

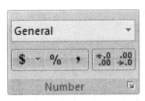

Figure 5
The Number group of the Ribbon's Home tab includes commands for applying number formatting options.

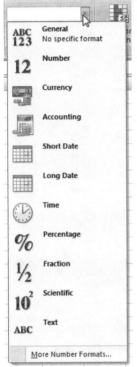

Figure 6
The Number Format drop-down list offers several predefined number formats.

To apply number formatting with Number group options

To apply one of the predefined number formats, choose an option from the Number Format drop-down list (**Figure 6**) or click the button for the format you want to apply (**Figure 5**):

◆ **Accounting Number Format** displays the number as currency, with a currency symbol, commas, and two decimal places.

◆ **Percent Style** displays the number as a percentage with a percent symbol and two decimal places.

◆ **Comma Style** displays the number with a comma and two decimal places.

Figure 7 shows examples of some of these formats.

✔ Tip

■ The Accounting Number Format button is also a menu. Click the triangle on the button to choose from additional options (**Figure 8**).

To change the number of decimal places

Click one of the Decimal buttons in the Number group of the Ribbon's Home tab (**Figure 5**):

◆ **Increase Decimal** displays an additional decimal digit.

◆ **Decrease Decimal** displays one less decimal digit.

General	0.015	1163.2	-12.785
Accounting Number Format	$ 0.02	$1,163.20	$ (12.79)
Percent Style	2%	116320%	-1279%
Comma Style	0.02	1,163.20	(12.79)

Figure 7 Three different values, each with one of the Number group's number formats applied.

Figure 8
The Accounting Number Format button is also a menu.

To apply number formatting with the Format Cells dialog

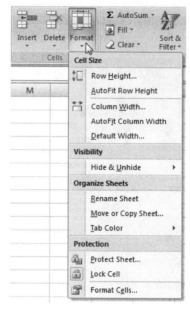

Figure 9
The Format menu offers access to many of the formatting commands discussed in this chapter.

1. Choose Home > Cells > Format > Format Cells (**Figure 9**), press Ctrl 1, or click the dialog box launcher button in the lower-right corner of the Number group (**Figure 5**).

2. If necessary, in the Format Cells dialog that appears, click the Number tab to display its options (**Figure 10**).

3. Choose a number format category from the Category list.

4. Set options in the dialog. The options vary for each category; **Figures 10** through **17** show examples. Check the Sample area to see the number in the active cell with the formatting options you selected applied.

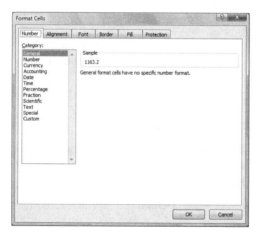
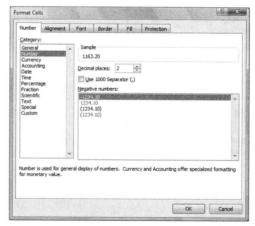

Figures 10 & 11 Examples of options in the Number tab of the Format Cells dialog.

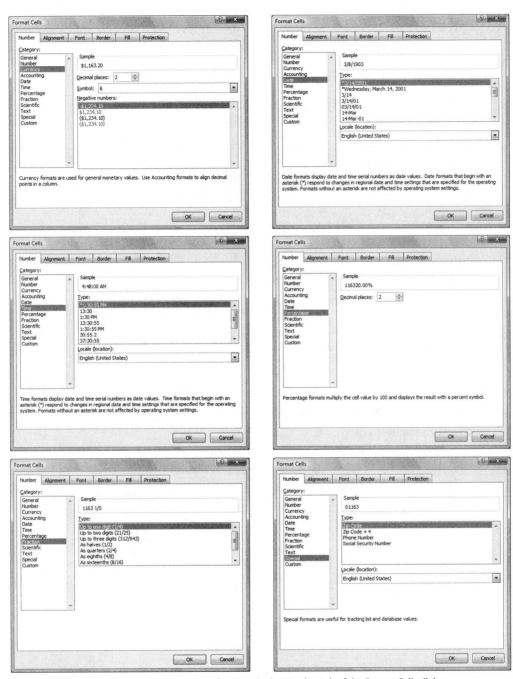

Figures 12, 13, 14, 15, 16, & 17 More examples of options in the Number tab of the Format Cells dialog.

Alignment

Excel offers a wide variety of options to set the way characters are positioned within a cell (**Figure 18**):

◆ **Text Alignment** options position the text within the cell.

◆ **Orientation** options control the angle at which text appears within the cell.

◆ **Text Control** options control how text appears within the cell.

◆ **Right-to-left** options control the reading order of cell contents. This option is useful for languages that read characters from right-to-left rather than left-to-right.

You can change alignment settings for selected cells with the Alignment group of the Ribbon's Home tab (**Figure 19**) or the Alignment tab of the Format Cells dialog (**Figure 21**).

✔ Tips

■ By default, within each cell, Excel left aligns text and right aligns numbers. This is called General alignment.

■ Although it's common to center headings over columns containing numbers, the work-sheet may actually look better with headings right aligned. **Figure 20** shows an example.

■ The Merge & Center option for text control is handy for centering worksheet titles over the cells in use.

General	a
Left Aligned	V n
Centered	e d
Right Aligned	r
FillFillFillFillFillFillFillFill	t M
Top Aligned	i e
	c r
Center Aligned	a g
	l e
Bottom Aligned	d
Wrap text with full horizontal justification. Note the way text wraps and is justifed.	
Merged and Centered	
Merged Only	

Figure 18 Examples of cells with different alignment options applied.

Figure 19 The Alignment group of the Ribbon's Home tab offers a number of alignment options.

Jan	Feb
1,254	1,256
1,865	1,736
1,614	1,284
1,987	1,908
6,720	6,184

Figure 20 Headings sometimes look better when they're right aligned (right) rather than centered (left) over columns of numbers.

ALIGNMENT BASICS

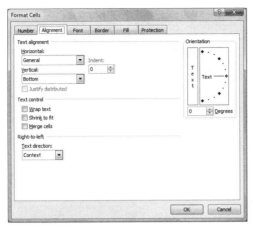

Figure 21 The Alignment tab of the Format cells dialog.

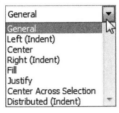

Figure 22
Options on the
Horizontal drop-
down list.

To set text alignment with Alignment group options

1. To set vertical alignment, click the Alignment group button for the type of alignment you want to apply (**Figure 19**):

   ▲ **Top align** aligns cell contents against the top of the cell.

   ▲ **Middle align** centers cell contents between the top and bottom of the cell.

   ▲ **Bottom align** aligns cell contents against the bottom of the cell.

2. To set horizontal alignment, click the Alignment group button for the type of alignment you want to apply (**Figure 19**):

   ▲ **Align Left** aligns cell contents against the left side of the cell.

   ▲ **Center** centers cell contents between the left and right sides of the cell.

   ▲ **Align Right** aligns cell contents against the right side of the cell.

To set text alignment with the Format Cells dialog

1. Choose Home > Cells > Format > Format Cells (**Figure 9**), press Ctrl 1, or click the dialog box launcher button in the lower-right corner of the Alignment group (**Figure 19**).

2. The Format Cells dialog appears. If necessary, click the Alignment tab to display its options (**Figure 21**).

3. To set horizontal text alignment, choose an option from the Horizontal drop-down list (**Figure 22**):

   ▲ **General** applies default alignment.

   ▲ **Left (Indent)** aligns cell contents against the left side of the cell. It also allows you to indent cell contents.

Continued on next page...

SETTING TEXT ALIGNMENT

Continued from previous page.

▲ **Center** centers cell contents between the left and right sides of the cell.

▲ **Right (Indent)** aligns cell contents against the right side of the cell.

▲ **Fill** repeats the cell contents to fill the cell.

▲ **Justify** stretches multiple lines of text across the cell so all lines except the last fill the cell from left to right.

▲ **Center Across Selection** centers the active cell's contents across the selected cells.

▲ **Distributed (Indent)** distributes the cell's contents horizontally within the cell.

4. To set vertical text alignment, choose an option from the Vertical drop-down list (**Figure 23**):

▲ **Top** aligns cell contents against the top of the cell.

▲ **Center** centers cell contents between the top and bottom of the cell.

▲ **Bottom** aligns cell contents against the bottom of the cell.

▲ **Justify** stretches multiple lines of text from the top to the bottom of the cell.

▲ **Distributed** distributes the cell's contents vertically within the cell.

5. Click OK.

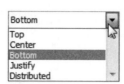

Figure 23
Options on the Vertical drop-down list.

Figure 24 This cell's contents were indented by clicking the Increase Indent button twice.

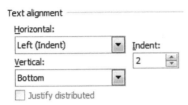

Figure 25 To indent text, set Text alignment options like this.

To indent cell contents with Alignment group options

Click the Alignment group button for the indentation change you want:

◆ **Decrease Indent** decreases the amount of indentation.

◆ **Increase Indent** increases the amount of indentation (**Figure 24**).

To indent cell contents with the Format Cells dialog

1. Choose Home > Cells > Format > Format Cells (**Figure 9**), press [Ctrl][1], or click the dialog box launcher button in the lower-right corner of the Alignment group (**Figure 19**).

2. In the Format Cells dialog that appears, click the Alignment tab to display its options (**Figure 21**).

3. Choose Left (Indent) from the Horizontal drop-down list (**Figure 25**).

4. In the Indent text box, enter the number of characters by which you want to indent cell contents (**Figure 25**).

5. Click OK.

INDENTING CELL CONTENTS

To wrap text with Alignment group options

Click the Wrap text button to enable text wrapping within a cell (**Figure 19**).

To set text control options with the Format Cells dialog

1. Choose Home > Cells > Format > Format Cells (**Figure 9**), press Ctrl 1, or click the dialog box launcher button in the lower-right corner of the Alignment group (**Figure 19**).

2. In the Format Cells dialog that appears, click the Alignment tab to display its options (**Figure 21**).

3. Turn on any valid combination of the check boxes in the Text control area.

4. Click OK.

✔ Tip

■ As shown in **Figures 26** through **28**, the Wrap text and Shrink to fit options can be used to fit cell contents within a cell.

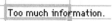

Figure 26 Select a cell with too much information.

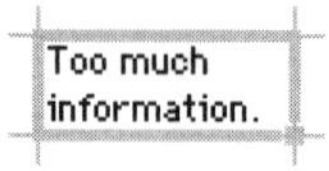

Figure 27 Here's the cell from **Figure 26** with Wrap text applied.

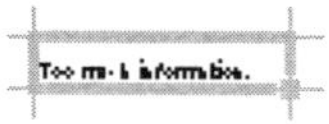

Figure 28 Here's the cell from **Figure 26** with Shrink to fit applied.

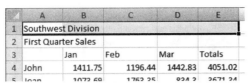

Figure 29 Select the cells you want to merge and center.

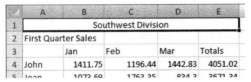

Figure 30 The cells are merged together and the cell contents are centered in the merged cell.

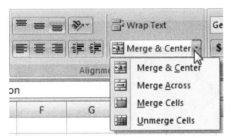

Figure 31 The Merge & Center button is also a menu with related options.

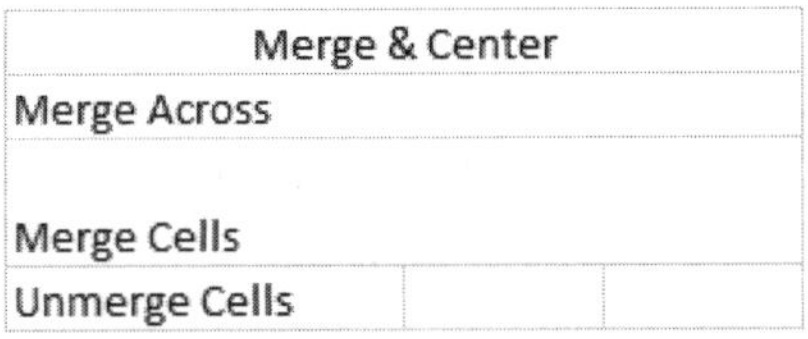

Merge & Center
Merge Across
Merge Cells
Unmerge Cells

Figure 32 The Merge & Center button menu's options, illustrated.

✔ Tip

■ You can get similar results by choosing Center Across Selection from the Horizontal drop-down list (**Figure 22**) in step 4 and skipping step 5. The cells, however, are not merged, so an entry into one of the adjacent cells could obscure the centered contents.

To merge & center cells with Alignment group options

1. Select the cell(s) whose contents you want to center, along with the cells of the columns to the right that you want to center across (**Figure 29**).

2. Click the Merge & Center button on the Alignment group of the Ribbon's Home tab. The cell contents shift so they're centered between the left and right sides of the selected area (**Figure 30**).

✔ Tip

■ The Merge & Center button is also a menu. Click its triangle to choose from other options (**Figure 31**), each of which is illustrated in **Figure 32**.

To merge & center cells with the Format Cells dialog

1. Select the cell(s) whose contents you want to center, along with the cells of the columns to the right that you want to center across (**Figure 29**).

2. Choose Home > Cells > Format > Format Cells (**Figure 9**), press ⌃1, or click the dialog box launcher button in the lower-right corner of the Alignment group (**Figure 19**).

3. In the Format Cells dialog that appears, click the Alignment tab to display its options (**Figure 21**).

4. Choose Center from the Horizontal drop-down list (**Figure 22**).

5. Turn on the Merge cells check box.

6. Click OK. The cell contents shift so they're centered between the left and right sides of the selected area (**Figure 30**).

MERGING & CENTERING CELLS

To change cell orientation with Alignment group options

Choose an option from the Orientation button's menu (**Figure 33**). **Figure 34** shows examples of each of the options.

✔ Tips

- Rotated text appears better when printed than it does on screen (**Figure 34**).

- Changing the orientation of a cell's contents can change the height and width of the cell's row (**Figure 34**).

To change cell orientation with the Format Cells dialog

1. Choose Home > Cells > Format > Format Cells (**Figure 9**), press Ctrl 1, or click the dialog box launcher button in the lower-right corner of the Alignment group (**Figure 19**).

2. In the Format Cells dialog that appears, click the Alignment tab to display its options (**Figure 21**).

3. Set options in the Orientation area (**Figure 35**) using one of these methods:
   - ▲ To display text characters one above the other, click the Vertical Orientation button.
   - ▲ To display text characters at an angle, drag the red diamond in the rotation area or enter an angle value in the Degrees box.

4. Click OK.

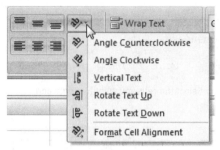

Figure 33 The Orientation button is a menu with various orientation options.

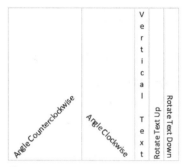

Figure 34 You can achieve a variety of orientation effects.

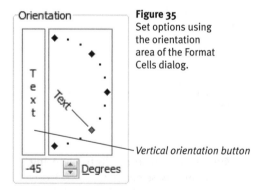

Figure 35 Set options using the orientation area of the Format Cells dialog.

Vertical orientation button

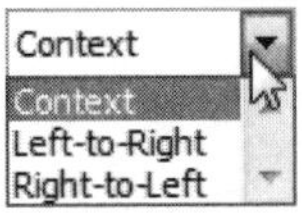

Figure 36
Use this drop-down list to set text direction options.

✔ Tips

- You cannot set orientation options if Center Across Selection is chosen from the Horizontal drop-down list (**Figure 22**). Choose another option before you set orientation.

- You can enter either a positive or negative value in the Degrees box (**Figure 35**).

- Rotated text appears better when printed than it does on screen (**Figure 34**).

- Changing the orientation of a cell's contents can change the height and width of the cell's row (**Figure 34**).

- Rotating the text in column headings often enables you to decrease column width, thus enabling you to fit more information on screen or on paper. I tell you how to change column width later in this chapter.

To change text direction

1. Choose Home > Cells > Format > Format Cells (**Figure 9**), press Ctrl 1, or click the dialog box launcher button in the lower-right corner of the Alignment group (**Figure 19**).

2. In the Format Cells dialog that appears, click the Alignment tab to display its options (**Figure 21**).

3. Choose an option from the Text Direction drop-down list (**Figure 36**):

   ▲ **Context** sets text direction based on the cell content's context or language.

   ▲ **Left-to-Right** enables you to enter text from left to right.

   ▲ **Right-to-Left** enables you to enter text from right to left.

✔ Tip

- In most cases, you will have no need to change text direction options.

CHANGING CELL ORIENTATION, TEXT DIRECTION

Font Formatting

Excel uses 11 point Calibri as the default font or typeface for worksheets. You can apply a variety of font formatting options to cells, some of which are shown in **Figure 37**:

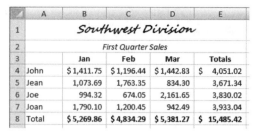

Figure 37 This example shows font, font size, and font style applied to the contents of cells.

- ◆ **Font** is the typeface used to display characters. This includes all fonts properly installed in your system.

- ◆ **Font style** is the weight or angle of characters. Options usually include Regular, Bold, Italic, and Bold Italic.

- ◆ **Size** is the size of characters, expressed in points.

- ◆ **Underline** is character underlining. Don't confuse this with borders, which can be applied to the bottom of a cell, regardless of its contents.

- ◆ **Color** is character color.

- ◆ **Effects** are special effects applied to characters.

You can apply font formatting with the Font group of the Ribbon's Home tab (**Figure 38**), shortcut keys, and the Format Cells dialog.

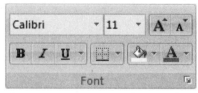

Figure 38 The Font group of the Ribbon's Home tab.

✔ Tip

- ■ You can change the formatting of individual characters within a cell. Just double-click the cell to make it active, select the characters you want to change (**Figure 39**), and use the appropriate font formatting technique to change the characters (**Figure 40**).

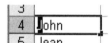

Figure 39 You can also select individual characters within a cell ...

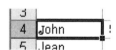

Figure 40 ... and apply formatting to them.

Figure 41
The Font drop-down list in the Font group of the Ribbon's Home tab lists all of the fonts installed in your system.

Figure 42
You can choose a size from the Font Size drop-down list.

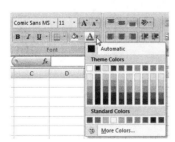

Figure 43 The Font Color menu on the Formatting toolbar enables you to apply color to characters.

To apply font formatting with Font group options or shortcut keys

1. To change the font:
   - ▲ Choose a font from the Font drop-down list (**Figure 41**).
   - ▲ Click on the Font box to select its contents, type in the name of the font you want to apply, and press Enter.

2. To change the character size:
   - ▲ Choose a size from the Font Size drop-down list (**Figure 42**).
   - ▲ Click on the Font Size box to select its contents, type in a size, and press Enter.
   - ▲ Click the Increase Font Size or Decrease Font Size buttons to increment or decrement the font size by one pixel.

3. To change the character style, click any combination of font style buttons or press corresponding shortcut keys:
   - ▲ **Bold** or Ctrl B makes characters appear bold.
   - ▲ *Italic* or Ctrl I makes characters appear slanted.
   - ▲ Underline or Ctrl U applies a single underline to characters.

4. To change the character color, choose a color from the Font Color menu (**Figure 43**).

✔ Tips

- ■ Font size must be between 1 and 409 points in half-point increments. (In case you're wondering, 72 points equals 1 inch.)

- ■ The Automatic color option (**Figure 43**) tells Excel to automatically apply color based on other formatting options.

APPLYING FONT FORMATTING

To apply font formatting with the Format Cells dialog

1. Choose Home > Cells > Format > Format Cells (**Figure 9**), press Ctrl 1, or click the dialog box launcher button in the lower-right corner of the Font group (**Figure 38**).

2. In the Format Cells dialog that appears, click the Font tab to display its options (**Figure 44**).

3. Set options as desired:
   - ▲ Select a font from the Font list or type a font name into the text box above the list.
   - ▲ Select a style from the Font style list or type a style name into the text box above the list.
   - ▲ Select a size from the Size list or type a size into the text box above the list.
   - ▲ Choose an underline option from the Underline drop-down list (**Figure 45**).
   - ▲ Choose a font color from the Color drop-down list (**Figure 46**).
   - ▲ Turn on check boxes in the Effects area to apply font effects.

4. When the sample text in the Preview area looks just the way you want, click OK.

✔ Tips

- ■ To return a selection to the default font, turn on the Normal font check box in the Format Cells dialog (**Figure 44**).

- ■ The accounting underline options in the Underline drop-down list (**Figure 45**) stretch almost the entire width of the cell.

- ■ The Automatic color option (**Figure 46**) tells Excel to automatically apply color based on other formatting options.

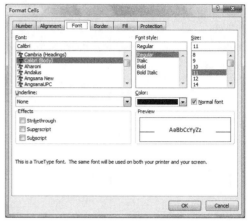

Figure 44 The Font tab of the Format Cells dialog.

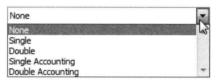

Figure 45 Excel offers several underlining options.

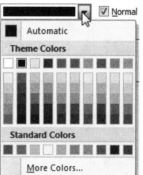

Figure 46 The Color drop-down list in the Format Cells dialog.

	A	B	C	D	E
1	*Southwest Division*				
2		*First Quarter Sales*			
3		Jan	Feb	Mar	Totals
4	John	$ 1,411.75	$ 1,196.44	$ 1,442.83	$ 4,051.02
5	Jean	1,073.69	1,763.35	834.30	3,671.34
6	Joe	994.32	674.05	2,161.65	3,830.02
7	Joan	1,790.10	1,200.45	942.49	3,933.04
8	Total	$ 5,269.86	$ 4,834.29	$ 5,381.27	$ 15,485.42

Figure 47 Use borders to place lines under headings and above and below column totals.

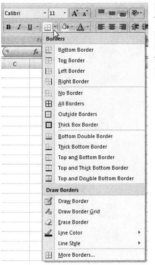

Figure 48
The Borders menu in the Font group of the Ribbon's Home tab.

Borders

Excel offers many border styles that you can apply to separate cells or a selection of cells (**Figure 47**).

Use the Font group of the Ribbon's Home tab or the Format Cells dialog to add and format borders.

To add borders with the Font group's Border button

1. Select the cell(s) you want to add borders to.

2. Choose the type of border you want to apply from the Borders menu (**Figure 48**).

✔ Tips

- To remove borders from a selection, choose No Border from the Border menu (**Figure 48**). If the border does not disappear, it may be applied to a cell adjoining the one you selected.

- The accounting underline options on the Underline drop-down list in the Format Cells dialog (**Figure 45**) are not the same as borders. They do not stretch across the entire width of the cell and they only appear when the cell is not blank.

ADDING BORDERS

To add borders with the Format Cells dialog

1. Choose Home > Cells > Format > Format Cells (**Figure 9**), press Ctrl 1, or click the dialog box launcher button in the lower-right corner of the Font group (**Figure 38**).

2. In the Format Cells dialog that appears, click the Border tab to display its options (**Figure 49**).

3. Select a line style in the Line area.

4. If desired, select a color from the Color drop-down list, which looks just like the one in **Figure 46**.

5. Set individual borders for the selected cells using one of these methods:

   ▲ Click one of the buttons in the Presets area to apply a predefined border. (None removes all borders from the selection.)

   ▲ Click a button in the Border area to add a border to the corresponding area.

   ▲ Click between the lines in the illustration in the Border area to place corresponding borders.

6. Repeat steps 3, 4, and 5 until all the desired borders for the selection are set.

7. Click OK.

✔ Tip

■ To get the borders in your worksheet to look just the way you want, be prepared to make several selections and trips to the Border tab of the Format Cells dialog.

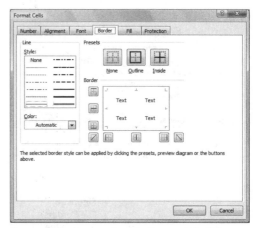

Figure 49 The Border tab of the Format Cells dialog with several cells selected.

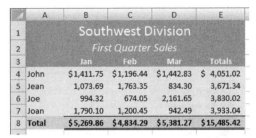

Figure 50 Use Excel's cell shading feature to add fill colors and patterns to cells.

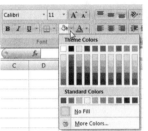

Figure 51 The Fill Color menu in the Font group of the Ribbon's Home tab.

Cell Shading

Excel's shading feature lets you add color to cells (**Figure 50**), either with or without patterns. You can do this with the Fill Color menu on the Font group (**Figure 51**) of the Ribbon's Home tab or in the Format Cells dialog.

✔ Tips

- By combining two colors with a pattern, you can create various colors and levels of shading.

- Be careful when adding shading to cells! If the color is too dark, cell contents may not be legible.

- To improve the legibility of cell contents in shaded cells, try making the characters bold.

- For a different look, use a dark color for the cell and make its characters white (**Figure 50**).

To apply shading with the Font group's Fill Color menu

1. Select the cell(s) to which you want to apply shading.

2. Choose a color from the Fill Color menu (**Figure 51**).

✔ Tip

- To remove colors from a selection, choose No Fill from the Fill Color menu (**Figure 51**).

To apply shading with the Format Cells dialog

1. Choose Home > Cells > Format > Format Cells (**Figure 9**), press $\boxed{\text{Ctrl}}\boxed{1}$, or click the dialog box launcher button in the lower-right corner of the Font group (**Figure 38**).

2. In the Format Cells dialog that appears, click the Fill tab to display its options (**Figure 52**).

3. Select a color from the Background Color palette.

4. If desired, choose a foreground color from the Pattern Color drop-down list (**Figure 53**) and a pattern from the Pattern Style drop-down list (**Figure 54**).

5. When the Sample area of the dialog looks just the way you want your selection to look, click OK.

✔ Tips

- You can use the Fill Effects and More Colors button to apply a gradient or select from other background colors.

- Use fill patterns with care! If there isn't enough contrast between cell contents and a patterned fill, the cell contents may be impossible to read.

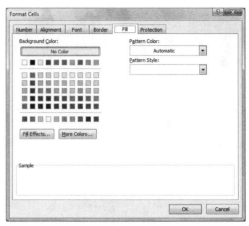

Figure 52 The Fill tab of the Format Cells dialog.

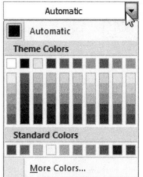

Figure 53
Use the Pattern Color drop-down list to choose a foreground color for a patterned fill …

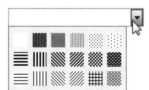

Figure 54
… and then use the Pattern Style drop-down list to choose a pattern.

Southwest Division				
First Quarter Sales				
	Jan	Feb	Mar	Totals
John	1411.75	1196.44	1442.83	4051.02
Jean	1073.69	1763.35	834.3	3671.34
Joe	994.32	674.05	2161.65	3830.02
Joan	1790.1	1200.45	942.49	3933.04
Total	5269.86	4834.29	5381.27	15485.42

Figure 55 An unformatted worksheet with the default Office theme applied.

Southwest Division				
First Quarter Sales				
	Jan	Feb	Mar	Totals
John	1411.75	1196.44	1442.83	4051.02
Jean	1073.69	1763.35	834.3	3671.34
Joe	994.32	674.05	2161.65	3830.02
Joan	1790.1	1200.45	942.49	3933.04
Total	5269.86	4834.29	5381.27	15485.42

Figure 56 The same worksheet shown above but with the Civic theme applied. Note the different font applied.

Themes & Cell Styles

Excel includes two related features to help you apply professional-looking formatting to your worksheet files:

◆ **Themes** are collections of color-coordinated formatting options that affect the overall design of an entire worksheet (**Figures 55** and **56**). Excel includes 20 built-in themes, but you can find and install others from the Microsoft Office Online Web site (office.microsoft.com). You can even make changes to an existing theme and save them as a new theme.

◆ **Cell Styles** are collections of formatting options based on the currently applied theme. Cell styles are designed for specific purposes—for example, for cells containing worksheet headings, values, or links. Cell Styles can include all formatting options discussed up to this point: number formatting, alignment, font, border, and fill. You can use the predefined cell styles or create your own.

There are three main benefits to using themes and cell styles to format your worksheets:

◆ They make it very quick and easy to format a worksheet.

◆ They ensure consistent formatting throughout a worksheet.

◆ They can give your worksheets a professional, polished appearance.

To use themes and cell styles:

1. Choose a theme for the active worksheet (**Figures 55** and **56**).

2. Select one or more cells and choose a cell style to apply to the selection.

3. Repeat step 2 until you've applied all the styles you want to use.

4. Apply other formatting options as desired to complete the worksheet formatting process formatting (**Figure 57**).

In this part of the chapter, I explain how to use the themes and cell styles features.

✔ Tips

■ It's important to note that themes work best on worksheets with no formatting applied. Applying a different theme will not change the appearance of cells that have conflicting formatting applied. For example, if you change the font of some cells in your worksheet and then apply a different theme, the theme's font will not be applied to those cells with the different font manually applied.

■ Themes can be applied to all Microsoft Office programs—not just Excel. So you can use the same theme in Excel, Word, and PowerPoint to maintain a consistent look for all of your Microsoft Office documents.

■ The themes and cell styles features are heavily dependent on color. If you plan to print your work and don't have access to a color printer, you may want to stick to more basic formatting options.

Figure 57 When you're finished applying cell styles and other formatting options, the worksheet might look like this.

Figure 58 Don't like the overall look of your formatted worksheet? No problem. Just change the theme. Here's the same worksheet with the Paper theme applied.

■ Once you get the hang of using Excel's formatting options and cell styles, you may want to experiment with creating your own cell styles. This advanced feature of Excel is beyond the scope of this book, but you can find articles about it on the book's support Web site, www.marialanger.com/excelquickstart/.

■ Once you have applied cell styles to a worksheet, changing the theme simply applies different theme elements to it. **Figure 58** shows how the worksheet in **Figure 57** might look with another theme applied.

Figure 59 You can find the Theme menu on the Ribbon's Page Layout tab.

To apply a theme

1. Activate the worksheet you want to apply the theme to (**Figure 55**).

2. Choose Page Layout > Themes > Themes to display the Theme menu (**Figure 59**).

3. Click to select the theme you want to apply. The appearance of the worksheet changes to reflect the theme's settings (**Figure 56**).

✔ Tip

■ Three menu commands at the bottom of the Themes menu (**Figure 59**) offer additional options for using themes:

   ▲ **More Themes on Microsoft Office Online** uses your default Web browser to display the templates page on the Microsoft Office Online Web site, which offers free themes you can download and use with Excel.

   ▲ **Browse for Themes** enables you to open a theme file already saved on your hard disk or a network location.

   ▲ **Save Current Theme** enables you to save the current theme as a new theme. Use this option if you have customized a theme and want to use the customized version again and again.

APPLYING THEMES

To customize a theme

1. Apply the theme you want to customize.

2. Choose an option from any combination of menus in the Themes group of the Page Layout tab (**Figure 60**):

   ▲ **Colors** (**Figure 61**) enables you to choose a color scheme for the theme.

   ▲ **Fonts** (**Figure 62**) enables you to choose a combination of fonts for the theme.

   ▲ **Effects** (**Figure 63**) enables you to choose a combination of lines and fill effects.

   Your changes are applied immediately.

✔ Tips

■ You can create your own custom color scheme for a theme. Choose Page Layout > Themes > Colors > Create New Theme Colors (**Figure 61**) to get started.

■ You can also create a new set of theme fonts. Choose Page Layout > Themes > Fonts > Create New Theme Fonts (**Figure 62**) to get started.

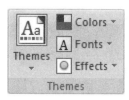

Figure 60
The Themes group on the Page Layout tab.

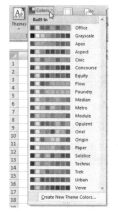

Figure 61 The Colors menu displays color schemes for all themes.

Figure 62 The Fonts menu lists all theme font combinations.

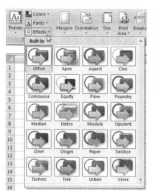

Figure 63
The Effects menu lets you choose from the line and fill effects combinations used by themes.

Figure 64 Select the cell you want to apply formatting to.

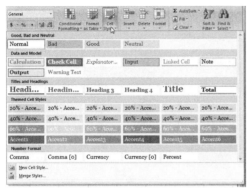

Figure 65 The Cell Styles menu offers a wide variety of predefined styles.

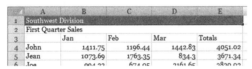

Figure 66 Here's the Accent1 style applied to a cell.

✔ Tips

■ You can combine styles from multiple cell style categories to combine formatting effects. Some styles, however, will overwrite others.

■ You can always modify the appearance of a cell with a cell style applied by manually applying other formatting options as discussed in the first half of this chapter.

■ To remove all styles from a cell, choose Home > Styles > Cell Styles > Normal.

To apply cell styles

1. Select the cell(s) you want to apply the formatting to (**Figure 64**).

2. Choose Home > Styles > Cell Styles to display the Cell Styles menu (**Figure 65**).

3. Click to select the style you want to apply. Styles are broken down into five different categories:

   ▲ Good, Bad and Neutral are formats you may want to apply to highlight certain cells in your worksheet.

   ▲ Data and Model are formats to indicate certain types of cell contents.

   ▲ Titles and Headings are formats for worksheet titles, column headings, and column totals.

   ▲ Themed Cell Styles are formats combining font and fill formatting that directly correspond to the currently applied theme.

   ▲ Number Format are standard, commonly used number formats.

   The option you choose is immediately applied to the selected cell(s) (**Figure 66**).

4. Repeat steps 1 through 3 to format the worksheet as desired.

■ The Cell Styles menu includes two other options you can use to work with cell styles:

   ▲ **New Cell Style** enables you to create a new style. Once created, it will appear at the top of the Cell Style menu.

   ▲ **Merge Styles** enables you to import styles from another Excel Workbook file into the current file.

Conditional Formatting

Excel's Conditional Formatting feature enables you to set up special formatting that is automatically applied by Excel only when cell contents meet certain criteria.

For example, say you have a worksheet containing the total sales for each member of your company's sales staff. You want to display all sales over $1,500 in bold, blue type with a light blue background and black border. You can use Conditional Formatting to automatically apply the desired formatting in cells containing values over 1,500 (**Figure 67**).

	A	B	C	D	E
1	Southwest Division				
2	*First Quarter Sales*				
3		Jan	Feb	Mar	Totals
4	John	$ 1,411.75	$ 1,196.44	$ 1,442.83	$ 4,051.02
5	Jean	1,073.69	1,763.35	834.30	3,671.34
6	Joe	994.32	674.05	2,161.65	3,830.02
7	Joan	1,790.10	1,200.45	942.49	3,933.04
8	Total	$ 5,269.86	$ 4,834.29	$ 5,381.27	$ 15,485.42

Figure 67 Conditional Formatting instructs Excel to format cells based on their contents.

The conditional formatting feature has been revised and improved in Excel 2007 to make it more flexible than ever before. You can now create and apply rules to a selection to determine when conditional formatting will be applied. There are six types of rules:

◆ **Format all cells based on their values** applies fill colors to cells depending on their values. For example, you can set low numbers to be orange and high values to be yellow with values in between colored with colors on a gradient.

◆ **Format only cells that contain** applies formatting to only those cells that meet certain criteria you specify.

◆ **Format only top or bottom ranked values** applies formatting to only those cells containing the highest or lowest values.

◆ **Format only values that are above or below average** applies formatting to the cells containing values that are above or below the average of all the cells, as calculated by Excel.

◆ **Format only unique or duplicate values** applies formatting to only those cells containing unique or duplicate values.

◆ **Use a formula to determine which cells to format** only formats those cells containing results that match the results of a formula you specify.

Clearly, there are many different ways you can use this feature to format worksheet contents—far too many to cover in detail in this book.

In this section, I explain how to use some basic conditional formatting options. You can apply what you learn here to other conditional formatting tasks.

Figure 68
The Highlight Rules submenu on the Conditional Formatting Menu.

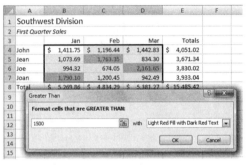

Figure 69 The Greater Than dialog with the selected cells behind it.

Figure 70
Excel offers several predefined formatting options.

Figure 71 Use the Format Cells dialog to set up custom formatting options.

To format cells with contents above a certain value

1. Select the cells you want to be considered for conditional formatting.

2. Choose Home> Styles > Conditional Formatting > Highlight Cells Rules > Greater Than (**Figure 68**) to display the Greater Than dialog (**Figure 69**).

3. Enter a value in the box on the left side of the dialog. As the value changes, Excel highlights different cells in the selection (**Figure 69**).

4. Choose a predefined formatting option from the drop-down list in the Greater Than dialog (**Figure 70**).

   or

   Choose Custom Format from the drop-down list in the Greater Than dialog (**Figure 70**), set options in the Format Cells dialog that appears (**Figure 71**), and click OK.

5. Click OK in the Greater Than dialog to save your settings and apply the formatting (**Figure 67**).

✔ Tip

■ The value that appears by default in the Greater Than dialog (**Figure 69**) is the average of all selected cells.

To add data bars to cells

1. Select the cells you want to be considered for conditional formatting.

2. Choose Home> Styles > Conditional Formatting > Data Bars to display a submenu of data bar colors (**Figure** 72) and choose a color.

   Data bars indicating values appear within each cell of the selection (**Figure** 73).

✔ Tip

■ The Color Scales and Icon Sets options offer two other ways for using color or images to indicate values in a cell. Data bars are my favorite, however, because I think they're least intrusive and maintain the readability of cell contents.

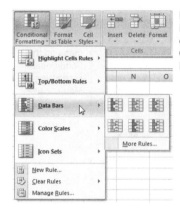

Figure 72
Data Bars options for Conditional Formatting.

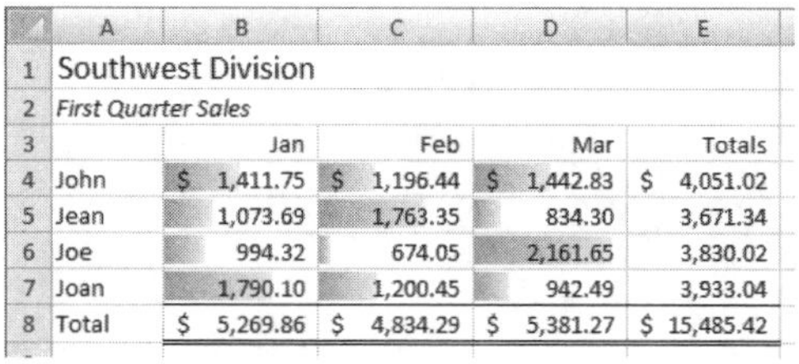

	A	B	C	D	E
1	Southwest Division				
2	*First Quarter Sales*				
3		Jan	Feb	Mar	Totals
4	John	$ 1,411.75	$ 1,196.44	$ 1,442.83	$ 4,051.02
5	Jean	1,073.69	1,763.35	834.30	3,671.34
6	Joe	994.32	674.05	2,161.65	3,830.02
7	Joan	1,790.10	1,200.45	942.49	3,933.04
8	Total	$ 5,269.86	$ 4,834.29	$ 5,381.27	$ 15,485.42

Figure 73 Data Bars are a cool way to visualize numbers, right in your worksheet.

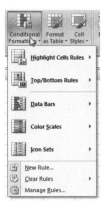

Figure 74
The Conditional
Formatting menu.

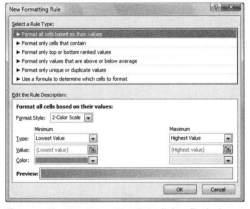

Figure 75 The New Formatting Rule dialog displaying options for the rule to format all cells based on their values.

Figure 76 Selecting a different rule type displays different options.

To create a custom rule

1. Select the cells you want to be considered for conditional formatting.

2. Choose Home > Styles > Conditional Formatting > New Rule (**Figure 74**). The New Formatting Rule dialog appears (**Figure 75**).

3. Select one of the rule types in the top half of the dialog. The bottom half of the dialog changes to offer applicable options (**Figure 76**).

4. Set options in the bottom half of the dialog.

5. If custom formatting is available for the rule, click the Format button. Then use the Format Cells dialog that appears (**Figure 71**) to set formatting options for the cells that match the criteria and click OK.

6. Click OK in the New Formatting Rule dialog to save your settings and apply the formatting.

✔ Tip

- Two other Conditional Formatting menu options can help you work with the Conditional Formatting feature:

  ▲ **Clear Rules** enables you to clear conditional formatting rules from selected cells, the entire worksheet, or other groups of Excel cells.

  ▲ **Manage Rules** displays the Conditional Formatting Rules Manager, which enables you to create, edit, and delete conditional formatting rules.

CREATING CUSTOM RULES

The Format Painter

The Format Painter lets you copy cell formatting and apply it to other cells. This can help you format worksheets quickly and consistently.

Cut
Copy
Paste
Format Painter
Clipboard

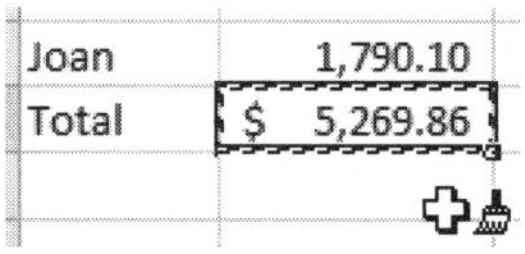

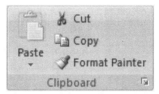

Figure 77 The Home tab's Clipboard group.

To use the Format Painter

1. Select a cell with the formatting you want to copy.
2. Click Home > Clipboard > Format Painter (**Figure 77**). The mouse pointer turns into a little plus sign with a paintbrush beside it and a marquee appears around the original selection (**Figure 78**).
3. Use the Format Painter pointer to select the cells you want to apply the formatting to (**Figure 79**). When you release the mouse button, the formatting is applied (**Figure 80**).

Joan
1,790.10
Total
$ 5,269.86

Figure 78 When you click the Format Painter button, a marquee appears around the original selection and the mouse pointer turns into the Format Painter pointer.

Joan 1,790.10 1,200.45 942.49 3,933.04
Total $ 5,269.86 4834.29 5381.27 5485.42

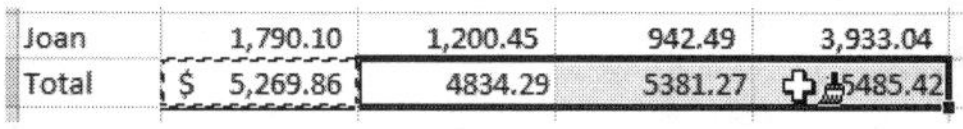

Figure 79 Drag to select the cells to which you want to copy formats.

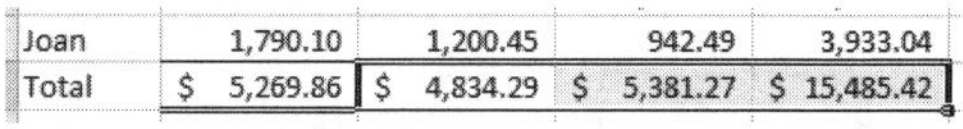

Joan 1,790.10 1,200.45 942.49 3,933.04
Total $ 5,269.86 $ 4,834.29 $ 5,381.27 $ 15,485.42

Figure 80 When you release the mouse button, the formatting is applied.

✔ Tips

- You can double-click the Format Painter button in step 1 to continue applying a copied format throughout the worksheet. Press Esc or click the Format Painter button again to stop applying the format and return the mouse pointer to normal.
- You can also use the Clipboard group's Copy and Paste > Paste Special commands to copy the formatting of selected cells and paste it into other cells.

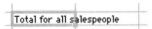

Figure 81 When text doesn't fit in a cell, it appears to overlap into the cell beside it ...

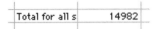

Figure 82 ... unless the cell beside it isn't blank.

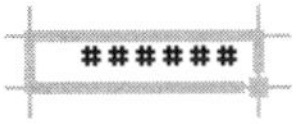

Figure 83 When a number doesn't fit in a cell, the cell fills with # signs.

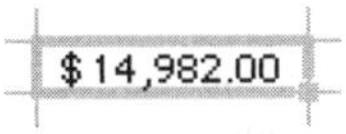

Figure 84 You can make the number fit by making the cell wider ...

Figure 85 ... or by changing the number's formatting to remove decimal places.

Column Width & Row Height

If the data you enter into a cell doesn't fit, you can make the column wider to accommodate all the characters. You can also make columns narrower to use worksheet space more efficiently. And although Excel automatically adjusts row height when you increase the font size of cells within the row, you can increase or decrease row height as desired.

Excel offers two ways to change column width and row height: with the mouse and with Format menu commands.

✔ Tips

- If text typed into a cell does not fit, it appears to overlap into the cell to its right (**Figure 81**). Even though the text may appear to be in more than one cell, all of the text is really in the cell in which you typed it. (You can see for yourself by clicking in the cell to the right and looking at the formula bar—it will not contain any part of the text!) If the cell to the right of the text is not blank, the text appears truncated (**Figure 82**). Don't let appearances fool you. The text is still all there; the missing part is just hidden by the contents of the cell beside it.

- If a number doesn't fit in a cell, the cell fills up with pound signs (#) (**Figure 83**). To display the number, make the column wider (**Figure 84**) or change the number formatting to omit symbols and decimal places (**Figure 85**). I tell you how to make columns wider on the next page and how to change number formatting earlier in this chapter.

- Setting column width or row height to 0 (zero) hides the column or row.

To change column width or row height with the mouse

1. Position the mouse pointer on the line right after the column letter(s) (**Figure 86**) or right below the row number (**Figure 87**) of the column or row you want to change. The mouse pointer turns into a line with two arrows coming out of it.

2. Press the mouse button and drag:

   ▲ To make a column narrower, drag to the left.

   ▲ To make a column wider, drag to the right.

   ▲ To make a row taller, drag down.

   ▲ To make a row shorter, drag up.

   As you drag, a dotted line moves along with the mouse pointer (**Figure 88**) and the width or height of the column or row appears in a little box.

3. Release the mouse button. The column width or row height changes.

✔ Tips

- When you change column width or row height, you change the width or height for the entire column or row, not just selected cells.

- To change column width or row height for more than one column or row at a time, select multiple columns or rows and drag the border of one of them. I explain how to select entire columns and rows in **Chapter 2**.

Figure 86 Position the mouse pointer on the right border of a column heading ...

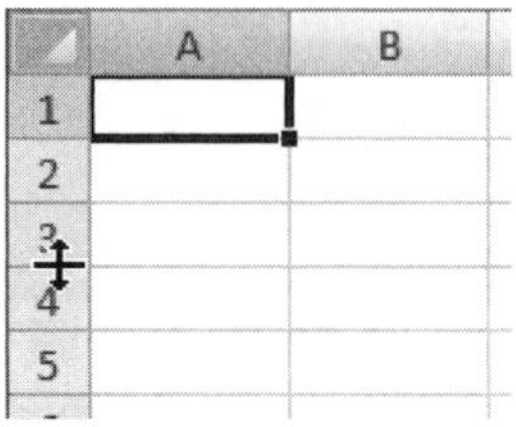

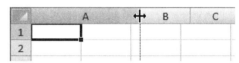

Figure 87
... or on the bottom border of a row heading.

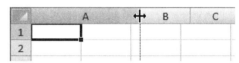

Figure 88 Drag to reposition the border, thus changing the width of the column (as shown here) or height of the row.

- If you drag a column or row border all the way to the left or all the way up, you set the column width or row height to 0, hiding the column or row from view. I tell you more about hiding columns and rows next.

- To quickly set the width or height of a column or row to fit its contents, double-click the column or row heading border. I tell you more about this AutoFit feature later in this chapter.

CHANGING COLUMN WIDTH & ROW HEIGHT

Figures 89 & 90 The Column Width (left) and Row Height (right) dialogs.

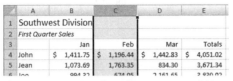

Figure 91 Select the column that you want to hide.

Figure 92
The Hide & Unhide submenu on the Format menu.

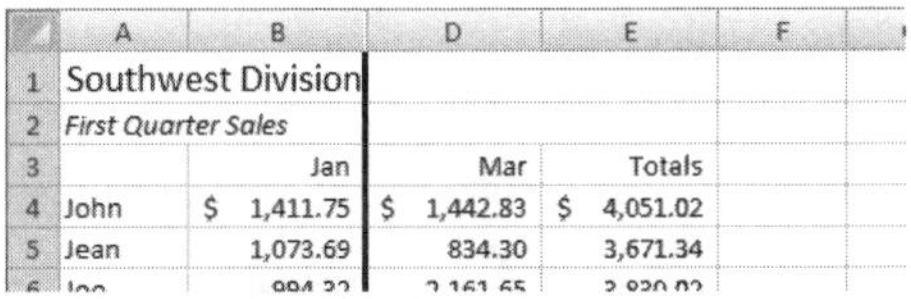

Figure 93 When you choose the Hide Columns command, the column disappears.

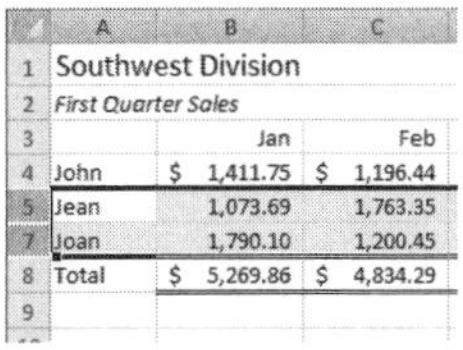

Figure 94 Select the rows above and below the hidden row.

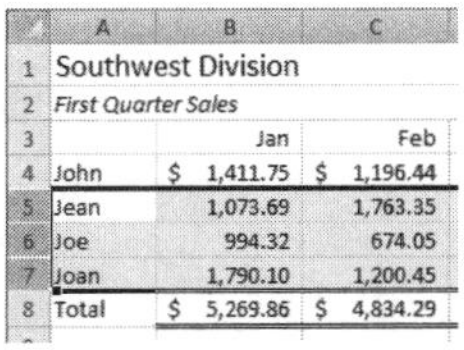

Figure 95 When you choose Unhide Rows, the hidden row reappears.

To change column width or row height with menu commands

1. Select the column(s) or row(s) whose width or height you want to change.

2. Choose Home > Cells > Format > Column Width or Home > Cells > Format > Row Height (**Figure 9**).

3. In the Column Width dialog (**Figure 89**) or Row Height dialog (**Figure 90**), enter a new value. Column width is expressed in standard font characters while row height is expressed in points.

4. Click OK to change the selected columns' width or rows' height.

To hide columns or rows

1. Select the column(s) (**Figure 91**) or row(s) you want to hide.

2. Choose Home > Cells > Format > Hide & Unhide > Hide Columns or Home > Cells > Format > Hide & Unhide > Hide Rows (**Figure 92**). The selected column(s) or row(s) disappear (**Figure 93**).

✔ Tip

■ Hiding a column or row is not the same as deleting it. Data in a hidden column or row still exists in the worksheet and can be referenced by formulas.

To unhide columns or rows

1. Select the columns or rows on both sides of the hidden column(s) or row(s) (**Figure 94**).

2. Choose Home > Cells > Format > Hide & Unhide > Unhide Columns or Home > Cells > Format > Hide & Unhide > Unhide Rows (**Figure 92**).

   The hidden column(s) or row(s) reappear (**Figure 95**).

AutoFit

Excel's AutoFit feature automatically adjusts a column's width or a row's height so it's only as wide or as high as it needs to be to display the information within it. This is a great way to adjust columns and rows to use worksheet space more efficiently.

To use AutoFit

1. Select the column(s) or row(s) for which you want to change the width or height (**Figure 96**).

2. Choose Home > Cells > Format > AutoFit Column Width or Home > Cells > Format > AutoFit Row Height (**Figure 9**).

   or

   Double-click on the border to the right of the column heading (**Figure 86**) or below the row heading (**Figure 87**).

   The column width or row height changes to fit cell contents (**Figure 97**).

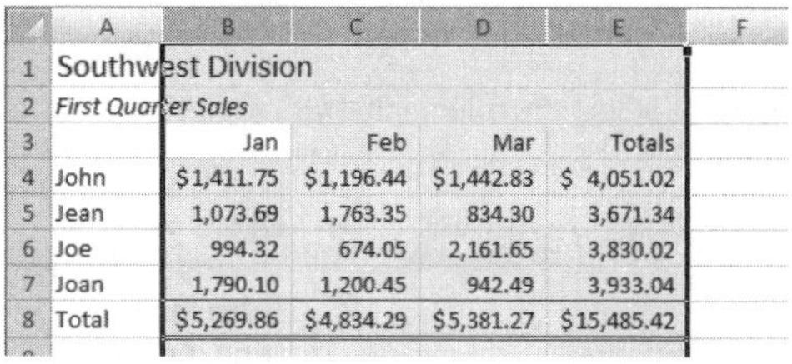

✔ Tips

■ To adjust a column's width without taking every cell into consideration—for example, to exclude a cell containing a lot of text—select only the cells for which you want to adjust the column (**Figure 98**). When you choose Home > Cells > Format > AutoFit Column Width (**Figure 9**), only the cells you selected are measured for the AutoFit adjustment (**Figure 99**).

■ Use the Wrap text and AutoFit features to keep your columns narrow. I tell you about Wrap text earlier in this chapter.

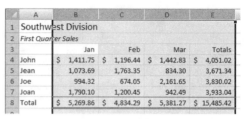

Figure 96 Select the columns for which you want to change the width.

Figure 97 When you choose the AutoFit Column Width command, the width of the columns changes so they're only as wide as they need to be to fit cell contents.

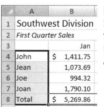

Figure 98 Select the cells that you want Excel to measure for the AutoFit feature.

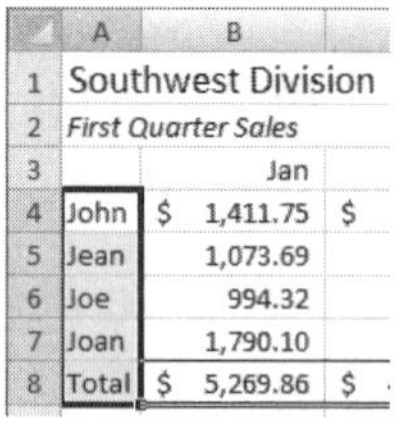

Figure 99 When you choose the AutoFit Column Width command, Excel resizes the entire column based on the width of the contents in the selected cells.

	A	B	C	D	E
1	Southwest Division				
2	*First Quarter Sales*				
3		Jan	Feb	Mar	Totals
4	John	$ 1,411.75	$ 1,196.44	$ 1,442.83	$ 4,051.02
5	Jean	1,073.69	1,763.35	834.30	3,671.34
6	Joe	994.32	674.05	2,161.65	3,830.02
7	Joan	1,790.10	1,200.45	942.49	3,933.04
8	Total	$ 5,269.86	$ 4,834.29	$ 5,381.27	$ 15,485.42

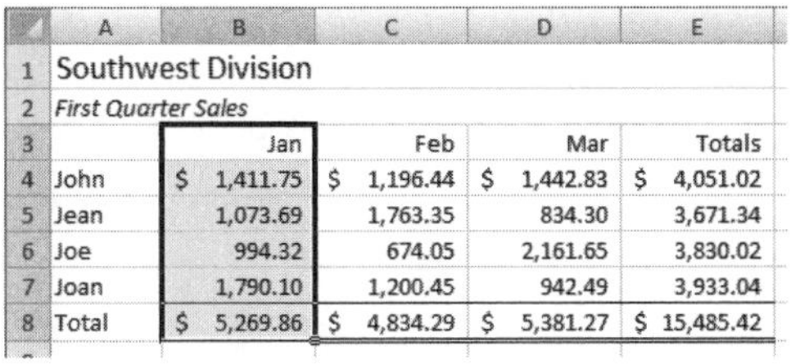

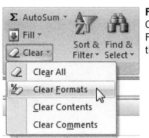

Figure 100 Select the cells you want to remove formatting from.

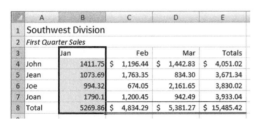

Figure 101 Choose Clear Formats from the Clear menu.

	A	B	C	D	E
1	Southwest Division				
2	*First Quarter Sales*				
3		Jan	Feb	Mar	Totals
4	John	1411.75	$ 1,196.44	$ 1,442.83	$ 4,051.02
5	Jean	1073.69	1,763.35	834.30	3,671.34
6	Joe	994.32	674.05	2,161.65	3,830.02
7	Joan	1790.1	1,200.45	942.49	3,933.04
8	Total	5269.86	$ 4,834.29	$ 5,381.27	$ 15,485.42

Figure 102 The formatting is removed but the cell contents remain.

Removing Formatting from Cells

You can use the Clear Formats command on the Editing Group's Clear menu (**Figure 101**) to remove formatting from cells, leaving cell contents—such as values and formulas—intact.

✔ Tips

- When you remove formats from a cell, you return font formatting to the normal font and number formatting to the General format. You also remove borders or shading added to the cell.
- Removing formatting does not affect column width or row height.

To remove formatting from cells

1. Select the cell(s) you want to remove formatting from (**Figure 100**).
2. Choose Home > Editing> Clear > Clear Formats (**Figure 101**). The formatting is removed but cell contents remain (**Figure 102**).

Working with Graphic Objects

7

Graphic Objects

The Insert tab of Microsoft Excel's Ribbon includes buttons and menus that make it easy to add a variety of graphic objects to your worksheets and charts:

◆ **Picture** lets you add your own images, such as a company logo or product illustration.

◆ **Clip Art** enables you to insert professionally created graphic images.

◆ **Shapes** enables you to draw a variety of interesting and useful shapes, lines, and connectors quickly and easily.

◆ **SmartArt**, which is new in Excel 2007, offers a wide variety of graphic elements that you can use to visually communicate information.

◆ **WordArt** enables you to add highly stylized text to your documents.

◆ **Text boxes** offer a flexible way to add annotations to a document.

This chapter explains how you can include all of these types of graphic objects in your Excel documents.

Inserting Pictures

Excel enables you to insert pictures from files saved on disk into your Excel worksheets and chart sheets. This makes it possible to include a company logo, product photo, line drawing, or some other custom graphic image.

✔ Tips

- Excel supports most image file formats.

- Another way to insert a picture into an Excel document is to open the picture in a graphics program, select it, and use the program's Copy command to copy it to the Windows clipboard. Then switch to the Excel document and use Excel's Paste command to paste the contents of the clipboard into the document. I tell you more about using the Copy and Paste commands in **Chapter 3**.

To insert a picture from a file

1. Click Insert > Illustrations > Picture (**Figure 1**) to display the Insert Picture dialog (**Figure 2**).

2. Locate and select the file you want to insert.

3. Click Insert. The picture file is inserted and the Picture Tools Format tab appears (**Figure 3**).

✔ Tips

- The Picture Tools Format tab (**Figure 3**) includes tools for working with a selected picture. I tell you more about many of these tools later in this chapter.

- To limit the list of images in the Insert Picture dialog (**Figure 2**) to a specific file format, choose an option from the pop-up menu after File name (**Figure 4**).

Figure 1
The Illustrations group of the Ribbon's Insert tab.

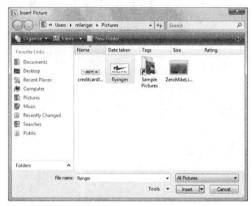

Figure 2 Use this dialog to locate, select, and insert the image you want to include in your document.

Figure 3 When an inserted picture is selected, the Picture Tools Format tab appears on the Ribbon.

Figure 4
Choose the type of picture you want listed in the Insert Picture dialog by choosing an option from this pop-up menu.

Figure 5
The Clip Art pane before a search.

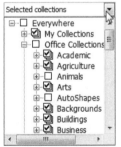

Figure 6
Select the collections you want to search.

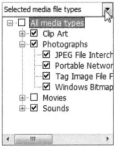

Figure 7
Indicate the type of media you're interested in.

Inserting Clip Art

Microsoft Office comes with a collection of clip art images that you can use in your documents. These images are accessible from the Office Clip Organizer, which is available to all Microsoft Office programs.

✔ Tip

■ Additional images are available online on the Microsoft Office Online Web site for you to download and install into the Office Clip organizer.

To insert clip art

1. Choose Insert > Illustrations > Clip Art (**Figure 1**) to display the Clip Art pane (**Figure 5**).

2. Enter a search word in the Search for box.

3. To search only some collections of clip art, display the Search in drop-down list (**Figure 6**) and click check boxes to toggle search location options on or off. You can click the + button beside a category to display options within it.

4. To specify the type of media you want to find, display the Results should be drop-down list (**Figure 7**) and click check boxes to toggle media type options on or off. You can click the + button beside a category to display options within it.

5. Click Go.

Continued on next page...

Continued from previous page.

6. Wait while Excel searches for clip art that matches the criteria you specified. When it's done, it displays matches in the Clip Art pane (**Figure 8**).

7. Click the thumbnail view of a clip art item to insert it in the document (**Figure 9**).

✔ Tips

- After step 5, a dialog may appear, asking whether you want to include thousands of additional images from Microsoft Office Online. If you have a live Internet connection, you can click Yes; otherwise, click No.

- The Picture Tools Format tab (**Figure 9**) includes tools for working with a selected picture. I tell you more about many of these tools later in this chapter.

Figure 8
The items that match your search criteria appear in the Clip Art pane.

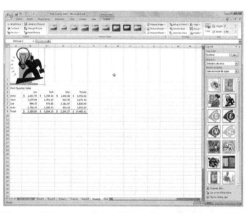

Figure 9 When you click a Clip Art item, it is inserted in your document.

Figure 10
The Shapes menu includes buttons for all kinds of lines and shapes.

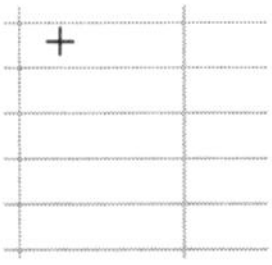

Drawing Shapes, Lines, & Connectors

The Shapes menu on the Insert tab's Illustrations group (**Figure 10**) makes it easy to draw predefined shapes, lines, and connectors on your worksheets or charts.

To draw a line, arrow, or connector

1. Click Insert > Illustrations > Shapes to display the Shapes menu (**Figure 10**).

2. Click the button for the line, arrow, or connector you want to insert to activate the appropriate drawing tool. The mouse pointer turns into a crosshairs pointer (**Figure 11**) or, in the case of the Scribble button, a pencil (**Figure 12**).

3. Position the mouse pointer where you want to begin drawing.

4. To draw a straight line, arrow, or double arrow, press the mouse button down and drag. As you move the mouse, a line is drawn (**Figure 13**). Release the mouse button to stop drawing (**Figures 14** and **15**).

   or

   To draw a curve, move the mouse to stretch a line (**Figure 13**) and click where you want the curve to appear (**Figure 16**). Repeat this process to draw as many curves as desired. Then either click the starting point or double-click the ending point to stop drawing (**Figure 17**).

   or

Continued on next page...

Figure 11
When you click a Shape menu button, the mouse pointer changes into a crosshairs pointer ...

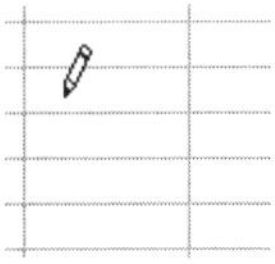

Figure 12
... or, in the case of the Scribble tool, a pencil pointer.

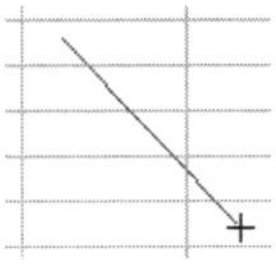

Figure 13
Drag to draw a line.

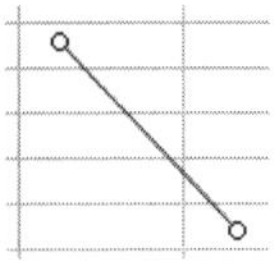

Figure 14
A freshly drawn line.

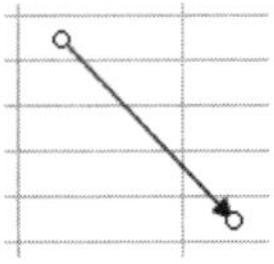

Figure 15
A freshly drawn arrow.

DRAWING LINES, ARROWS, & CONNECTORS

145

Continued from previous page.

To draw a freeform shape, combine clicking and dragging to draw straight lines and freeform lines: click from point to point to draw straight lines and drag (with a pencil tool that appears automatically) to draw freeform lines (**Figure 18**). Either click the starting point or double-click the ending point to stop drawing (**Figure 19**).

or

To draw a scribble, press the mouse button down and drag the pencil pointer to get the desired line shape (**Figure 20**). Release the mouse button to stop drawing (**Figure 21**).

or

To draw a connector, press the mouse button down and drag a line between the items you want to connect (**Figure 22**). When you release the mouse button, the connector appears (**Figure 23**).

✔ Tips

■ You can point to a button on the Shapes menu to learn its name and distinguish between plain lines and connectors.

■ To draw a line or arrow that's perfectly vertical, horizontal, or at a 45° angle, hold down (Shift) in step 4.

■ The small white circles in **Figures 14**, **15**, **17**, **19**, **21**, and **23** are selection handles. I tell you more about selection handles later in this chapter.

Figure 16
Using the Curve tool, click to indicate where the curve should appear.

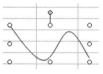

Figure 17
A curved line with two curves.

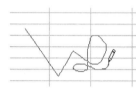

Figure 18 Using the Freeform tool, click to draw straight lines and drag to draw freeform lines.

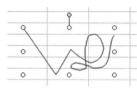

Figure 19
Double-clicking ends the line without creating a closed-in shape.

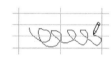

Figure 20
To use the Scribble tool, hold the mouse button down and drag the pencil pointer.

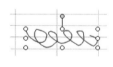

Figure 21
Releasing the mouse button completes the scribble.

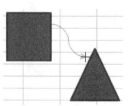

Figure 22
To use a connector tool, just drag from the starting point to the ending point.

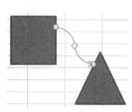

Figure 23
When you release the mouse button, the connector is drawn.

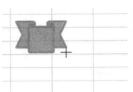

Figure 24
Drag to draw
the shape.

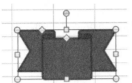

Figure 25
A freshly drawn
shape.

To draw a shape

1. Click Insert > Illustrations > Shapes to display the Shapes menu (**Figure 10**).

2. Click the button for the shape you want to insert to activate the appropriate drawing tool. The mouse pointer turns into a crosshairs pointer (**Figure 11**).

3. Position the crosshairs where you want to begin drawing the shape or line.

4. Press the mouse button and drag. As you move the mouse, the shape or line begins to take form (**Figure 24**).

5. Release the mouse button to complete the shape (**Figure 25**).

✔ Tips

■ The shape tools makes it easy to draw complex shapes. (Do you think I could draw something like what you see in **Figure 25**? No way!)

■ As discussed in the previous section, you can use connectors to draw lines between two shapes (**Figure 23**).

Inserting SmartArt

Excel's new SmartArt feature makes it very easy to insert complex graphic elements that you can use to created visualized representations of information. SmartArt graphics include lists, diagrams, and organization charts.

To insert a SmartArt graphic

1. Click Insert > Illustrations > SmartArt (**Figure 1**) to display the Choose a SmartArt Graphic dialog.

2. In the left column of the dialog, click the category of SmartArt you want to insert.

3. In the middle of the dialog, click the button for the art you want to insert. A description of the art you selected appears on the right side of the dialog (**Figure 26**).

4. Click OK. The art appears in the worksheet window, along with the Text pane, which you can use to enter or edit art contents (**Figure 27**).

5. In the Text pane, replace the placeholder text with the text you want to appear in the art.

6. Modify the art's basic structure as follows:
   ▲ To insert another text box, press Enter after the previous text box.
   ▲ To delete a text box, click the text box and press Backspace.

7. When you're finished making changes, click outside the SmartArt graphic. The Text pane disappears (**Figure 28**)

✔ Tip

■ To edit a completed SmartArt graphic, click it to display the Text pane.

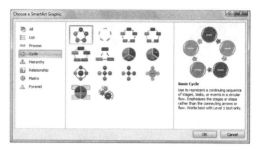

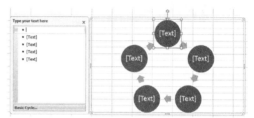

Figure 26 The Choose a SmartArt Graphic dialog.

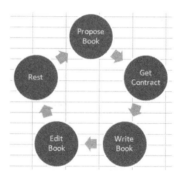

Figure 27 A Text pane appears beside the freshly inserted SmartArt graphic so you an modify its contents.

Figure 28 A completed cycle chart. (A writer's life is an endless cycle.)

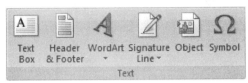

Text Box | Header & Footer | WordArt | Signature Line | Object | Symbol

Text

Figure 29 The Text group on the Ribbon's Insert tab.

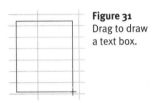

Figure 30
The mouse pointer turns into a special crosshairs pointer when you click the Text Box button.

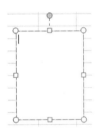

Figure 31
Drag to draw a text box.

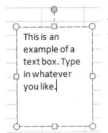

Figure 32
When you release the mouse button, the text box appears with a blinking insertion point inside it.

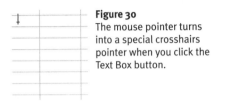

Figure 33
You can type whatever text you like in the text box.

This is an example of a text box. Type in whatever you like.

Adding Text Boxes

Text boxes offer a flexible way to add comments or other text to a worksheet or chart. A text box can be any size and can include any amount of text. And, like a graphic, it can be positioned anywhere on a worksheet or chart.

To add a text box

1. Click Insert > Text > Text Box (**Figure 29**). The mouse pointer turns into a special crosshairs pointer (**Figure 30**).

2. Position the crosshairs where you want to begin drawing the text box.

3. Press the mouse button and drag. As you move the mouse, the text box begins to take form (**Figure 31**).

4. Release the mouse button to complete the text box. An insertion point appears within it (**Figure 32**).

5. Enter the text you want in the text box (**Figure 33**).

✔ Tips

- A text box is like a little word processing document within an Excel sheet. Once created, you can enter and format text within it.

- Text boxes offer more flexibility than worksheet cells when entering long passages of text.

- To edit text in a text box, double-click inside it to select one or more characters. Then use the arrow keys to move the insertion point. Use standard editing techniques to modify text.

ADDING TEXT BOXES

Inserting WordArt

WordArt offers a way to add highly stylized and colorful text to a worksheet or chart. You might find it useful for adding titles or labels to your work.

To insert WordArt

1. Click Insert > Text > WordArt to display the WordArt menu (**Figure 34**).

2. Click the text style you want to use. A selected block of sample text appears in your document (**Figure 35**).

3. With the sample text still selected, type in the text you want to appear. The sample text is replaced with your text (**Figure 36**).

4. Click outside the WordArt image to remove the selection box (**Figure 37**).

✔ Tip

■ Once you have created a WordArt image, you can use buttons on the WordArt toolbar to modify it. The toolbar only appears when the WordArt image is selected.

Figure 34 The WordArt menu offers a wide variety of text styles.

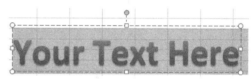

Figure 35 A sample text block appears.

Figure 36 Type in your text to replace the sample.

Figure 37 When you click outside the WordArt image, the selection box and handles disappear.

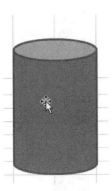

Figure 38
When you position the mouse pointer on an object, a four-headed arrow appears with the mouse pointer arrow.

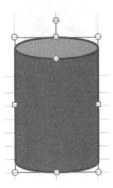

Figure 39
Selection handles appear around selected objects.

Figure 40 Hold down [Shift] and click to select other objects.

Selecting & Deselecting Objects

Once you have drawn or inserted a graphic object into your Excel document, you must select it to work with it.

To select an object

1. Position the mouse pointer on the object. A four-headed arrow appears beneath the mouse pointer arrow (**Figure 38**).

2. Click. Selection handles appear around the object (**Figure 39**).

✔ Tip

■ If a shape does not have any fill, you must click on its border to select it. I tell you about fill color later in this chapter.

To select multiple objects

1. Follow the instructions above to select the first object (**Figure 39**).

2. Hold down [Shift] and continue to click objects until all have been selected (**Figure 40**).

✔ Tip

■ To deselect objects from a multiple selection, hold down [Shift] while clicking on the objects you want to deselect.

To deselect an object

Click on any other object or anywhere else in the window. The selection handles disappear.

Grouping & Ungrouping Objects

Grouping multiple objects enables you to select, move, and modify all of the objects in the group by clicking any one of them.

To group objects

1. Select all the objects you want to include in the group (**Figure 40**).

2. Click Drawing Tools > Format > Arrange > Group > Group (**Figure 41**).

   The objects are grouped together, with only one set of selection handles (**Figure 42**).

✔ Tips

■ In addition to grouping individual objects, you can also group groups of objects.

To ungroup objects

1. Select the grouped objects you want to ungroup (**Figure 42**).

2. Click Drawing Tools > Format > Arrange > Group > Ungroup (**Figure 41**).

   Separate selection handles appear for each object (**Figure 40**).

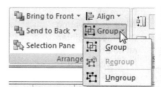

Figure 41
The Group menu lets you group and ungroup items.

Figure 42 The objects selected in **Figure 40** after grouping them. Note that the clip art image of the man with the light bulb was not selected and is not part of the group—even though it appears that it is.

Figure 43
Position the mouse pointer on the object.

Figure 44
Drag to move the object.

Figure 45
The Clipboard group.

Moving Objects

In many cases, when you insert or draw a graphic object, it doesn't end up exactly where you want it. No problem; you can always move it.

To move an object by dragging

1. Position the mouse pointer on the object or on the edge of the object so that the four-headed arrow appears (**Figure 43**).

2. Press the mouse button and drag. An outline of the object moves along with the mouse pointer (**Figure 44**).

3. When the object's outline is in the desired position, release the mouse button. The object moves.

✔ Tips

- To restrict an object's movement so that it moves only horizontally or vertically, hold down Shift while dragging.

- To restrict an object's movement so that it snaps to the worksheet gridlines, hold down Alt while dragging.

To move an object with the Cut & Paste commands

1. Select the object you want to move.

2. Choose Home > Clipboard > Cut (**Figure 45**) or press Ctrl X. The object disappears.

3. To paste the object into a different sheet, switch to that sheet.

4. Choose Home > Clipboard > Paste (**Figure 45**) or press Ctrl V. The object appears.

5. If necessary, drag the object into the desired position on the sheet.

✔ Tip

- This technique is most useful when moving an object to another sheet.

MOVING OBJECTS

Copying Objects

One way to get multiple identical objects is to simply copy one of them.

To copy an object by dragging

1. Position the mouse pointer on the object or on the edge of the object so that the four-headed arrow appears.

2. While holding down Ctrl, press the mouse button and drag. An outline of the object moves along with the mouse pointer (**Figure 46**).

3. When you release the mouse button, a copy of the object appears at the outline (**Figure 47**).

To copy an object with the Copy & Paste commands

1. Select the object you want to copy.

2. Choose Home > Clipboard > Copy (**Figure 45**) or press Ctrl C.

3. To paste the object into a different sheet, switch to that sheet.

4. Choose Home > Clipboard > Paste (**Figure 45**) or press Ctrl V.

Deleting Objects

If you decide you no longer want an object in your worksheet or chart, you can delete it.

To delete an object

1. Select the object(s) you want to delete.

2. Press Backspace.

    or

    Choose Home > Editing > Clear > Clear All (**Figure 48**).

    The object(s) disappear.

Figure 46 Hold down Ctrl while dragging ...

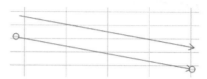

Figure 47 ... to copy an object.

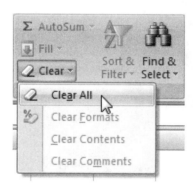

Figure 48 The Clear menu on the Editing group when an object is selected.

✔ Tip

■ If you select an object in a group, deleting that object will delete the entire group of objects. If you only want to delete one object in a group, you must ungroup the objects first. I explain how to group and ungroup objects earlier in this chapter.

COPYING & DELETING OBJECTS

Figure 49 Position the mouse pointer on a selection handle and it turns into a resizing pointer.

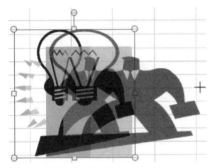

Figure 50 Drag to stretch (or shrink) the object.

Figure 51 When you release the mouse button, the object resizes.

Figure 52
The Format tab's Size group.

Resizing Objects

In many instances an object you draw or insert won't be the size you want it to be. Fortunately, Excel offers three ways to resize objects: by dragging, by setting options in the Size group, and by setting options in the Size tab of the Size and Properties dialog.

To resize an object by dragging

1. Select the object you want to resize.

2. Position the mouse pointer on a selection handle. The mouse pointer turns into a double-headed arrow (**Figure 49**).

3. Press the mouse button and drag to stretch or shrink the object. The mouse pointer turns into a crosshairs and an outline of the object moves with your mouse pointer as you drag (**Figure 50**).

4. When the outline of the object reflects the size you want, release the mouse button. The object is resized (**Figure 51**).

✔ Tips

- To resize an object or group proportionally, drag a corner selection handle.

- To resize multiple objects at the same time, select the objects, then resize one of them. All selected objects will be resized.

To resize an object with Size group options

1. Select the object you want to resize.

2. If necessary, click the Format tab to display its options.

3. Enter new values in the Shape Height and Shape Width boxes of the Size group (**Figure 52**).

    The object resizes immediately.

To resize an object with the Size and Properties dialog

1. Select the object you want to resize.

2. Click the Dialog Box Launcher button in the lower-right corner of the Format tab's Size group (**Figure 52**).

3. The Size and Properties dialog appears. If necessary, click the Size tab to display its options (**Figure 53**).

4. To set the object size to exact measurements, enter values in the Height and Width boxes under Size and rotate.

    or

    To set the object size as a percentage of the object's current size, enter values in the Height and Width boxes under Scale.

    The image is resized as you make your changes.

5. When you're finished setting object size, click Close to dismiss the dialog.

✔ Tips

- To resize an object proportionally, turn on the Lock aspect ratio check box in step 4.

- To resize a picture relative to its original size, turn on the Relative to original picture check box in step 4. This option is only available for some types of graphic objects.

- To reset an object's size to its original size, click the Reset button near the bottom of the dialog. This button is only available for some types of graphic objects.

- You can leave the Size and Properties dialog open while you select other objects to work with.

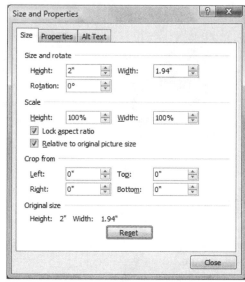

Figure 53 The Size tab of the Size and Properties dialog offers options for resizing and rotating graphic images.

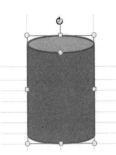

Figure 54
When you position the mouse pointer on the green rotation handle, it turns into a rotation pointer.

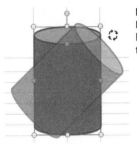

Figure 55
Drag the green handle to rotate the object.

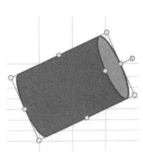

Figure 56
When you release the mouse button, the image is redrawn with the rotation you specified.

Rotating Objects

You can also rotate objects to adjust their position or achieve special graphic effects. Excel offers three ways to do this.

To rotate an object by dragging

1. Select the object you want to rotate.

2. Position the mouse pointer on the round green handle that appears outside its selection handles. The mouse pointer changes to a rotation pointer, which looks like an arrow on an arc (**Figure 54**).

3. Press the mouse button down and drag to the right or left. An outline of the object rotates (**Figure 55**).

4. When the object is in the desired position, release the mouse button. The object is redrawn with the rotation you specified (**Figure 56**).

To rotate or flip an object with Rotate menu commands

1. Select the object you want to rotate.

2. Click Format > Arrange > Rotate to display the rotate menu (**Figure 57**).

3. Choose the rotate or flip command you want. The image rotates or flips according to the command you chose.

✔ Tip

■ Rotating an image changes its angle. Flipping an image creates a mirror image.

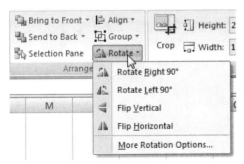

Figure 57 The Arrange group's Rotate menu includes commands for rotating or flipping objects.

To rotate an object with the Size and Properties dialog

1. Select the object you want to rotate.

2. Choose Format > Arrange > Rotate > More Rotation Options (**Figure 57**).

3. The Size and Properties dialog appears. If necessary, click the Size tab to display its options (**Figure 53**).

4. Enter a rotation value in the Rotation box in the Size and rotate area of the dialog. The value you enter should be an angle between 0 and 359.

   The object is rotated as you make your changes.

5. When you're finished click Close to dismiss the dialog.

✔ Tips

■ Entering a positive value in the Rotation box rotates clockwise; entering a negative value in the Rotation box rotates counter-clockwise.

■ To reset an object's rotation to its original angle, click the Reset button near the bottom of the dialog. This button is only available for some types of graphic objects.

■ You can leave the Size and Properties dialog open while you select other objects to work with.

ROTATING OBJECTS

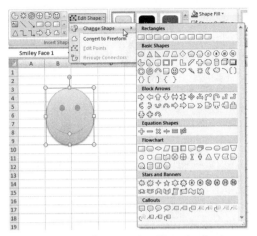

Figure 58 You can change an AutoShape by simply choosing a different one from the Change Shape submenu on the Edit Shape menu.

Drag a diamond to customize the shape.

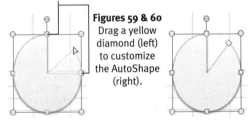

Figures 59 & 60
Drag a yellow diamond (left) to customize the AutoShape (right).

Drag the diamond to customize the shape.

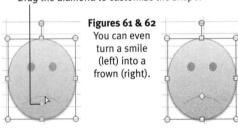

Figures 61 & 62
You can even turn a smile (left) into a frown (right).

Modifying AutoShapes

In addition to resizing and rotating, AutoShape objects can be modified in several other ways. For example, you can change the AutoShape to a different AutoShape or customize the AutoShape's settings.

To change an AutoShape

1. Select the AutoShape you want to change.

2. Click Format > Insert Shape > Edit Shape > Change Shape to display a menu of AutoShapes (**Figure 58**).

3. Click to select the AutoShape you want to change the currently selected shape to. The shape changes.

To customize an AutoShape by dragging

1. Select the AutoShape you want to customize.

2. Position the mouse pointer on the yellow diamond-shaped handle. The mouse pointer turns into a hollow white arrowhead pointer.

3. Drag the yellow diamond. As you drag, the outline of the customized shape moves with the mouse pointer (**Figures 59** and **61**).

4. Release the mouse button. The shape changes (**Figures 60** and **62**).

✔ Tip

- This technique can only be used on AutoShape lines or shapes that display one or more yellow diamonds when selected.

MODIFYING AUTOSHAPES

Aligning Objects

The Align menu in Excel's Arrange group makes it easy to set alignment for multiple selected objects.

To align objects

1. Select the objects you want to align (**Figure 63**).

2. Click Format > Arrange > Align to display the Align menu (**Figure 64**).

3. Choose one of the six alignment commands at the top of the menu.

   The objects are aligned according to the option you chose (**Figure 65**).

✔ Tips

- If the objects you selected include both drawn objects and pictures, you may see two Format tabs in step 2 (**Figure 66**). You can work with either one.

- If your results after step 3 aren't what you expected, use the Undo command or press Ctrl Z to revert back to the original alignment of the objects. Then try again. Sometimes it's easier to start over than to fix an error. I tell you about the Undo command in **Chapter 3**.

- Choosing one of the Distribute options in step 3 distributes space evenly between selected objects, either horizontally (**Figure 67**) or vertically.

Figure 63
Start by selecting the objects you want to align.

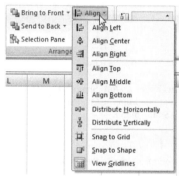

Figure 64
Choose an option from the Align menu.

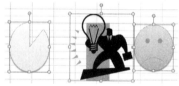

Figure 65
Align Middle aligns the vertical middles of objects.

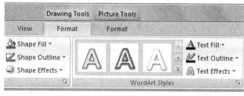

Figure 66 It is possible to see two Format tabs!

Figure 67
Distribute Horizontally puts equal space between objects.

Figure 68
Because each object is drawn in a separate layer, objects can be obscured by other objects "on top" of them.

Figure 69
To change an object's layer, start by selecting it.

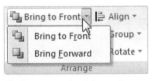

Figure 70 Use the Bring to Front button and menu to bring a selected object to the top of the stack.

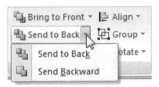

Figure 71 Use the Send to Back button and menu to send a selected object to the bottom of the stack.

Figure 72
A selected object can be brought to the top layer ...

Figure 73
... or sent to the bottom layer.

Changing Stacking Order

Each time you draw a shape or insert a picture, Excel puts it on a new drawing layer. When one object overlaps another object, the first object may be partially obscured by the one "on top" of it (**Figure 68**).

To change stacking order

1. Select the object(s) you want to move to another layer (**Figure 69**).

2. Click an option on the Format tab's Arrange group (**Figures 70** and **71**):

   ▲ Format > Arrange > Bring to Front moves the object(s) to the top layer (**Figure 72**).

   ▲ Format > Arrange > Bring to Front > Bring Forward moves the object(s) up one layer.

   ▲ Format > Arrange > Send to Back moves the object(s) to the bottom layer (**Figure 73**).

   ▲ Format > Arrange > Send to Back > Send Backward moves the object(s) down one layer.

✔ Tip

■ Once you've put objects in the stacking order you want, consider grouping them so they stay just the way you want them to. I tell you how to group objects earlier in this chapter.

Other Formatting Options

Excel offers a variety of other options for formatting drawn objects, such as shapes and WordArt, and pictures, such as clip art and inserted image files. All of these options can be found on groups under the Drawing Tools Format tab or Picture Tools Format tab when the object is selected.

In this section, I provide a brief overview of some of the other options available for formatting graphic objects in your Excel worksheets and charts.

To apply shape styles

1. Select the shape you want to modify.

2. Click Format to display the Format tab's Shape Styles group (**Figure 74**).

3. Click to select options to modify the shape:

   ▲ **Theme** buttons, which appear in a one-line scrolling list, enable you to apply a set of predefined formatting combinations.

   ▲ **Shape Fill** (**Figure 75**) lets you choose colors, pictures, gradients, or textures to apply to the interior of the shape.

   ▲ **Shape Outline** (**Figure 76**) enables you to set the color, line thickness or weight, line style, and arrow formatting for a shape outline or line.

   ▲ **Shape Effects** (**Figure 77**) enables you to apply special effects to the shape.

   or

   Click the Dialog Box Launcher button in the bottom-right corner of the Shape Styles group (**Figure 74**) to display the Format Shape dialog (**Figure 78**), set options for categories as desired, and click Close.

Figure 74 The Shape Styles group on the Drawing Tools' Format tab.

Figure 75 The Shape Fill menu offers options for formatting the interior of a shape.

Figure 76 The Shape Outline menu includes options for formatting a shape's outline or a line.

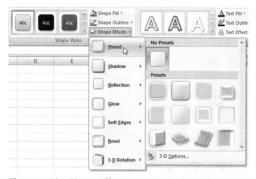

Figure 77 The Shape Effects menu includes submenus full of special effects.

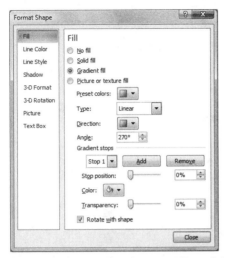

Figure 78 You can also use the Format Shape dialog to set formatting options for shapes and lines.

Figure 79 The WordArt Styles group on the Drawing Tools' Format tab.

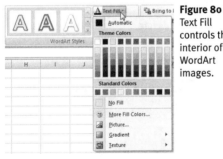

Figure 80
Text Fill controls the interior of WordArt images.

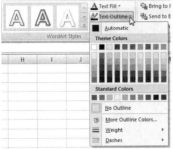

Figure 81
Text Outline controls the outline of WordArt images.

To apply WordArt styles

1. Select the WordArt image you want to modify.

2. Click Format to display the Format tab's WordArt Styles group (**Figure 79**).

3. Click to select options to modify the WordArt image:

   ▲ **Theme** buttons, which appear in a one-line scrolling list, enable you to apply a set of predefined formatting combinations.

   ▲ **Text Fill** (**Figure 80**) lets you choose colors, pictures, gradients, or textures to apply to the interior of the WordArt image.

   ▲ **Text Outline** (**Figure 81**) enables you to set the color, line thickness or weight, and lines style for the WordArt image outline.

   ▲ **Text Effects** (**Figure 82**) enables you to apply special effects to the WordArt image.

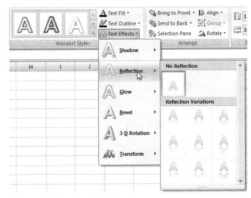

Figure 82 The Text Effects menu includes submenus of special effects that can be applied to WordArt images.

APPLYING WORDART STYLES

To adjust picture settings

1. Select the picture you want to modify.

2. Click Format to display the Format tab's Adjust group (**Figure 83**).

3. Click to select options to modify the picture:

   ▲ **Brightness** (**Figure 84**) lets you adjust the picture's brightness.

   ▲ **Contrast** (**Figure 85**) lets you adjust the picture's contrast.

   ▲ **Recolor** (**Figure 86**) enables you to choose color variations or set one color as transparent.

   ▲ **Compress Picture** enables you to set image compression options, so the image takes up less disk space.

   ▲ **Change Picture** displays the Insert Picture Dialog (**Figure 2**) so you can replace the picture with a different one.

   ▲ **Reset Picture** restores the picture to its original settings.

Figure 83 The Adjust group on the Picture Tools' Format tab.

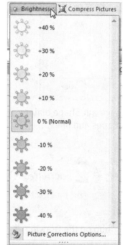

Figure 84 Use the Brightness menu to set the brightness of the picture.

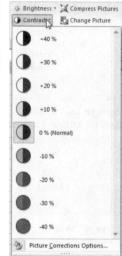

Figure 85 The Contrast menu offers options for setting picture contrast.

Figure 86 You can apply different color settings with the Recolor menu's options.

Figure 87 The Picture Styles group on the Picture Tools' Format tab.

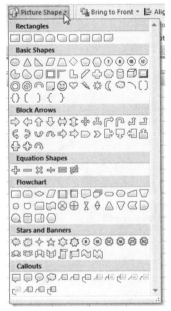

Figure 88
The Picture Shape menu lets you specify a shape for the picture.

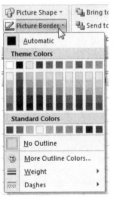

Figure 89
Use the Picture Border menu to set border options for a picture.

To apply picture styles

1. Select the picture you want to modify.

2. Click Format to display the Format tab's Picture Styles group (**Figure 87**).

3. Click to select options to modify the picture:

   ▲ **Theme** buttons, which appear in a one-line scrolling list, enable you to apply a set of predefined formatting combinations.

   ▲ **Picture Shape** (**Figure 88**) enables you to select a shape for your picture. The picture's image will only appear in the interior of the shape.

   ▲ **Picture Border** (**Figure 89**) enables you to set the color, line thickness or weight, and line style for the picture's border.

   ▲ **Picture Effects** (**Figure 90**) enables you to apply special effects to the picture.

Continued on next page...

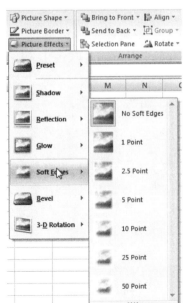

Figure 90
The picture Effects menu offers a range of special effects for pictures.

Continued from previous page.

or

Click the Dialog Box Launcher button in the bottom-right corner of the Picture Styles group (**Figure 87**) to display the Format Picture dialog (**Figure 91**), set options for categories as desired, and click Close.

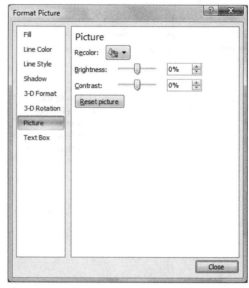

Figure 91 Use the Format Picture dialog to set all kinds of options for a selected picture.

Creating Charts

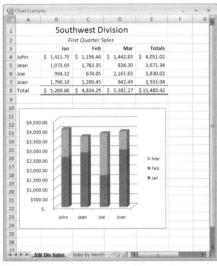

Figure 1 Here's a 3-D stacked column chart embedded in a worksheet file.

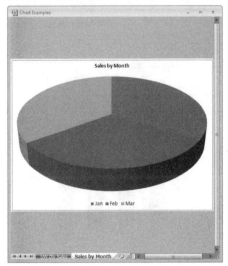

Figure 2 Here's a 3-D pie chart on a chart sheet of its own.

Charts

A chart is a graphic representation of data. A chart can be embedded in a worksheet (**Figure 1**) or can be a chart sheet of its own (**Figure 2**).

With Microsoft Excel, you can create many different types of charts. The 3-D stacked column chart and 3-D pie chart shown here (**Figures 1** and **2**) are only two examples. Since each type of chart has at least one variation and you can customize any chart you create, there's no limit to the number of ways you can present data graphically with Excel.

✔ Tips

- Include charts with worksheets whenever you want to emphasize worksheet results. Charts can often communicate information like trends and comparative results better than numbers alone.

- A skilled chartmaker can, through choice of data, chart format, and scale, get a chart to say almost anything about the data it represents!

Inserting a Chart

The Insert tab's Charts group (**Figure 3**) makes it easy to insert a chart based on worksheet data. You start by selecting the cells containing the data you want your chart to be based upon, then choose the type of chart you want to create. Excel creates a default version of the chart and inserts it in the worksheet window.

Column
Line
Pie
Bar
Area
Scatter
Other Charts
Charts

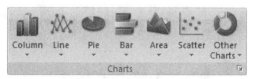

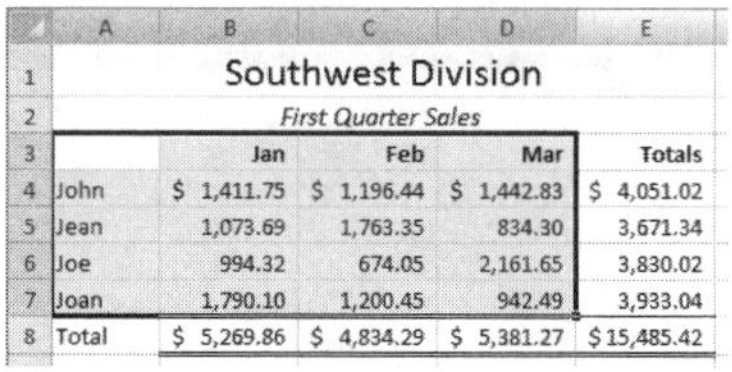

Figure 3 The Charts group on the Insert tab.

To insert a chart

1. Select the data you want to include in the chart (**Figure 4**).
2. Click the Insert tab to display the Charts group (**Figure 3**).
3. Click the button for the type of chart you want to insert to display a menu of chart subtypes (**Figure 5**).
4. Click the button for the chart you want to insert. The chart appears in the worksheet window (**Figure 6**).

✔ Tip

- In step 1, if you include column or row headings in your selection (**Figure 4**), those headings will be used as data series names, axis labels, and legend labels in the chart (**Figure 6**).

Southwest Division
First Quarter Sales
Jan Feb Mar Totals
John $ 1,411.75 $ 1,196.44 $ 1,442.83 $ 4,051.02
Jean 1,073.69 1,763.35 834.30 3,671.34
Joe 994.32 674.05 2,161.65 3,830.02
Joan 1,790.10 1,200.45 942.49 3,933.04
Total $ 5,269.86 $ 4,834.29 $ 5,381.27 $ 15,485.42

Figure 4 Select all the data you want to include in the chart.

2-D Column
3-D Column
Cylinder
Cone
Pyramid
All Chart Types...

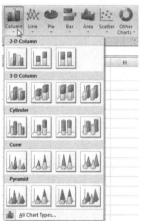

Figure 5 Clicking one of the buttons in the Charts group displays a menu of chart subtypes.

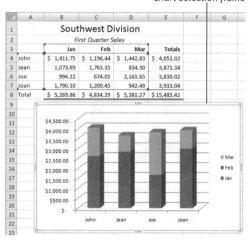

Chart selection frame
Southwest Division
First Quarter Sales
Jan Feb Mar Totals
John $ 1,411.75 $ 1,196.44 $ 1,442.83 $ 4,051.02
Jean 1,073.69 1,763.35 834.30 3,671.34
Joe 994.32 674.05 2,161.65 3,830.02
Joan 1,790.10 1,200.45 942.49 3,933.04
Total $ 5,269.86 $ 4,834.29 $ 5,381.27 $ 15,485.42
Mar
Feb
Jan
John
Jean
Joe
Joan

Figure 6 A default version of the chart is inserted in the worksheet window.

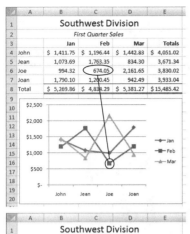

Figures 7 & 8
A linked worksheet and chart before (top) and after (bottom) a change to a cell's contents.

Worksheet & Chart Links

When you create a chart based on worksheet data, the worksheet and chart are linked. Excel knows exactly which worksheet and cells it should look at to plot the chart. If the contents of one of those cells changes, the chart changes accordingly (**Figures 7** and **8**).

✔ Tips

- Excel's Range Finder feature places a color-coded box around ranges in a selected chart (**Figure 9**), making them easy to spot.

- You can see (and edit) the links between a chart and a worksheet by activating the chart, selecting one of the data series, and looking at the formula bar. In the formula bar, you should see a formula with a SERIES function that specifies the sheet name and absolute cell references for the range making up that series. **Figure 9** shows an example.

- If you delete worksheet data or an entire worksheet that is linked to a chart, Excel warns you with a dialog like the one in **Figure 10**. Click OK and then, if you removed the data by mistake, use the Undo command or press ⌷Ctrl⌷ ⌷Z⌷ to get the deleted data back. I tell you about the Undo command in **Chapter 3**.

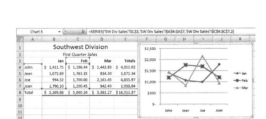

Figure 9 This illustration shows both the Range Finder feature and the SERIES formula.

Figure 10 If you delete cells linked to a chart, you may see a dialog like this.

Working with Chart Objects

An inserted chart is an object very similar to the graphic objects discussed in **Chapter 7**. It can be selected, resized , and moved.

To select a chart

Click the chart. A selection frame appears around it (**Figure 6**).

✔ Tips

- You must select a chart (or one of its elements, as explained later) to make changes to it.

- When a chart is selected, the Chart Tools tabs appear at the top of the Excel application window (**Figure 11**).

To deselect a chart

Click anywhere other than on the chart. The selection frame disappears (**Figure 1**).

To resize a chart

1. Select the chart you want to resize.

2. Position the mouse pointer on one of the selection handles on the chart's frame. The mouse pointer turns into a two-headed arrow (**Figure 12**).

3. Press the mouse button and drag. The frame stretches or shrinks as you drag it (**Figure 13**).

4. Release the mouse button. The chart resizes (**Figure 14**).

Figure 11 When a chart is selected, the Chart Tools tabs appear at the top of the window.

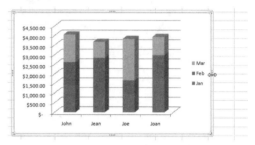

Figure 12 Position the mouse pointer on a selection handle of the chart's frame.

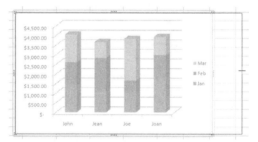

Figure 13 Drag the selection handle to stretch the frame.

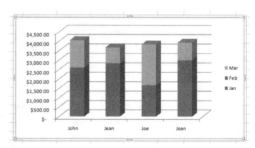

Figure 14 When you release the mouse button, the chart resizes.

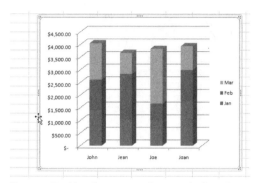

Figure 15 Position the mouse pointer on the frame's edge.

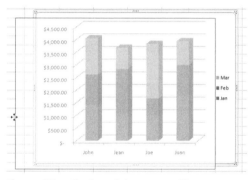

Figure 16 Drag the frame into a new position.

Figure 17 Use this dialog to move a chart to another sheet.

To move a chart within the worksheet

1. Select the chart you want to move.

2. Position the mouse pointer on the chart border anywhere except on a selection handle. The mouse pointer turns into a four-headed arrow (**Figure 15**).

3. Press the mouse button and drag. The chart's frame moves with the mouse pointer (**Figure 16**).

4. When the chart is in the desired position, release the mouse button. The chart moves.

To move a chart to another sheet

1. Select the chart you want to move.

2. Click Design > Location > Move Chart to display the Move Chart dialog (**Figure 17**).

3. Select one of the option buttons:

    ▲ **New sheet** places the chart on its own chart sheet (**Figure 2**). If you select this option, you can enter a name for the sheet in the text box.

    ▲ **Object in** places the chart as an object in an existing sheet. Choose a sheet from the drop-down list of sheets in the current workbook.

4. Click OK. The sheet moves.

MOVING CHARTS

Chart Design Options

The Design tab offers a number of options to change the overall design of a selected chart. It includes five groups of options:

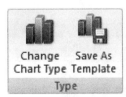

Figure 18
The Design tab's
Type group.

- ◆ **Type** (**Figure 18**) lets you change the chart type or save the current chart as a template for future charts.

- ◆ **Data** (**Figure 22**) enables you to switch the row and column data for a chart, thus changing the data layout and to select new or different data for a chart.

- ◆ **Chart Layouts** (**Figure 28**) offers a number of predefined layouts for chart elements such as titles and elements.

- ◆ **Chart Styles** (**Figure 30**) enables you to apply color-coordinated formatting to your chart.

- ◆ **Location** lets you move a chart to another sheet, as I discuss on the previous page.

In this part of the chapter I explain how to use these options to set the overall appearance of a chart.

✔ Tip

- ■ The Design tab is only available when a chart or chart element is selected.

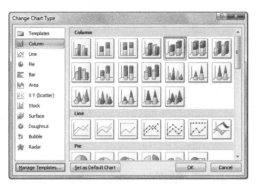

Figure 19 Use the Change Chart Type dialog to select a new type for the selected chart.

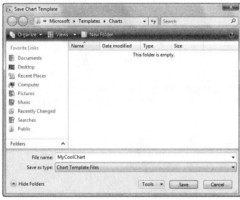

Figure 20 Use the Save Chart Template dialog to save the selected chart as a design template that can be applied to other charts.

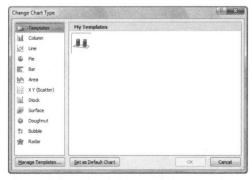

Figure 21 Once a chart has been saved as a template, it appears in the Change Chart Type dialog.

To change a chart's type

1. Select the chart you want to change.

2. Click Design > Type > Change Chart Type (**Figure 18**). The Change Chart Type dialog appears (**Figure 19**).

3. In the list on the left side of the dialog, select a main chart type.

4. In the main part of the dialog, click the icon for the chart subtype you want.

5. Click OK. The chart changes to the subtype you specified.

To save a chart as a template

1. Customize a chart as discussed throughout this chapter.

2. Select the chart.

3. Click Design > Type > Save As Template (**Figure 18**).

4. In the Save Chart Template dialog that appears (**Figure 20**), enter a name for the template and click Save.

✔ Tips

■ Once a chart has been saved as a template, it appears in the Templates folder of the Change Chart Type dialog (**Figure 21**). This makes it easy to apply its settings to other chartes.

■ The chart template feature can save you time if you often create charts with the same customized settings.

USING CHART TYPE OPTIONS

To switch row & column data

1. Select the chart you want to modify.

2. Click Design > Data > Switch Row/Column (**Figure 22**). The row and column data is switched (**Figure 23**).

✔ Tips

- This option is only available for certain types of charts.

- If you are unpleasantly surprised by the results of step 2, you can use the Undo command or press Ctrl Z to revert back to the original data display. I tell you about the Undo command in **Chapter 3**.

To change, add, or remove a data series

1. Select the chart you want to modify.

2. Click Design > Data > Select Data (**Figure 22**). The Select Data Source dialog appears (**Figure 24**).

3. To change the entire chart data range, click anywhere in the Chart data range box to position the insertion point there, then use your mouse to select the new range. As you drag to select, the Select Data Source dialog collapses to move out of the way (**Figure 25**). When you release the mouse button, the dialog is restored with the range you selected inserted in the Chart data range box.

4. To change just one series, click the name of the series in the bottom half of the dialog, and click the Edit button above it. The Edit Series dialog appears (**Figure 26**). Position the insertion point in the field you want to change, then click or drag in the worksheet window to enter the series in the dialog. Click OK to save your changes.

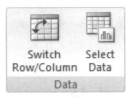

Figure 22
The Data group offers two commands for working with a chart's data.

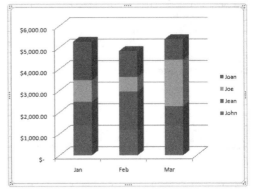

Figure 23 Clicking the Switch Row/Column button changes the chart in **Figure 1** so it looks like this.

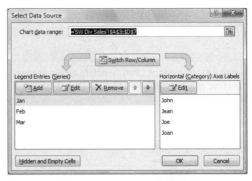

Figure 24 The Select Data Source dialog offers a way to change, add, or remove a chart's data series.

Figure 25 When you begin to select cells, the Select Data Source dialog collapses to get out of your way.

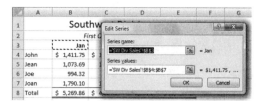

Figure 26 Use the Edit Series dialog to specify cells containing a series name or data.

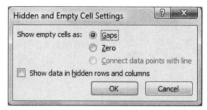

Figure 27 You can use this dialog to indicate how hidden and empty cells should appear in a chart.

✔ Tips

■ Although you can use the Select Data Source dialog to build a chart from scratch, it's much easier to simply select the cells to be charted when inserting a chart, as discussed at the beginning of this chapter.

■ Changes you make in the Select Data Source dialog are immediately reflected in your chart. If you make a mistake and really mess things up, just click Cancel instead of OK to restore the chart to its condition before you made changes.

5. To add a legend data series, click the Add button. Then use the Edit Series dialog that appears to enter cell references for the series name and series values. Click OK to save your settings.

6. To remove a data series, select the series you want to remove and click Remove. The data series is removed from the dialog and the chart.

7. To rearrange a chart's data:

   ▲ Click Switch Row/Column to switch the two data series. This is the same as clicking Design > Data > Switch Row/Column (**Figure 22**) as discussed on the previous page.

   ▲ To move a legend series up or down in the presentation order, select the series you want to move and click the up or down arrow above it. The data is rearranged in the dialog and in the chart.

8. When you are finished making changes, click OK.

■ To specify how hidden and empty cells should appear in a chart, click the Hidden and Empty Cells button in the Select Data Source dialog. Then use the Hidden and Empty Cell Settings dialog (**Figure 27**) to set options for displaying these special cells.

WORKING WITH CHART DATA

To set a chart layout

1. Select the chart you want to modify.

2. Click the Design tab to display the Chart Layouts group (**Figure 28**).

3. Click to select one of the options that appear in the single-line scrolling list (**Figure 28**).

   or

   Click the menu button in the bottom-right corner of the list (**Figure 28**) to display a menu of all chart layouts (**Figure 29**) and click to select the one you want.

✔ Tip

■ Chart layouts include elements such as legends, titles, and access titles—all of which can be modified, as explained later in this chapter.

To set a chart style

1. Select the chart you want to modify.

2. Click the Design tab to display the Chart Styles group (**Figure 30**).

3. Click to select one of the options that appear in the single-line scrolling list (**Figure 30**).

   or

   Click the menu button in the bottom-right corner of the list (**Figure 30**) to display a menu of all chart styles (**Figure 31**) and click to select the one you want.

✔ Tip

■ Chart styles change the colors of a chart's data series.

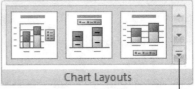

Figure 28 The Chart Layouts group is a single-line scrolling list of options. *Click here to display a menu*

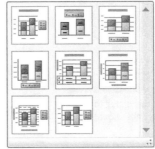

Figure 29 A click displays all options in a menu.

Figure 30 The Chart Styles group offers a variety of color-coordinated styles for your chart.

Figure 31 Clicking the menu button in the Chart Styles group displays all available options in a menu.

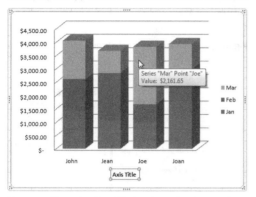

Figure 32 The Layout tab offers groups of options for modifying the appearance of individual chart elements.

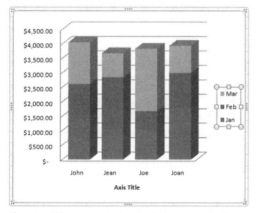

Figure 33 Chart tips identify the chart elements and values you point to.

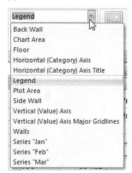

Figure 34 When you select a chart element, selection handles or a box (or both) appear around it.

Figure 35 The Current Selection group displays the name of the currently selected chart element.

Legend
Back Wall
Chart Area
Floor
Horizontal (Category) Axis
Horizontal (Category) Axis Title
Legend
Plot Area
Side Wall
Vertical (Value) Axis
Vertical (Value) Axis Major Gridlines
Walls
Series "Jan"
Series "Feb"
Series "Mar"

Figure 36 Choose a chart element from the Chart Element drop-down list.

Chart Elements

Each chart is made up of multiple *elements*, each of which can be selected, then modified or formatted to fine-tune the appearance of a chart.

The Layout tab (**Figure 32**) offers groups of options to add, remove, and modify a chart's elements.

To identify a chart element

Point to the element you want to identify. Excel displays the name (and values, if appropriate) for the element in a Chart Tip box (**Figure 33**).

To select a chart element

Click the element you want to select. Selection handles or a selection box (or both) appear around it (**Figure 34**).

Or

1. Click the Layout tab to display the Current Selection group (**Figure 35**).

2. Choose the chart element you want to format from the Chart Element drop-down list (**Figure 36**).

✔ Tips

■ To select a single data point, select the data series and then click the point you want to select.

■ Excel displays the name of a selected chart element in the Chart Element drop-down list in the Current Selection group of the Layout tab (**Figure 35**).

To remove a chart element

1. Select the chart element.

2. Press (Backspace). The chart element disappears.

Labels

Labels are textual labels that appear in specific locations on a chart. You can add, remove, or modify labels with options in the Labels group of the Layout tab (**Figure 37**).

The Labels group offers menus for five types of labels:

◆ **Chart Title** is a title for the chart.

◆ **Axis Titles** are labels for a chart's axes, if present.

◆ **Legend** is a list of color-coded labels identifying a chart's data series.

◆ **Data Labels** provide additional information about specific data points.

◆ **Data Table** is a table of the worksheet data that is plotted in the chart.

To set the chart title

1. Click Layout > Labels > Chart Title to display a menu of chart title options (**Figure 38**).

2. Choose an option to determine where the chart title should appear:

▲ **None** does not display the chart title. If one is already displayed, when you choose this option it is removed.

▲ **Centered Overlay Title** displays a centered title that's overlaid on top of the chart's plot area (**Figure 39**).

▲ **Above Chart** displays a centered title above the chart's plot area.

Figure 37 The Layout tab's Labels group.

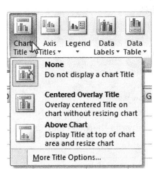

Figure 38
You can set basic chart title options by choosing an option from this menu.

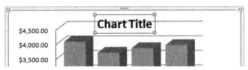

Figure 39 The Centered Overlay Title option puts a title over the chart's plot area.

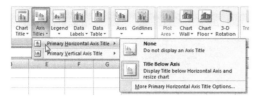

Figure 40 Use the Primary Horizontal Axis Title to set the title for a chart's horizontal axis.

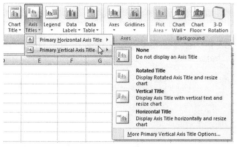

Figure 41 A title below the axis.

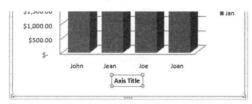

Figure 42 Use the Primary Vertical Axis Title submenu to set the title for a chart's vertical axis.

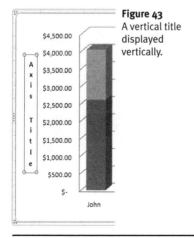

Figure 43
A vertical title displayed vertically.

To set the horizontal axis title

1. Click Layout > Labels > Axis Titles > Primary Horizontal Axis Title to display a submenu of chart title options (**Figure 40**).

2. Choose a title location:

   ▲ **None** does not display a horizontal axis title.

   ▲ **Title Below Axis** displays a title below the horizontal axis (**Figure 41**).

To set the vertical axis title

1. Click Layout > Labels > Axis Titles > Primary Vertical Axis Title to display a submenu of chart title options (**Figure 42**).

2. Choose a title location:

   ▲ **None** does not display a vertical axis title.

   ▲ **Rotated Title** displays a vertical axis title rotated 90°.

   ▲ **Vertical Title** displays a vertical axis with text reading from top to bottom (**Figure 43**).

   ▲ **Horizontal Title** displays a vertical axis title displayed horizontally.

SETTING AXES TITLES

To set a legend

1. Click Layout > Labels > Legend to display a menu of chart legend options (**Figure 44**).

2. Choose a legend location:

   ▲ **None** doesn't display a legend.

   ▲ **Show Legend at Right** displays the legend vertically, to the right of the chart (**Figure 34**).

   ▲ **Show Legend at Top** displays the legend horizontally, above the chart.

   ▲ **Show Legend at Left** displays the legend vertically, to the left of the chart.

   ▲ **Show Legend at Bottom** displays the legend horizontally at the bottom of the chart (**Figure 45**).

   ▲ **Overlay Legend at Right** displays the legend on the right, overlapping the chart's plot area.

   ▲ **Overlay Legend at Left** displays the legend on the left, overlapping the chart's plot area.

To set data labels

1. If you only want data labels on a specific data series or data point, select that series or point.

2. Click Layout > Labels > Data Labels to display a menu of data labels options (**Figure 46**).

3. Choose a data labels option:

   ▲ **None** doesn't display data labels for the selection.

   ▲ **Show** displays data labels on the selection (**Figure 47**).

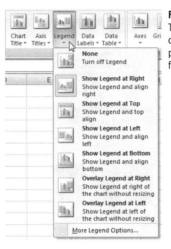

Figure 44
The Legend menu offers a variety of position options for chart legends.

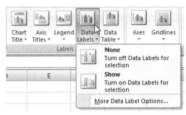

Figure 45 Here's an example of a legend at the bottom of a chart.

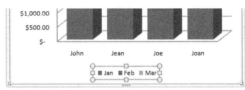

Figure 46
Use the Data Labels menu to set whether data labels are displayed.

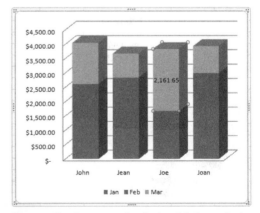

Figure 47 Here's an example of a data label on a single selected data point.

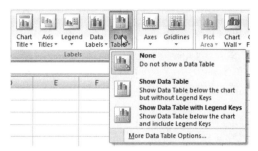

Figure 48 The Data Table menu.

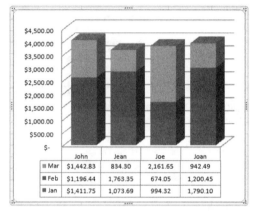

Figure 49 Here's an example of a chart wth a data table with legend keys.

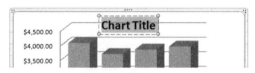

Figure 50 Select the default title text.

Figure 51 Type in the text you want to appear.

To set a data table

1. Click Layout > Labels > Data Table to display a menu of chart data table options (**Figure 48**).

2. Choose a data table option:
   - ▲ **None** doesn't display a data table.
   - ▲ **Show Data Table** displays a data table below the chart without legend keys.
   - ▲ **Show Data Table with Legend Keys** displays a data table and legend keys below the chart (**Figure 49**).

To customize label text

1. Select the text within the label's selection box (**Figure 50**).

2. Type in the text you want to appear (**Figure 51**).

Axes & Gridlines

Axes are the bounding lines of a chart. 2-D charts have two axes: horizontal and vertical. 3-D charts have three axes: horizontal, vertical, and depth. Pie and doughnut charts do not have axes at all.

Gridlines, which work with axes, are lines indicating major and minor scale points along a chart's walls. They can make it easier to follow chart points to their corresponding values on a chart axis. Pie and doughnut charts do not have gridlines.

The Layout tab's Axes group (**Figure 52**) offers two menus of options:

◆ **Axes** offers commands for displaying horizontal, vertical, and depth axis options, including labels and corresponding tick marks.

◆ **Gridlines** offers commands for displaying horizonta, vertical, and depth major and minor gridlines.

To set axis options

1. Click Layout > Axes > Axes > Primary Horizontal Axis to display a submenu of horizontal axis options (**Figure 53**).

2. Choose a horizontal axis option:

▲ **None** does not display a horizontal axis.

▲ **Show Left to Right Axis** displays an axis with labels and tick marks that begins on the left and goes to the right. This is a standard horizontal axis (**Figure 56**).

▲ **Show Axis without labeling** displays an axis without labels or tick marks.

▲ **Show Right to Left Axis** displays an axis with labels that begins on the right and goes to the left.

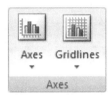

Figure 52
The Layout tab's Axes group.

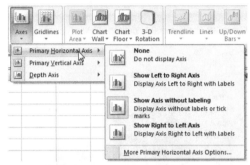

Figure 53 Use the Primary Horizontal Axis submenu to choose a horizontal axis option.

Figure 54 Use the Primary Vertical Axis submenu to set vertical axis options.

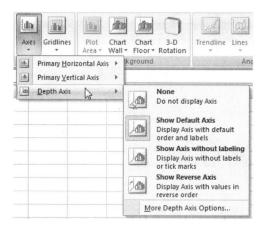

Figure 55 If you're formatting a 3-D chart, you can set options for its depth axis.

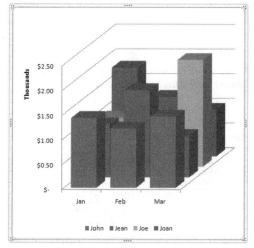

Figure 56 Here's an example of a 3-D chart with a left to right horizontal axis, a vertical axis with numbers in thousands, and an unlabeled depth access. In this example, a legend is a good replacement for the depth axis.

3. Click Layout > Axes > Axes > Primary Vertical Axis to display a submenu of vertical axis options (**Figure 54**).

4. Choose a vertical axis option:

   ▲ **None** does not display a vertical axis.

   ▲ **Show Default Axis** displays a vertical axis with default settings calculated by Excel (**Figure 1**).

   ▲ **Show Axis in Thousands** displays a vertical axis with numbers in thousands (**Figure 56**).

   ▲ **Show Axis in Millions** displays a vertical axis with numbers in millions.

   ▲ **Show Axis in Billions** displays a vertical axis with numbers in billions.

   ▲ **Show Axis with Log Scale** displays a vertical axis with numbers in a logarithmic scale.

5. Click Layout > Axes > Axes > Depth Axis to display a submenu of depth axis options (**Figure 55**).

6. Choose a depth axis option:

   ▲ **None** does not display a depth axis.

   ▲ **Show Default Axis** displays a depth axis with default settings calculated by Excel.

   ▲ **Show Axis without labeling** displays an axis without labels or tick marks (**Figure 56**).

   ▲ **Show Reverse Axis** displays an axis with label values in reverse order.

✔ Tip

■ Remember not all charts have axes and only 3-D charts have a depth axis. If an axis option cannot be selected, that option is simply not available for the type of chart you have selected.

To set gridlines

1. Click Layout > Axes > Gridlines > Primary Horizontal Gridlines to display a submenu of horizontal gridline options (**Figure 57**).

2. Choose the gridline option you want:

   ▲ **None** does not display any gridlines.

   ▲ **Major Gridlines** displays gridlines that correspond to major tick mark units for the axis scale.

   ▲ **Minor Gridlines** displays gridlines that correspond to minor tick mark units for the axis scale.

   ▲ **Major & Minor Gridlines** displays gridlines that correspond to both the major and minor tick mark units for the axis scale.

3. Click Layout > Axes > Gridlines > Primary Vertical Gridlines to display a submenu of vertical gridline options (**Figure 58**).

4. Repeat step 2; the options are the same but for the vertical axis.

5. Click Layout > Axes > Gridlines > Depth Gridlines to display a submenu of depth gridline options (**Figure 59**).

6. Repeat step 2; the options are the same but for the depth axis.

✔ Tips

■ I explain how to set the scale for an axis later in this chapter.

■ Although gridlines can make a chart's data easier to read, too many gridlines can clutter a chart's walls, making data impossible to read.

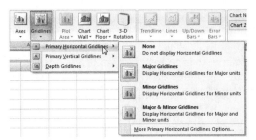

Figure 57 The Primary Horizontal Gridlines submenu offers options for setting the horizontal gridlines.

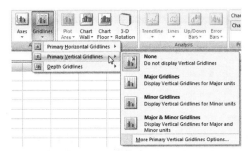

Figure 58 You can set vertical gridline options with the Primary Vertical Gridlines submenu.

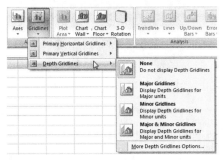

Figure 59 If you're working with a 3-D chart, you can set gridlines for the depth axis.

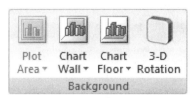

Figure 60 The Background group with a 3-D chart selected. If a 2-D chart is selected, only the Plot Area menu is available.

Figure 61 The Plot Area menu offers options for the background of a 2-D chart.

Background Fill

The Layout tab's Background group (**Figure 60**) includes three menus of options for formatting a chart's background:

◆ **Plot area** is the part of a 2-D chart where the data is plotted.

◆ **Chart Wall** is the background of the chart. This is basically the same as plot area, but for a 3-D chart, which has two walls.

◆ **Chart Floor** is the bottom plot area for a 3-D chart.

You can use options on these menus to remove fill or display the default fill color.

✔ Tips

■ Since the default fill color is white for many charts, if you remove the fill, the chart may look the same as it does with the default fill.

■ The options on these menus enable you to turn the fill on or off. I explain how to change the color of the fill later in this chapter.

To set a 2-D chart's background

1. Click Layout > Background > Plot Area to display a menu of plot area options (**Figure 61**).

2. Choose one of the options:
   ▲ **None** removes the fill from the plot area.
   ▲ **Show Plot Area** displays the default fill color for the plot area.

To set a 3-D chart's background

1. Click Layout > Background > Chart Wall to display a menu of chart wall options (**Figure 62**).

2. Choose one of the options:
   - ▲ **None** removes the fill from the chart walls.
   - ▲ **Show Chart Wall** displays the default fill color for the chart wall.

3. Click Layout > Background > Chart Floor to display a menu of chart floor options (**Figure 63**).

4. Choose one of the options:
   - ▲ **None** removes the fill from the chart walls.
   - ▲ **Show Chart Floor** displays the default fill color for the chart floor.

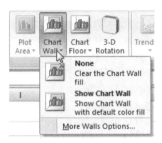

Figure 62 Use the Chart Wall menu to set the background for a 3-D chart.

Figure 63 You can also set the floor fill for a 3-D chart.

Figure 64 The Format Legend dialog offers options for formatting a chart legend.

Formatting Chart Elements

Excel can display a special Format dialog (**Figured 64**) for every kind of element in a chart. The dialog offers only those options that apply to the element you want to format in the type of chart that is selected.

Although many chart elements share the same formatting options, some options are specific to a single type of chart element. As a result, the Format dialog has dozens of combinations of options, many of which are covered in the remaining pages of this chapter.

✔ Tips

- The name of the dialog varies depending on the item being formatted.

- **Table 1** provides a list of the kinds of options available for each type of chart element.

Table 1

Format dialog options for various chart elements

Options	Chart Title	Axis Title	Legend	Data Labels	Data Table	Axes	Gridlines	Plot Area	Chart Wall	Chart Floor
Legend Options			√							
Label Options				√						
Data Table Options					√					
Axis Options						√				
Fill	√	√	√	√	√	√		√	√	√
Border Color	√	√	√	√	√			√	√	√
Border Styles	√	√	√	√	√			√	√	√
Line Color						√	√			
Line Style						√	√			
Shadow	√	√	√	√	√	√	√	√	√	√
Alignment	√	√		√		√				
Number				√		√				
3-D Format	√	√		√	√	√		√	√	√
3-D Rotation								√	√	√

To open the Format dialog for a chart element

1. Select the chart element you want to format.

2. If necessary, click the Layout tab to display the Current Selection group (**Figure 35**).

3. Click Format Selection. The Format dialog appears for the currently selected chart element (**Figure 64**).

Or

Choose the More Options command at the bottom of any Layout tab menu or submenu.

To use the Format dialog

1. In the list on the left side of the Format dialog (**Figure 64**), click the name of the type of formatting you want to change.

2. Make changes in the main part of the dialog. Your changes take affect immediately.

3. Repeat steps 1 and 2 for each type of change you want to make.

4. When you're finished making changes, click close to dismiss the dialog.

✔ Tip

■ You can keep the Format dialog open while you select and work with other chart elements. The options in the dialog change each time you select a different element to format.

USING THE FORMAT DIALOG

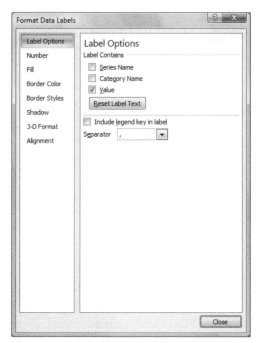

Figure 65 The Label Options pane of the Format dialog.

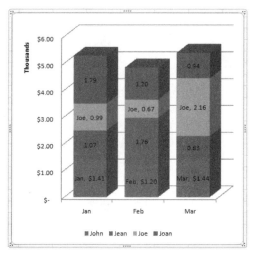

Figure 66 In this stacked column chart example, all segments include the value. The second segment down also includes the series name while the bottom segment includes the category name. As you can see, you can get pretty creative with the labels.

Legend Options

The Legend Options pane of the Format dialog (**Figure 64**) offers the following options for the placement of a legend:

◆ **Legend Position** determines the position of the legend: Top, Bottom, Left, Right, or Top Right.

◆ **Show the legend without overlapping the chart** positions the legend so that it does not overlap other chart elements. This may cause the chart's plot area to resize.

✔ Tip

■ To prevent the plot area from resizing when a legend is displayed, turn the Show the legend without overlapping the chart check box off.

Label Options

The Label Options pane of the Format dialog (**Figure 65**) enables you to specify what should be included in a selected series' or point's data label. It offers the following options, some of which are illustrated in **Figure 66**:

◆ **Label Contains** offers three possible options for display: Series Name, Category Name, Value. You can turn on any combination of these check boxes.

◆ **Reset Label Text** enables you to reset a selected label's text to the default option. You might find this useful if you manually modified a label and want to restore it to the settings in the dialog.

◆ **Include legend key in label** displays the legend color with the label.

◆ **Separator** is the character to place between components of the label if more than one option is selected.

Data Table Options

The Data Table Options (**Figure 67**) enable you to specify whether a data table should include borders and legend keys:

◆ **Table Borders** enables you to hide or display Horizontal, Vertical, and Outline borders.

◆ **Show legend keys** deterines whether a color-coded legend key should be included in the table.

Axis Options

The Axis Options (**Figures 68**, **69**, and **70**) control formatting of the tick marks, labels, and other features of an axis. Excel displays a different set of options depending on the axis you are formatting.

Excel distinguishes between four types of axes:

◆ **Category axis** is the axis on which categories of information are displayed. This is normally the horizontal axis, but can be the vertical axis for some chart types.

◆ **Time scale axis** is a category axis with the axis type set to time.

◆ **Value axis** is the axis on which values are displayed. This is normally the vertical axis but can be the horizontal axis for some chart types.

◆ **Series axis** is normally the depth axis on 3-D charts.

Here's a look at the options for category, value, and series axes.

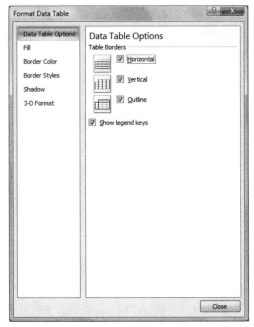

Figure 67 The Data Table Options control the display of borders and a legend key.

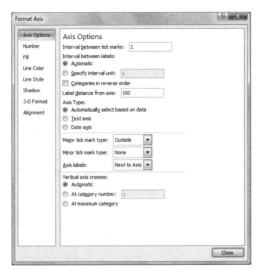

Figure 68 The category axis options for a typical category axis. Other options may appear for some chart types.

Category axis options

Axis Options for a typical category axis (**Figure 68**) include:

◆ **Interval between tick marks** is the number of units between tick marks.

◆ **Interval between labels** is the number of tickmarks between labels. Automatic lets Excel determine where labels should go based on available space.

◆ **Categories in reverse order** displays data in the reverse order on the axis.

◆ **Label distance** determines how far a label is from the axis. Enter a higher number to move the label farther away; enter a lower number to bring it closer.

◆ **Axis Type** lets you set the type of axis: text or date. Automatic lets Excel decide for you.

◆ **Major tick mark type** and **Minor tick mark type** enable you to specify whether tick marks should appear inside, outside, across the axis, or not at all.

◆ **Axis labels** determines where the axis labels should appear in relation to the axis or whether they should appear at all.

◆ **Vertical axis crosses** enables you to specify where the vertical axis should cross the horizontal axis; leave it set to Automatic to let Excel decide for you.

✔ Tip

■ You may see more or fewer options in this dialog depending on the type of chart you're formatting. This example shows the most commonly found options.

Value axis options

Axis Options for a typical value axis (**Figure 69**) include:

◆ **Minimum**, **Maximum**, **Major unit**, and **Minor unit** enable you to specify values for the axis scale or let Excel determine values for you.

◆ **Values in reverse order** displays data in the reverse order on the axis.

◆ **Logarithmic scale** displays the axis in a logarithmic scale using the base you specify.

◆ **Display units** enables you to set the scale's units—for example, hundreds, thousands, billions. This can help keep your chart's axis neat when charting large values.

◆ **Show display units label on chart** displays the option you chose from the Display units drop-down list so it's clear what units are being displayed.

◆ **Major tick mark type** and **Minor tick mark type** enable you to specify whether tick marks should appear inside, outside, across the axis, or not at all.

◆ **Axis labels** determines where the axis labels should appear in relation to the axis or whether they should appear at all.

◆ **Vertical axis crosses at** or **Floor crosses at** enables you to specify where another axis should cross this axis; leave it set to Automatic to let Excel decide for you.

Figure 69 Value axis options for a 3-D column chart.

✔ Tip

■ You may see different options in this dialog depending on the type of chart you're formatting. This example shows options for a 3-D column chart.

Figure 70 Series axis options for a 3-D column chart.

Series axis options

Axis Options for a typical series axis (**Figure 70**) include:

◆ **Interval between tick marks** is the number of units between tick marks.

◆ **Interval between labels** is the number of tickmarks between labels. Automatic lets Excel determine where labels should go based on available space.

◆ **Series in reverse order** displays data in the reverse order on the axis.

◆ **Major tick mark type** and **Minor tick mark type** enable you to specify whether tick marks should appear inside, outside, across the axis, or not at all.

◆ **Axis labels** determines where the axis labels should appear in relation to the axis or whether they should appear at all.

Fill Options

Fill options, which are available for most chart options, enable you to specify a fill color, gradient, picture, or texture. The options that appear vary depending on the option button you select at the top of the Fill Options pane.

◆ **No fill** does not fill the element at all. There are no other options.

◆ **Solid fill** (**Figure 71**) enables you to set the color and transparency for the fill. Choose a color from the pop-up menu (**Figure 72**) and use the slider to set a transparency value.

◆ **Gradient fill** (**Figure 73**) enables you to set up a fill with one or more gradient stops. Start by choosing one of the Preset colors (**Figure 74**), then set other options in the dialog to customize the gradient as desired.

◆ **Picture or texture fill** enables you to use a texture, graphic file, clipboard contents, or clip art as fill. You can set options to identify the image, tile it, and specify transparency.

◆ **Automatic** lets Excel decide how to fill the element based on other settings. There are no other options.

Figure 71 The Fill options when Solid fill is selected.

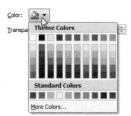

Figure 72
Use this pop-up menu to choose a color.

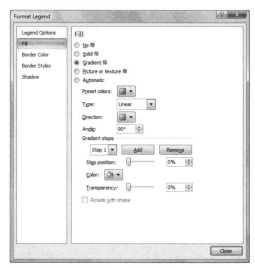

Figure 73 Excel offers many options for setting up a gradient fill.

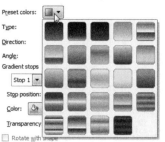

Figure 74
The Preset colors pop-up menu makes it easy to set up some colorful gradients.

Figure 75 Border Color options for a solid line.

Border Color or Line Color

All types of chart elements offer either Border Color or Line Color options. (These two sets of options are virtually identical, so in an effort to save space, I just show Border Color options here.) The options that appear vary depending on the option button you select at the top of the pane.

◆ **No line** does not display a line. There are no other options. This option is not available for all types of chart elements.

◆ **Solid line** (**Figure 75**) enables you to set the color and transparency for the line. Choose a color from the pop-up menu (**Figure 72**) and use the slider to set a transparency value.

◆ **Gradient line** enables you to set options for a gradient line. This option is not available for most types of chart elements.

◆ **Automatic** lets excel determine the line color based on other settings. There are no other options.

BORDER & LINE COLOR OPTIONS

Border Style or Line Style

All types of chart elements offer either Border Style or Line Style options. These two sets of options are virtually identical, so in an effort to save space, I just show Line Style options here (**Figure 76**).

- ◆ **Width** is the thickness of the line, in points.

- ◆ **Compound type** is the style for lines consisting of multiple parallel lines.

- ◆ **Dash type** is the style for dashed lines.

- ◆ **Cap type** is the style for the end of the line.

- ◆ **Join type** is the style for line intersections.

- ◆ **Arrow settings** enable you to set styles for the beginning and ending arrows on lines. This option is not available for borders.

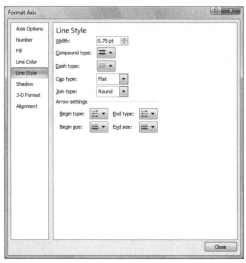

Figure 76 The Line Style pane offers options for customizing a line.

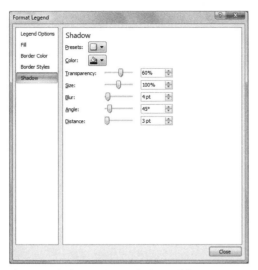

Figure 77 Shadow options make it possible to create fully customized shadows.

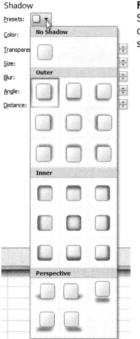

Figure 78
Start by choosing one of the preset shadow options.

Shadow Options

All types of chart elements offer Shadow formatting options (**Figure 77**). Using these options can give your charts an interesting, 3-D effect—even if they aren't 3-D charts.

◆ **Presets** (**Figure 78**) enables you to choose from among many preset shadow options. You must chose an option other than No Shadow to display a shadow for the element. You can then customize the shadow with the remaining options.

◆ **Color** (**Figure 72**) enables you to select a color for the shadow.

◆ **Transparency** determines how much you can see through the shadow.

◆ **Size** is the size of the shadow in relation to the chart element. Normally, this will be 100%.

◆ **Blur** is the thickness of the shadow.

◆ **Angle** is the angle of the shadow in relation to the object.

◆ **Distance** is the distance between the element and the shadow.

Alignment Options

Some types of chart elements offer Alignment formatting options (**Figure 79**):

◆ **Text layout** controls how text is positioned and aligned:

▲ **Vertical alignment** controls how text is aligned vertically on the chart.

▲ **Text direction** controls how text characters read: horizontally or vertically—rotated or stacked.

▲ **Custom Angle** enables you to specify an angle to display text.

◆ **Autofit** can resize the text to fit its shape. This option is only available if a shape has been applied to the element.

◆ **Internal margin** enables you to set the spacing between the text and its borders.

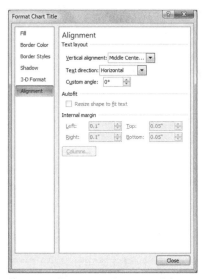

Figure 79 Alignment options control the positioning and alignment of text elements.

Number Options

You can use Number options to format chart elements that display values. As shown in **Figure 80**, these options are virtually identical to Number formatting options available for worksheet cells. You can learn more about these options in **Chapter 6**.

Figure 80 Number options for a chart element are the same as number options for a worksheet cell.

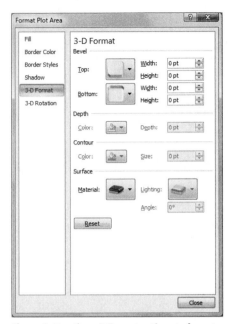

Figure 81 Use the 3-D Format options to format any three dimensional chart element.

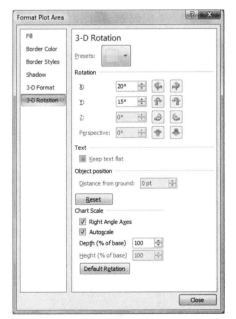

Figure 82 You can use the 3-D Rotation options to set the orientation for a three dimensional chart.

3-D Formatting Options

Excel offers two kinds of 3-D formatting options for chart elements:

◆ **3-D Format** options (**Figure 81**) enable you to format any three dimensional chart element. Set options in this dialog to specify bevel, depth, contour, and surface options. You'll find these options most useful for formatting 3-D filled images, such as columns in a column chart.

◆ **3-D Rotation** options (**Figure 82**) enable you to set the rotation of true 3-D charts. Enter the number of degrees in the X and Y boxes to change the rotation.

The best way to work with these two option panes is to experiment. Try out the settings to see how they affect your chart elements. You can always use the Undo command or press [Ctrl] [Z] to restore the element to its original appearance.

3-D Format & Rotation Options

Printing

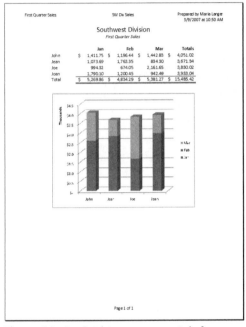

Figure 1 Print Preview lets you see reports before you commit them to paper.

✔ Tips

- When you save a document, Excel saves many print-related options with it.

- This chapter assumes that your computer is already set up for printing. If it is not, consult the documentation that came with your printer for setup information.

Printing

In most cases, when you create a worksheet or chart, you'll want to print it. With Microsoft Excel, you can print all or part of a sheet, multiple sheets, or an entire workbook—all at once.

Excel gives you control over page size, margins, headers, footers, page breaks, orientation, scaling, page order, and content. Its Print Preview feature (**Figure 1**) shows you what your report will look like when printed, so you can avoid wasteful, time-consuming reprints.

Printing is basically a three-step process:

1. Use Excel's Page Setup, Scale to Fit, and Sheet Options groups to set up your report for printing. (You can skip this step if you set the report up the first time you printed it and don't need to change the setup.)

2. Use the Page Layout and Print Preview features to take a look at your report before committing it to paper. You can skip this step if you already know what the report will look like.

3. Use the Print command to send the desired number of copies to the printer for printing.

In this chapter, I explain each of these steps.

Page Setup Options

The Page Layout tab's Page Setup (**Figure 2**), Scale to Fit (**Figure 3**), and Sheet Options (**Figure 4**) groups and the Page Setup dialog (**Figures 5**, **11**, **12**, **13**, **21**, and **28**) offer options you can use to set up a document for printing.

The Page Setup group (**Figure 2**) includes seven menus or buttons:

◆ **Margins** (**Figure 10**) offers basic options to set document's margins and the distance a header or footer should be from the edge of the paper.

◆ **Orientation** (**Figure 6**) enables you to set the document's print direction.

◆ **Size** (**Figure 8**) offers a list of standard paper sizes.

◆ **Print Area** (**Figure 20**) enables you to specify what part of the document should print.

◆ **Breaks** (**Figure 33**) enables you to insert, remove, or reset all page breaks.

◆ **Background** enables you to specify a background image.

◆ **Print Titles** displays the Sheet tab of the Page Setup dialog (**Figure 21**) so you can set column or row headings as titles that repeat on every page.

The Scale to Fit group (**Figure 3**) includes drop-down lists to set the width and height of a document in pages and the print scale of a document.

The Sheet Options group (**Figure 4**) enables you to specify whether you want to view or print gridlines and headings.

Figure 2 The Page Layout tab's Page Setup group.

Figure 3
The Scale to Fit group.

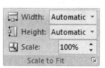

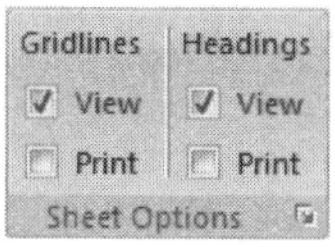

Figure 4
The Sheet Options group.

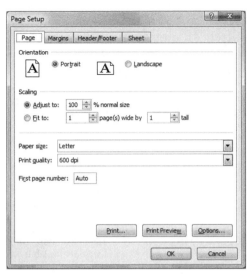

Figure 5 The Page tab of The Page Setup dialog.

In the Page Setup dialog, options are organized under the following tabs:

◆ **Page** (**Figure 5**) lets you set the orientation, scaling, first page number, paper size, and print quality.

◆ **Margins** (**Figures 11** and **12**) lets you set the page margins, the distance the header and footer should be from the edge of the paper, and the positioning of the document on the paper.

◆ **Header/Footer** (**Figure 13**) lets you select a standard header and footer or create custom ones.

◆ **Sheet** (**Figure 21**) lets you specify the print area, print titles, items to print, and page order. If a chart sheet is active when you choose Page Setup, you'll see a Chart tab (**Figure 28**) rather than a Sheet tab. Use it to specify the print quality and indicate if you want the chart to print in black and white.

In this part of the chapter I explain how to set all of these options with Page Layout tab groups and the Page Setup dialog.

To open the Page Setup dialog

1. Click the Page Layout tab to display its options.

2. Click the Dialog Box Launcher button in the bottom-right corner of the Page Setup group (**Figure 2**), the Scale to Fit group (**Figure 3**), or the Sheet Options group (**Figure 4**).

   The Page Setup dialog appears.

✔ Tip

■ The tab of the Page Setup dialog that appears depends on which group's Dialog Box Launcher button you clicked. You can always click a tab to go to the one you want.

To set orientation with the Page Setup group

1. Click Page Layout > Page Setup > Orientation to display the Orientation menu (**Figure 6**).

2. Choose the option you want:

   ▲ **Portrait**, the default option for worksheets, prints vertically down the page.

   ▲ **Landscape**, the default option for chart sheets, prints horizontally across the page.

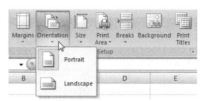

Figure 6 The Orientation menu enables you to set a document for Portrait or Landscape orientation.

To set scaling options with the Scale to Fit group

To scale the document to a specific magnification, enter a percent value in the Scale box in the Scale to Fit group (**Figure 3**).

Or

To scale the document so it fits on a certain number of pages, choose options from the Width (**Figure 7**) and Height drop-down lists in the Scale to Fit group (**Figure 3**).

✔ Tips

■ You will not see any magnification changes onscreen when you set these options. The scale options affect printed documents only.

■ The options you choose from the Width and Height drop-down lists represent the maximum number of pages.

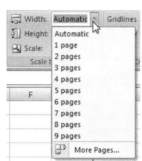

Figure 7
Choose the number of pages you want the document to fit on horizontally from the Width drop-down list. The Height drop-down list is identical, but works for the number of pages vertically.

To set paper size with the Scale to Fit group

1. Click Page Layout > Page Setup > Size to display the Size menu (**Figure 8**). These options vary depending on your printer.

2. Choose the paper size on which you want to print.

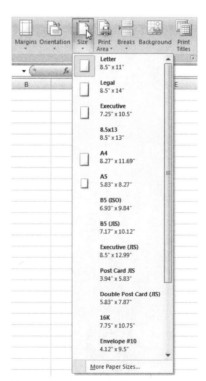

Figure 8 You can use the Size menu to choose a paper size.

SETTING PAGE OPTIONS

Figure 9 The Paper Size drop-down list.

✔ Tips

■ Neither scaling option is available for chart sheets. You can change the scaling for a chart sheet on the Chart tab of the Page Setup dialog, which I discuss later in this chapter.

■ The options that appear in this dialog vary from printer to printer. To learn more about the options for your printer, consult the documentation that came with the printer.

To set all Page options in the Page Setup dialog

1. In the Page Setup dialog, click the Page tab to display its options (**Figure 5**).

2. In the Orientation area, select the desired orientation option:

   ▲ **Portrait**, the default option for worksheets, prints vertically down the page.

   ▲ **Landscape**, the default option for chart sheets, prints horizontally across the page.

3. For a worksheet only, in the Scaling area, select the desired scaling option:

   ▲ **Adjust to** enables you to specify a percentage of the normal size for printing. Be sure to enter a value in the text box. This option is selected by default with 100 in the text box.

   ▲ **Fit to** instructs Excel to shrink the report so it fits on the number of pages you specify. Be sure to enter values in the two text boxes.

4. Choose an option from the Paper size drop-down list (**Figure 9**). These options vary depending on your printer.

5. Choose an option from the Print quality drop-down list. These options vary depending on your printer.

6. If desired, in the First page number box, enter a value that should be used as the page number on the first page of the report. This enables you to start page numbering at a value other than 1.

7. Click OK to save your settings.

SETTING ALL PAGE OPTIONS

To set margins with the Page Setup group

1. Click Page Layout > Page Setup > Margins to display the Margins menu (**Figure 10**).

2. Choose the margin option you want.

   or

   Choose Custom Margins to display the Margins tab of the Page Setup dialog (**Figures 11** and **12**). Then follow the steps in the next section to set margins.

✔ Tip

■ The margins menu includes only a few common options. If you want to customize your margins, use the Margins tab of the Page Setup dialog (**Figures 11** and **12**) as discussed next.

To set margins & centering options with the Page Setup dialog

1. In the Page Setup dialog, click the Margins tab to display its options (**Figure 11** or **12**).

2. Enter values in the Top, Left, Right, and Bottom text boxes to set the amount of space between the edge of the paper and the report content.

3. Enter values in the Header and Footer text boxes to set the amount of space between the edge of the paper and the header and footer content.

4. For a worksheet only, turn on the desired Center on page check boxes:

   ▲ **Horizontally** centers the report content between the left and right margins.

   ▲ **Vertically** centers the report content between the top and bottom margins.

5. Click OK to save your settings.

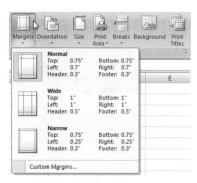

Figure 10 The Margin menu offers three basic margin combinations.

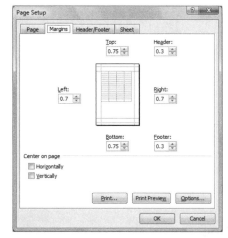

Figure 11 The Margins tab of the Page Setup dialog for a worksheet ...

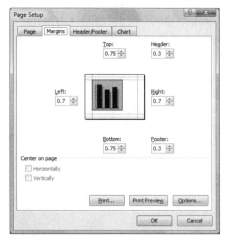

Figure 12 ... and for a chart sheet.

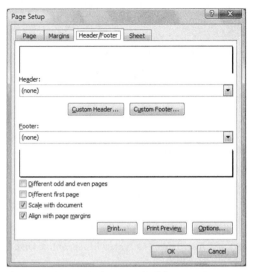

Figure 13 The Header/Footer tab of the Page Setup dialog.

Figure 14 The Header and Footer drop-down lists offer a number of predefined headers and footers.

Figure 15 The header and footer you select appear in the sample areas in the dialog.

✔ Tips

- As you make changes in this window, the preview area changes accordingly. This helps you get an idea of what the document will look like when previewed or printed.

- You can also set margins in the Print Preview window. I explain how later in this chapter.

- Do not set margins to smaller values than the Header and Footer values or Excel will print your report over the header or footer.

- Some printers cannot print close to the edge of the paper. If part of your report is cut off when printed, increase the margin, header, and footer values.

To add built-in headers & footers

1. In the Page Setup dialog, click the Header/Footer tab to display its options (**Figure 13**).

2. Choose options from the Header and Footer drop-down lists (**Figure 14**).

   The option(s) you selected appear in the sample area(s) in the dialog (**Figure 15**).

3. Click OK to save your settings.

✔ Tips

- The drop-down list for Footer is identical to the one for Header (**Figure 14**).

- Excel gets your name and company name from entries you made when you installed Excel. I explain how to change this information in **Chapter 15**.

- To change the formatting of text in the header or footer, you need to use the Custom Header or Custom Footer button in the Header/Footer tab of the Page Setup dialog. I tell you about that next.

To add custom headers & footers

1. In the Page Setup dialog, click the Header/Footer tab to display its options (**Figure 13**).

2. To add a header, click the Custom Header button to display the Header dialog (**Figure 16**).

3. Enter the text or codes that you want to appear in the header in the Left section, Center section, and Right section text boxes. You can use the buttons listed in **Table 1** to format selected text or insert codes for dynamic information. **Figure 17** shows an example.

4. Click OK to save your settings. The settings appear in the Page Setup dialog (**Figure 18**).

5. To add a footer, click the Custom Footer button. This displays the Footer dialog, which looks just like the Header dialog.

6. Repeat steps 3 and 4 for the footer.

7. Click OK in the Page Setup dialog to save your settings.

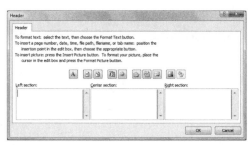

Figure 16 The Header dialog.

Figure 17 An example of a custom header entered into the Header dialog.

Figure 18 Here's the header from **Figure 17** in the Page Setup dialog.

Table 1

Buttons for Inserting Dynamic Information into Headers or Footers	
Button Name	**Function**
Format Text	Displays the Font dialog to format selected text. This dialog looks and works like the Font tab of the Format Cells dialog, which I tell you about in Chapter 6.
Insert Page Number	Inserts the &[Page] code to display the page number.
Insert Number of Pages	Inserts the &[Pages] code to display the total pages number.
Insert Date	Inserts the &[Date] code to display the print date.
Insert Time	Inserts the &[Time] code to display the print time.
Insert File Path	Inserts the &[Path]&[File] code to display the complete workbook pathname.
Insert File Name	Inserts the &[File] code to display the workbook name.
Insert Sheet Name	Inserts the &[Tab] code to display the sheet name.
Insert Picture	Displays the Insert Picture dialog so you can locate and select a picture to insert in the header. Then inserts the &[Picture] code, which is linked to the picture. I tell you about inserting pictures in Chapter 7.
Format Picture	Displays the Format Picture dialog so you can set picture formatting options for an inserted picture. I tell you about formatting pictures in Chapter 7.

ADDING CUSTOM HEADERS & FOOTERS

✔ Tips

- In step 3, to enter an ampersand (&) character in a header or footer, type && where you want it to appear.

- To specify the starting page number to be printed in the header or footer, enter a value in the First page number text box of the Page tab of the Page Setup dialog (**Figure 5**).

- *Dynamic information* changes automatically. For example, the page number changes on each page and the print date changes each day you print the file. Using the buttons or codes for dynamic information (**Table 1**) ensures header and footer contents are accurate.

To remove headers & footers

1. In the Page Setup dialog, click the Header/Footer tab to display its options (**Figure 13**).

2. To remove a header, choose (none) from the Header drop-down list (**Figure 14**). The header disappears from the dialog.

3. To remove a footer, choose (none) from the Footer drop-down list (**Figure 14**). The footer disappears from the dialog.

4. Click OK to save your settings.

REMOVING HEADERS & FOOTERS

To set additional header & footer options

1. In the Page Setup dialog, click the Header/Footer tab to display its options (**Figure 13**).

2. Toggle check boxes near the bottom of the dialog to set options as desired:

   ▲ **Different odd and even pages** enables you to specify a different header and footer for odd and even pages.

   ▲ **Different first page** enables you to specify a different header and footer for the first page of a printout.

   ▲ **Scale with document** applies the same scaling to the header and footer that is applied to the rest of the document when printed. I explain how to set scaling options earlier in this chapter.

   ▲ **Align with page margins** ensures that the header and footer are properly aligned with the document's left and right margins when printed.

3. Click OK to save your settings.

✔ Tip

■ Turning on the Different odd and even pages and Different first page check boxes display tabs in the Header (**Figure 19**) and Footer dialogs so you can specify the content for each header and footer.

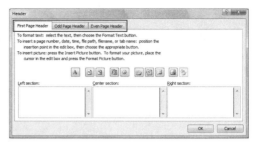

Figure 19 Tabs appear in the Header and Footer dialogs so you can specify the content for each header and footer in your document.

Figure 20 Use the Print Area menu to set and clear a worksheet's print area.

To set the print area with the Page Setup group

1. Select the part of the document you want to print.

2. Choose Page Layout > Page Setup > Print Area > Set Print Area (**Figure 20**).

✔ Tips

■ If you want to print an entire sheet, it is not necessary to set the print area—as long as a different print area has not already been set.

■ You can have a different print area active in every sheet of a workbook.

■ Excel remembers the print areas that were active when a workbook was saved. When you reopen a workbook the same print areas are active.

■ To print a different part of your worksheet, you must specify a different print area.

To clear a print area

Choose Page Layout > Page Setup > Print Area > Clear Print Area (**Figure 20**).

To set gridline & heading printing with the Sheet Options group

Toggle the Print check boxes in the Sheet Options group (**Figure 4**) as desired:

◆ **Print under Gridlines** prints the worksheet gridlines.

◆ **Print under Headings** prints the column and row headings.

✔ Tip

■ By default both of these check boxes are turned off so neither gridlines nor column and row headings print.

To set sheet options in the Page Setup dialog

1. In the Page Setup dialog, click the Sheet tab to display its options (**Figure 21**).

2. To print less than the entire worksheet, enter a range in the Print area box (**Figure 22**).

3. To display column or row titles on all pages of a lengthy report, enter row or column (or both) ranges in the Rows to repeat at top or Columns to repeat at left boxes (**Figure 22**). **Figures 23** through **25** show how this affects the printout.

4. Turn on check boxes in the dialog to set additional print options as desired:

   ▲ **Gridlines** prints worksheet gridlines.

   ▲ **Black and white** prints the worksheet in black and white. This can save time if you print on a color printer.

   ▲ **Draft quality** reduces printing time by omitting gridlines and most graphics.

   ▲ **Row and column headings** prints the column letters and row numbers with the worksheet.

5. To print worksheet comments, choose an option other than (None) from the Comments drop-down list (**Figure 26**).

6. To specify how cells containing errors should be printed, choose an option from the Cell errors as drop-down list (**Figure 27**).

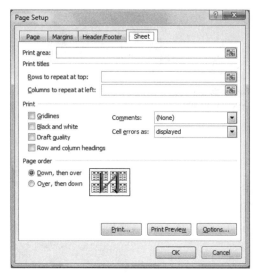

Figure 21 The Sheet tab of the Page Setup dialog.

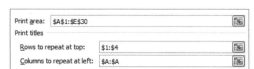

Figure 22 This example shows the proper way to enter ranges for the Print area and Print titles.

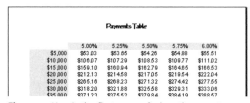

Figure 23 Here's the first page of a lengthy report.

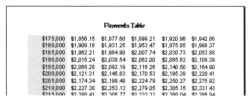

Figure 24 Without page titles, the headings don't appear on subsequent pages.

Figure 25 But with page titles set as they are in **Figure 22,** headings appear on every page.

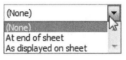

Figure 26
The Comments drop-down list.

Figure 27
The Cell errors as drop-down list.

Figure 28 The Chart tab of the Page Setup dialog.

7. Select a Page order option for a long or wide worksheet:

   ▲ **Down, then over** prints all rows of the first few columns first, then prints rows from subsequent columns.

   ▲ **Over, then down** prints all columns of the first bunch of rows first, then prints columns from subsequent rows.

8. Click OK to save your settings.

✔ Tips

- In steps 2 and 3, you can enter each range manually by typing it into the text box or have Excel enter it automatically for you by clicking in the text box, then selecting the range in the worksheet window.

- I tell you about worksheet comments in **Chapter 11.**

To set chart options with the Page Setup dialog

1. In the Page Setup dialog, click the Chart tab to display its options (**Figure 28**).

2. Turn on Printing quality check boxes as desired:

   ▲ **Draft quality** omits graphics from printouts. This increases printing speed and uses less printer memory.

   ▲ **Print in black and white** prints the chart in black and white with patterns replacing colors.

3. Click OK to save your settings.

Adding a Background Image

Excel now enables you to add an image to the background of your sheets. You do this with the Background button in the Page Setup group (**Figure 2**).

✔ Tip

■ I tell you more about inserting images in Excel sheets in **Chapter 7**.

To add a background image

1. Click Page Layout > Page Setup > Background (**Figure 2**).

2. The Sheet Background dialog appears (**Figure 29**). Use it to locate and select the image you want to use as a background.

3. Click Insert.

   The image is inserted as a background image in your worksheet. If the image is smaller than the page size, it is tiled as shown in **Figure 30**.

✔ Tip

■ For best results, choose a low-contrast or light-colored image. Otherwise, you may not be able to read worksheet contents placed above it.

To remove a background image

Click Page Layout > Page Setup > Delete Background (**Figure 31**). The background image is removed.

✔ Tip

■ To replace a background image with a different image, remove it as instructed here, then follow the instructions above to add a different background image.

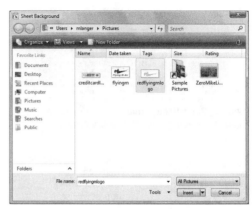

Figure 29 Use the Sheet Background dialog to locate, select, and insert an image.

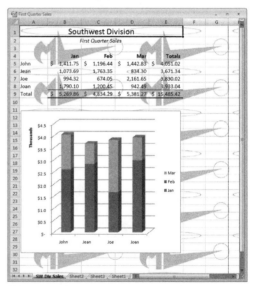

Figure 30 In this example, an image is tiled in the background of a sheet. (I like my company's logo, but not *that* much.)

Figure 31 Once an image has been inserted as a background, the Background button turns into a Delete Background button.

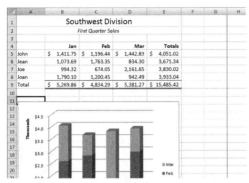

Figure 32 Select a cell to the right of and below where you want the page break to occur.

Figure 33 The Breaks menu offers several page break options.

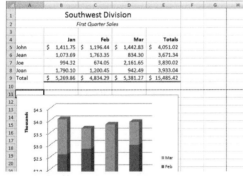

Figure 34 A manual page break is inserted to the left of and above the selected cell. In this case, the selected cell is in column A, so no page break is inserted to its left.

Adding Page Breaks

Once you start preparing your worksheet for printing, you may see black dashed lines within the worksheet window. (You can see an example to the right of column G in **Figures 30** and **32**.) These lines represent page breaks automatically inserted by Excel based on column widths, row heights, and margin settings.

Sometimes you might want a page to break in a specific place. You can insert your own vertical and horizontal page breaks as needed to ensure that page breaks occur where you want them to. You do this with the Breaks menu (**Figure 33**) or with Page Break Preview (**Figure 36**).

✔ Tip

- To remove one of Excel's automatically calculated page breaks, you must insert a manual page break to the left of or above it. Otherwise, you'll be adding a manual page break after the automatic page break.

To add a page break with the Breaks menu

1. Select the cell below and to the right of where you want a page break to occur (**Figure 32**).

2. Choose Page Layout > Page Setup > Breaks > Insert Page Break (**Figure 33**).

   A different dashed line appears, indicating the manual page break you inserted (**Figure 34**).

To remove manual page breaks with the Breaks menu

1. Select the cell to the right of and below the page break you want to remove (**Figure 34**).

2. Choose Page Layout > Page Setup > Breaks > Remove Page Break (**Figure 33**). The page break is removed.

Or

Choose Page Layout > Page Setup > Breaks > Reset All Page Breaks (**Figure 33**). All manual page breaks are removed.

To add page breaks with Page Break Preview

1. Click View > Workbook Views > Page Break Preview (**Figure 35**) to switch to Page Break Preview view (**Figure 36**).

2. Position the mouse pointer over one of the dashed, blue page break lines. The mouse pointer turns into a box with two triangles in its corners.

3. Press the mouse button and drag to make the change. A dark line moves with the mouse pointer (**Figure 37**).

4. Release the mouse button. The page break shifts to the new position and turns into a solid blue line (**Figure 38**). Any automatic page break to its right or below it also shifts.

5. To return to Normal view, click View > Workbook Views > Normal.

✔ Tips

■ The first time you use the Page Break Preview feature, a dialog with instructions appears (**Figure 36**). Click OK to dismiss the dialog before you can drag page breaks. Turn on the check box within the dialog if you don't want to see it again.

Figure 35 The Workbook Views group with Page Break Preview selected.

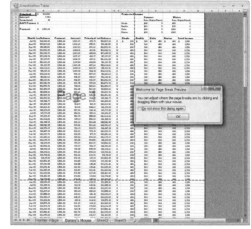

Figure 36 Page Break Preview view, with its instruction dialog.

Figure 37 Drag a page break to change it.

Figure 38 A manual page break looks like a thick blue line.

■ You may need to scroll within the window to see all page breaks for a large worksheet.

■ You can use this feature to change both vertical and horizontal page breaks.

WORKING WITH PAGE BREAKS

Page Layout View

Excel's new Page Layout view feature enables you to work with your worksheet in a view that shows you one or more pages at a time You can use Page Layout view (**Figure 39**) to fine-tune the appearance of your worksheet files.

✔ Tip

- Page Layout view is a fully functional view for working with worksheet contents. As you work with Excel, you may find that you prefer Page Layout view over Normal view for creating, formatting, and modifying your workbook files.

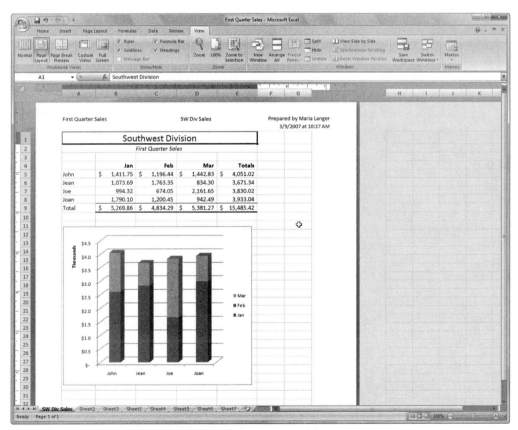

Figure 39 Page Layout view offers a fully functional view of your worksheets, page by page.

To switch to Page Layout view

Click View > Workbook Views > Page Layout (**Figure 40**). The document switches to Page Layout view (**Figure 39**).

To modify worksheet contents in Page Layout view

Make changes as desired to anything you see within the Excel window (**Figure 39**), including worksheet cells, charts, or the document header and footer.

Figure 40 The Workbook Views group with Page Layout selected.

Print Preview

Excel's Print Preview feature lets you see what a report will look like before you print it (**Figure 41**). If a report doesn't look perfect, you can use Page Setup or the Show Margins check box right inside the Print Preview window to make adjustments. When you're ready to print, click the Print button.

✔ Tip

■ Unlike Page Layout view, Print preview does not enable you to modify the contents of a report. You must be in Normal or Page Layout view to make changes to a worksheet's contents.

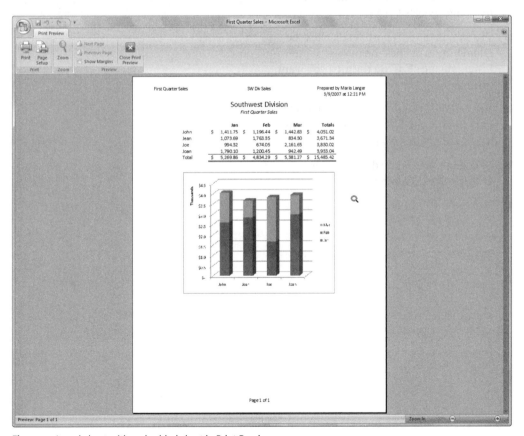

Figure 41 A worksheet with embedded chart in Print Preview.

To preview a report

Choose Microsoft Office > Print > Print Preview (**Figure 42**).

Or

Click the Print Preview button in the Page Setup dialog or the Preview button in the Print dialog.

A preview of the current sheet appears (**Figure 41**). It reflects all Page Setup settings.

✔ Tips

- To view the other pages of the report, click the Next Page or Previous Page button. (These buttons are inactive for one-page reports.)

- To zoom in to see report detail, click the Zoom button or click the mouse pointer (a magnifying glass) on the area you want to magnify.

- To open the Print dialog and print, click the Print button. I tell you about the Print dialog later in this chapter.

- To change Page Setup dialog options, click the Page Setup button.

- To close the Print Preview window, click the Close Print Preview button.

Figure 42 The Print submenu under the Microsoft Office menu.

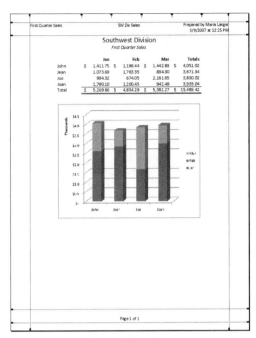

Figure 43 When you turn on the Show Margins check box, handles for margins, header, footer, and columns appear.

Figure 44 Position the mouse pointer on a handle and drag to change the measurement.

To change margin options & column widths

1. In the Print Preview window, turn on the Show Margins check box. Handles for margins, header and footer locations, and column widths appear around the report preview (**Figure 43**).

2. Position the mouse pointer over the handle or guideline for the margin, header, footer, or column you want to change. The mouse pointer turns into a line with two arrows coming out of it (**Figure 44**).

3. Press the mouse button and drag to make the change. A measurement for your change appears in the status bar as you drag.

4. Release the mouse button to complete the change. The report reformats automatically.

✔ Tips

- The changes you make by dragging handles in the Print Preview dialog will be reflected in the appropriate text boxes of the Page Setup dialog.

- I tell you how to change margins and header and footer locations with the Page Setup dialog earlier in this chapter. I tell you how to change column widths in the worksheet window or with the Column Width dialog in **Chapter 6**.

The Print Dialog

You use the Print dialog (**Figure 45**) to set options for a print job and send it to the printer.

To print

1. Choose Microsoft Office > Print > Print (**Figure 42**) or press (Ctrl)(P).

   or

   Click the Print button in the Page Setup dialog (**Figure 5, 11, 12, 13, 21,** or **28**) or Print Preview window (**Figure 41**).

   The Print dialog appears (**Figure 45**).

2. If desired, choose a different printer from the Name drop-down list near the top of the dialog.

3. Select a Print range option:

   ▲ **All** prints all pages in the report.

   ▲ **Page(s)** enables you to enter a page range. Enter the first and last page to print in the From and To text boxes.

4. Select a Print what option:

   ▲ **Selection** prints only the selected cells, sheet, or object.

   ▲ **Active sheet(s)** prints the currently selected sheets.

   ▲ **Entire workbook** prints all nonblank sheets in the workbook file.

   ▲ **Table** prints a database table on the worksheet. This option is only available if the worksheet includes a table.

5. Enter the number of copies you want to print in the Number of copies box. If you enter a value greater than 1, you can turn on the Collate check box to have Excel automatically collate copies as it prints.

6. Click OK. Excel sends the document to the printer.

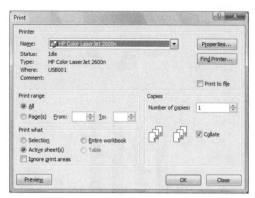

Figure 45 The Print dialog.

✔ Tips

- In step 4, to disregard any print areas set for the workbook or sheet, turn on the Ignore print areas check box.

- You can click the Properties button in the Print dialog to display a dialog full of options for your printer. Consult the documentation that came with your printer to learn more about these options.

PRINTING

Working with Tables

	A	B	C	D
1	First Name ▼	Last Name ▼	Phone Number ▼	Cases Solv ▼
2	Nancy	Drew	555-4256	215
3	Sherlock	Holmes	555-4584	983
4	Lew	Archer	555-6235	129
5	Sam	Spade	555-6845	39
6	Peter	Wimsey	555-1428	54
7	Jessica	Fletcher	555-1253	194
8	John	Aabbott	555-9871	2
9	Total			1616

Figure 1 Here's a tiny table with just a few records and fields. Note the table formatting automatically applied by Excel and the filter menus for each field.

Table Basics

Microsoft Excel's table feature (formerly known as its list or database feature) and related functions help make it a flexible tool for organizing, maintaining, and reporting data. With Excel, you can easily filter data, sort records, and generate subtotals for a table, all without affecting other information in the same worksheet file. You can use Excel's calculating, formatting, charting, and printing features on your table, too.

In Excel, a *table* is a range of worksheet cells with unique labels in the first row that has been identified as a table. **Figure 1** shows an example of a very small, basic table with header and total rows.

A table is organized into fields and records. A *field* is a category of information. In **Figure 1**, *First Name*, *Last Name*, and *Phone Number* are the first three fields. A *record* is a collection of fields for one thing. In **Figure 1**, *row 2* shows the record for *Nancy Drew* and *row 3* shows the record for *Sherlock Holmes*.

✔ Tips

- Fields are always in columns while records are always in rows.

- Excel 2007 includes many advanced features for working with tables, including the ability to publish them on a SharePoint server and to view data on servers in a table. A discussion of these features is beyond the scope of this book.

Creating Tables

There are two ways you can create a table in Excel:

◆ Select empty cells you want to include in the table and convert them to an empty table. Then fill the table with data.

◆ Select a range of cells already containing a list of data and convert it into a table.

Once a range of cells has been converted to a table, it doesn't have to stay that way. You can convert it back to a normal range of cells at any time.

✔ Tip

■ When you select one or more cells within a table, Excel displays the Table Tools' Design tab on the Ribbon. You can use buttons and menus on this tab to work with a selected table.

To create an empty table

1. Select a range of empty cells that you want to turn into a table (**Figure 2**). Make sure it includes enough columns for all fields of information.

2. Click Insert > Tables > Table (**Figure 3**).

3. In the Create Table dialog that appears (**Figure 4**), confirm that the range of cells in the text box corresponds to the range of cells you selected in step 1. If it does not or if you change your mind about the range of cells, select a new range.

4. If your table will have headers, turn on the My table has headers check box.

5. Click OK. Excel formats the cells as a table (**Figure 5**).

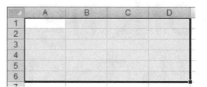

Figure 2 Select the cells you want to convert to a table.

Figure 3
The Insert tab's Tables group.

Figure 4 Use the Create Table dialog to identify the cells for your table.

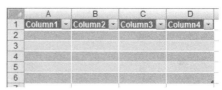

Figure 5 Excel converts the cells into a table. This example table includes headers.

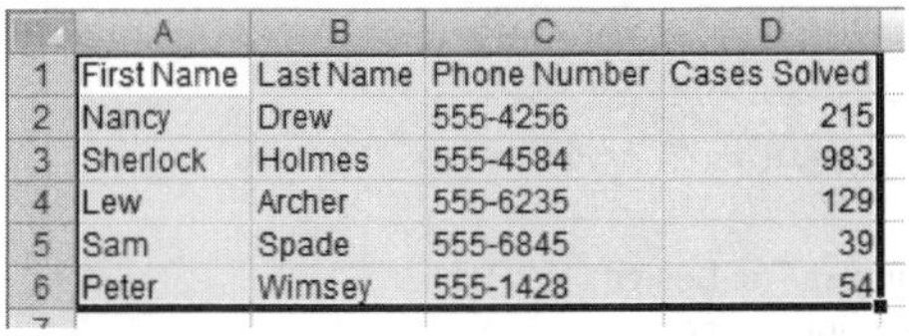

Figure 6 Select the cells you want to convert into a table.

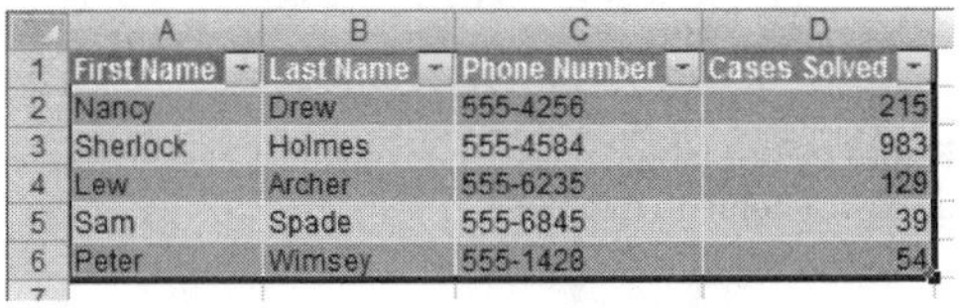

Figure 7 Excel turns the range of cells into a table.

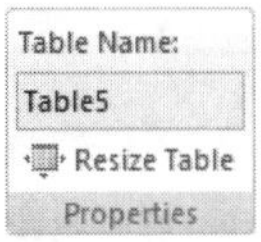

Figure 8
The Design tab's Properties group.

Figure 9 Use this dialog to specify a different range for an existing table.

Figure 10
The Design tab's Tools group.

Figure 11 Excel asks if you really want to convert the table to a normal range.

To convert a range or cells to a table

1. Select the cells you want to convert to a table (**Figure 6**).

2. Click Insert > Tables > Table (**Figure 3**).

3. In the CreateTable dialog that appears (**Figure 4**), confirm that the range of cells in the text box corresponds to the range of cells you selected in step 1. If it does not or if you change your mind about the range of cells, select a new range.

4. If the first row of the selection contains headers, turn on the My table has headers check box.

5. Click OK. Excel formats the cells as a table (**Figure 7**).

To resize a table

1. Click anywhere inside the table.

2. Click Design > Properties > Resize Table (**Figure 8**).

3. The Resize Table dialog appears (**Figure 9**). Enter a new range in the box or select a range in the worksheet to have Excel automatically enter it in the box.

4. Click OK. The table resizes to include the cells you specified.

To convert a table to a range of cells

1. Click anywhere inside the table.

2. Choose Design > Tools > Convert to Range (**Figure 10**).

3. Click Yes in the confirmation dialog that appears (**Figure 11**). The table is converted back into a normal range of Excel cells.

Setting Table Options

The Design tab's Table Style Options group (**Figure 12**) offers a number of options that determine table features and appearance. The Table Styles group (**Figure 13**) makes it easy to apply a color scheme to a table.

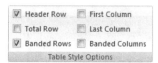

Figure 12 The Design tab's Table Style Options group.

✔ Tip

■ To use these commands simply click anywhere within the table to select it. Then apply the command you want. The change affects the entire table.

Figure 13 The Table Styles group makes it easy to apply a color scheme to a table.

To add a header row

1. Click the Design tab to display the Table Style Options group (**Figure 12**).

2. Turn on the Header Row check box. Excel adds a row above the table with default column names and filter menu buttons (**Figure 14**).

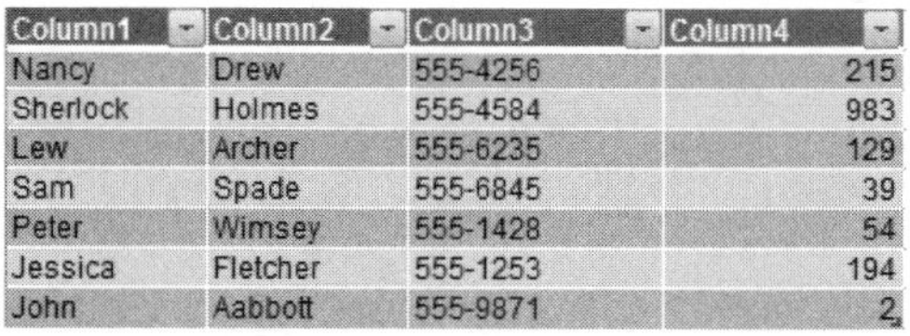

Column1	Column2	Column3	Column4
Nancy	Drew	555-4256	215
Sherlock	Holmes	555-4584	983
Lew	Archer	555-6235	129
Sam	Spade	555-6845	39
Peter	Wimsey	555-1428	54
Jessica	Fletcher	555-1253	194
John	Aabbott	555-9871	2

Figure 14 Here's a table with default column headers.

✔ Tip

■ By default, Excel adds a header row to all tables, using either the contents of the first row (if you indicate that your table has a header row; **Figure 7**) or the default column headers (**Figure 14**).

Nancy	Drew	555-4256	215
Sherlock	Holmes	555-4584	983
Lew	Archer	555-6235	129
Sam	Spade	555-6845	39
Peter	Wimsey	555-1428	54
Jessica	Fletcher	555-1253	194
John	Aabbott	555-9871	2

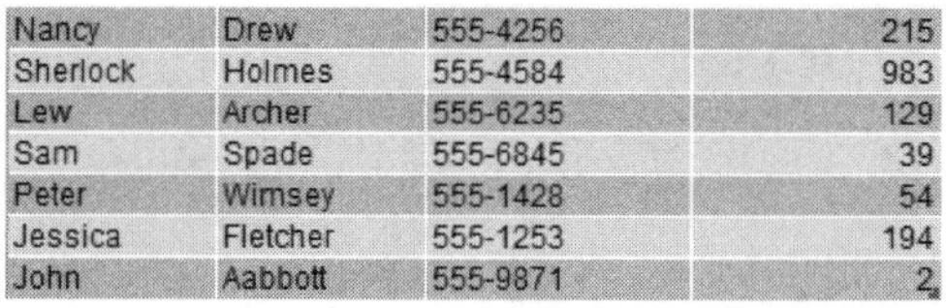

Figure 15 You can also remove headers from your table.

To remove a header row

1. Click the Design tab to display the Table Style Options group (**Figure 12**).

2. Turn off the Header Row check box. Excel removes the header row (**Figure 15**).

First Name ▾	Last Name ▾	Phone Number ▾	Cases Solved ▾
Nancy	Drew	555-4256	215
Sherlock	Holmes	555-4584	983
Lew	Archer	555-6235	129
Sam	Spade	555-6845	39
Peter	Wimsey	555-1428	54
Jessica	Fletcher	555-1253	194
John	Aabbott	555-9871	2
Total			1616

Figure 16 Excel instantly inserts a total row at the bottom of the table.

Total row

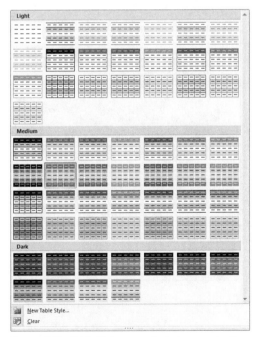

Figure 17 Here's an example of a table with banded rows and columns and special formatting for the first and last column.

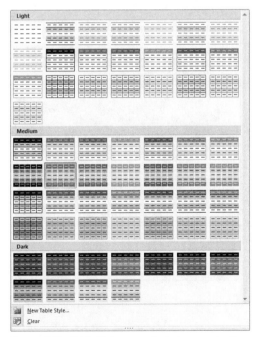

Figure 18 The Table Styles group includes a menu of color schemes for a table.

To add totals to a table

1. Click the Design tab to display the Table Style Options group (**Figure 12**).

2. Turn on the Total Row check box.

   Excel adds a total row with column totals for each column containing numerical values (**Figure 16**).

✔ Tip

- The totals in the total row automatically change when values in the database change.

To apply special formatting to columns and rows

1. Click the Design tab to display the Table Style Options group (**Figure 12**).

2. Toggle check boxes to set the table's formatting as desired:

   ▲ **Banded Rows** displays alternating shades of a color for each row.

   ▲ **Banded Columns** displays alternating shades of a color for each column.

   ▲ **First Column** displays special shading for the first column of the table.

   ▲ **Last Column** displays special shading for the last column of the table.

   Figure 17 shows an example of a larger table with all of these options enabled.

To change a table's color scheme

1. Click the Design tab to display the Table Styles group (**Figure 13**).

2. Click the button for the style you want to apply. You can also click the menu button in the lower-right corner of the group to display the full menu of options (**Figure 18**).

   The table's color scheme changes.

ADDING TOTALS, FORMATTING WITH STYLES

Entering Data into a Table

Entering data into an Excel table is very similar to entering data into an Excel worksheet. Simply select the cell, enter the text, value, or formula you want to appear, and press Enter.

Here are a few things to keep in mind:

- A quick way to enter data into a table is to press Tab to move from cell to cell in the same row. Then, when you finish entering data in the last column of the row, press Enter to advance to the first column of the next row.
- To insert a row or column in the middle of the table, select the row or column immediately after the row (**Figure 19**) or column you want to insert and click Home > Cells > Insert. A row (**Figure 20**) or column is inserted.
- To delete a row or column, select it and click Home > Cells > Delete.
- To add a row at the bottom of the table, click in the last cell of the table (before the total row, if one is present; **Figure 21**) and press Tab. A new row is inserted after that row (**Figure 22**).

✔ Tips

- If you enter a formula into a cell, that formula is automatically copied to all cells in the column.
- When you insert or delete a row, Excel changes the background color of other rows, if necessary, to maintain the banded shading. You can see this in **Figures 19** and **20**.
- If you created an empty table with a header row (**Figure 5**), be sure to replace the default column headings with unique heading names.

	A	B	C	D
1	First Name	Last Name	Phone Number	Cases Solv
2	Nancy	Drew	555-4256	215
3	Sherlock	Holmes	555-4584	983
4	Lew	Archer	555-6235	129
5	Sam	Spade	555-6845	39
6	Peter	Wimsey	555-1428	54
7	Total			1420
8				

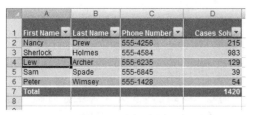

Figure 19 Select a cell in a row beneath where you want to insert a row.

	A	B	C	D
1	First Name	Last Name	Phone Number	Cases Solv
2	Nancy	Drew	555-4256	215
3	Sherlock	Holmes	555-4584	983
4				
5	Lew	Archer	555-6235	129
6	Sam	Spade	555-6845	39
7	Peter	Wimsey	555-1428	54
8	Total			1420

Figure 20 Excel inserts the row and adjusts the banding colors.

	A	B	C	D
1	First Name	Last Name	Phone Number	Cases Solved
2	Nancy	Drew	555-4256	215
3	Sherlock	Holmes	555-4584	983
4	Lew	Archer	555-6235	129
5	Sam	Spade	555-6845	39
6	Peter	Wimsey	555-1428	54
7	Total			1420

Figure 21 Select the last cell before the total row.

	A	B	C	D
1	First Name	Last Name	Phone Number	Cases Solved
2	Nancy	Drew	555-4256	215
3	Sherlock	Holmes	555-4584	983
4	Lew	Archer	555-6235	129
5	Sam	Spade	555-6845	39
6	Peter	Wimsey	555-1428	54
7				
8	Total			1420

Figure 22 When you press Tab, a new row is inserted above the total row.

AutoFilter menus

Figure 23 The AutoFilter feature displays a menu for each header cell in the table.

Figure 24
The Sort & Filter group on the Data tab.

Figure 25
Use the scrolling list in this menu to select the column contents you want to exactly match.

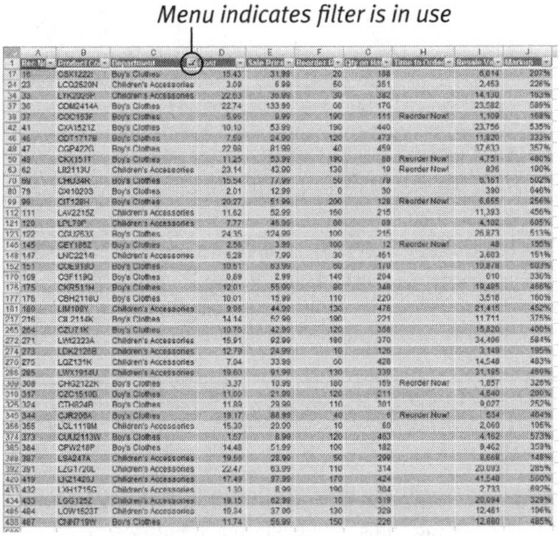

Menu indicates filter is in use

Figure 26 Excel displays only the records that match the criteria you specified.

AutoFilter

The AutoFilter feature displays filter menus in table headers (**Figure 23**). You can use these menus to display only those records that match the criteria you select for a column's contents. You can also use the filter menu to sort records.

✔ Tips

- If the filter menus do not appear in the column headers, click Data > Sort & Filter > Filter (**Figure 24**) to display it.

- The filter feature is extremely flexible, enabling you to match a field's contents with full contents, partial contents, and wildcards.

To match records with column contents

1. Click the AutoFilter button for the column you want to match data in. For example, if you wanted to find all records for a specific department, you'd click the Department column's AutoFilter button (**Figure 23**).

2. In the menu's scrolling list, turn on the check boxes for the contents you want to find (**Figure 25**).

3. Click OK.

    The table's display changes to show only those records matching the criteria you specified (**Figure 26**).

To use text or number filters

1. Click the AutoFilter button for the column you want to match data in.

2. Click Text Filters (**Figure 27**) or Number Filters (**Figure 28**) to display the appropriate filter submenu.

3. Choose the type of filter you want to use. The Custom AutoFilter dialog appears; **Figures 29** and **30** show examples for a text filter and a number filter, respectively.

4. Use the drop-down lists or text boxes to enter one or more criteria.

5. Select the And or Or option button to tell Excel whether it should match both criteria (And) or either criteria (Or).

6. Click OK. Excel filters the table to display only those records that match the criteria you specified.

✔ Tip

■ Criteria can include wildcard characters:
  ? matches any single character
  * matches any group of characters

To use multiple AutoFilters

Set criteria for multiple fields as desired. Excel displays only the records that match *all* of the filters (**Figure 31**).

To clear filters

Use one of the following techniques:

◆ To turn off a column's filter, select Clear Filter from "*column name*" in the Auto-Filter menu you used to filter the data (**Figure 26**).

◆ To clear all filters, click Design > Sort & Filter> Clear (**Figure 24**).

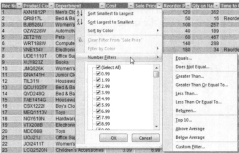

Figures 27 & 28 The Text Filters submenu for field containing text values (top) and the Number Filters submenu for a field containing numerical values (bottom).

Figures 29 & 30 The Custom AutoFilter dialog for a text filter (top) and a number filter (bottom).

Figure 31 Here's the filter results after filtering on two columns using the settings shown in **Figures 28** and **29**. Note that Excel matches both columns' criteria.

	A	B	C	D
1	First Name	Last Name	Phone Number	Cases Solv
2	Nancy	Drew	555-4256	215
3	Sherlock	Holmes	555-4584	983
4	Lew	Archer	555-6235	129
5	Sam	Spade	555-6845	39
6	Peter	Wimsey	555-1428	54
7	Jessica	Fletcher	555-1253	194
8	John	Aabbott	555-9871	2
9	Total			1616
10				

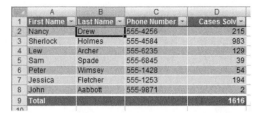

Figure 32 Start by selecting any cell in the column you want to sort by.

Icon indicates that table is sorted by this column

	A	B	C	D
1	First Name	Last Name	Phone Number	Cases Solv
2	John	Aabbott	555-9871	2
3	Lew	Archer	555-6235	129
4	Nancy	Drew	555-4256	215
5	Jessica	Fletcher	555-1253	194
6	Sherlock	Holmes	555-4584	983
7	Sam	Spade	555-6845	39
8	Peter	Wimsey	555-1428	54
9	Total			1616
10				

Figure 33 In this example, clicking the Sort A to Z button puts the records in alphabetical order by last name.

Sorting

You can sort an entire table or a filtered table by any column(s). Excel will quickly put table contents in the order you specify.

✔ Tips

- When you sort data in a table, the contents of cells in adjacent columns are not disturbed.
- If the results of a sort are not what you expected, click the Undo button on the Quick Access Toolbar or press Ctrl Z to restore the original sort order.

To sort with Sort commands

1. Select a cell in the column for the field by which you want to sort (**Figure 32**).
2. Click one of the buttons in the Data tab's Sort & Filter group (**Figure 24**):
   - ▲ **Sort A to Z** (for text) or **Sort Smallest to Largest** (for values) sorts from A to Z or from lowest to highest value
   - ▲ **Sort Z to A** (for text) or **Sort Largest to Smallest** (for values) sorts from Z to A or from highest to lowest value.

Or

1. Click the AutoFilter button for the column you want to sort by.
2. Select one of the commands at the top of the menu (**Figure 25**):
   - ▲ **Sort A to Z** (for text) or **Sort Smallest to Largest** (for values) sorts from A to Z or from lowest to highest value
   - ▲ **Sort Z to A** (for text) or **Sort Largest to Smallest** (for values) sorts from Z to A or from highest to lowest value.

   The data is sorted by the selected column and a sort icon appears in the filter menu's button (**Figure 33**).

To sort with the Sort dialog

1. Click Data > Sort & Filter > Sort (**Figure 24**) to display the Sort dialog (**Figure 34**).

2. Choose a primary sort field from the Sort by drop-down list (**Figure 35**).

3. Choose an option from the Sort On drop-down list (**Figure 36**).

4. Select a sort order option from the Order drop-down list. The wording of the options varies depending on whether the column you selected in step 2 contains text (**Figure 37**) or values.

5. To add a sort field, click the Add Level button to add another row of options to the dialog (**Figure 38**). Then follow steps 2 through 4 for that row.

6. Repeat step 5 as necessary to add as many sort fields as you like.

7. Click OK. Excel sorts the table as you specified (**Figure 39**).

✔ Tips

- Additional sort fields are "tie-breakers" and are only used if the previous sort field has more than one record with the same value. **Figure 38** shows how they can be used.

- If you select a cell in the column by which you want to sort, that column is automatically referenced in the Sort dialog when you open it.

Figure 34 The Sort dialog.

Figure 35 The Sort by drop-down list includes all table columns.

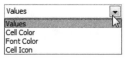

Figure 36 Use the Sort On drop-down list to specify what to sort on within the field.

Figure 37 Finally, specify the sort order.

Figure 38 If you click the Add Level button, you can add another sort field.

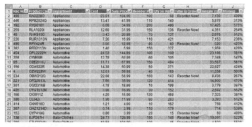

Figure 39 The beginning of the table in **Figure 17** sorted by Department, Price, and Cost.

Working with Others

Collaboration Features

In office environments, a document is often the product of multiple people. In the old days, a draft worksheet or financial report would be printed and circulated among reviewers. Along the way, it would be marked up with colored ink and covered with sticky notes full of comments. Some poor soul would have to make sense of all the markups and notes to create a clean document. The process was time consuming and was sometimes repeated through several drafts to fine-tune the document for publication.

Microsoft Excel, which is widely used in office environments, includes many features that make the collaboration process easier:

◆ **Properties** stores information about the document's creator and contents.

◆ **Comments** enables reviewers to enter notes about the document. The notes don't print—unless you want them to.

◆ **Change Tracking** enables reviewers to edit the document while keeping the original document intact. Changes can be accepted or rejected to finalize the document.

◆ **Document Protection** limits how a document can be changed.

◆ **Workbook sharing** enables multiple users to access a workbook file simultaneously via network.

◆ **Save options** protect documents from being opened or modified.

Document Properties

The Document Properties pane (**Figure 1**) enables you to store information about a document. This information, which is saved with the document, can be viewed by anyone who opens the document.

✔ Tip

- Information in the Document Properties pane is also used by Microsoft's search feature. A discussion of this feature is beyond the scope of this book, but you can see it in action by clicking Start and entering search criteria in the Start Search box.

To view, enter, or edit Document Properties information

1. Open the document for which you want to view or edit properties.

2. Choose Microsoft Office > Prepare > Properties (**Figure 2**). The Document Properties pane appears above the document (**Figure 1**).

3. Enter or edit information in each field as desired:

   ▲ **Author** is the person who created the document. This field may already be filled in based on information stored in Excel.

   ▲ **Title** is the title of the document. This does not have to be the same as the file name.

Figure 1 The Document Properties pane, which appears above the document window, offers text boxes for entering information about the document.

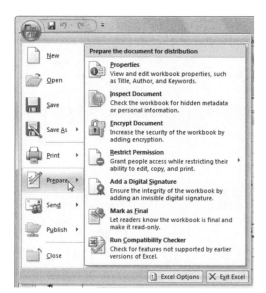

Figure 2 The Prepare submenu on the Microsoft Office menu.

Figure 3 The General tab of the Properties dialog for a workbook. Other tabs show additional information.

▲ **Subject** is the subject of the document.

▲ **Keywords** are important words related to the document.

▲ **Category** is a category name assigned to the document. It can be anything you like.

▲ **Status** is the document's status.

▲ **Comments** are notes about the document.

4. When you are finished viewing or editing Document Properties pane contents, click the pane's close button. Your changes are automatically saved.

✔ Tips

■ It is not necessary to enter information in every text box.

■ Excel's Properties dialog (**Figure 3**) offers additional information about a document. To open it, choose Advanced Properties from the Document Properties pop-up menu in the upper-left corner of the Document Properties pane.

Comments

Comments are annotations that you and other document reviewers can add to a document. These notes can be viewed onscreen but don't print unless you want them to.

To insert a comment

1. Select the cell for which you want to insert a comment (**Figure 4**).

2. Choose Review > Comments > New Comment (**Figure 5**).

   Two things happen: a comment marker (a tiny red triangle) appears in the upper-right corner of the cell and a box with your name and a blinking insertion point appears (**Figure 6**).

3. Type your comment into the box. It can be as long or as short as you like (**Figure 7**).

4. When you are finished, click anywhere else in the worksheet window. Your comment is saved and the box disappears.

✔ Tip

■ Word gets your name from the Excel Options dialog. I tell you more about that in **Chapter 15**.

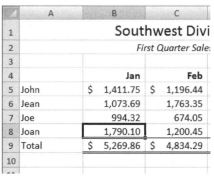

Figure 4 Start by selecting the cell you want to enter a comment for.

Figure 5 The Review tab's Comments group.

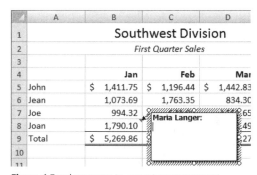

Figure 6 Excel prepares to accept your comment.

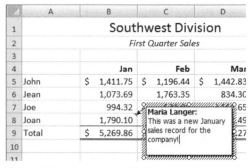

Figure 7 Enter your comment in the box.

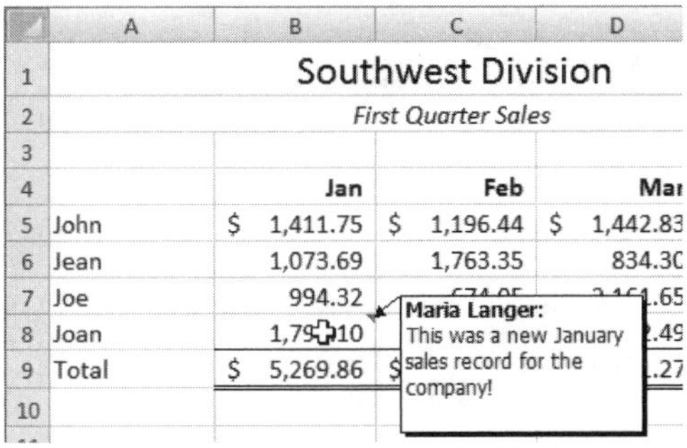

	A	B	C	D
1		Southwest Division		
2		*First Quarter Sales*		
3				
4		**Jan**	**Feb**	**Mar**
5	John	$ 1,411.75	$ 1,196.44	$ 1,442.83
6	Jean	1,073.69	1,763.35	834.30
7	Joe	994.32		.65
8	Joan	1,790.10		.49
9	Total	$ 5,269.86		.27
10				

Maria Langer:
This was a new January sales record for the company!

Figure 8 When you position the mouse pointer over a cell with a comment marker, the comment appears.

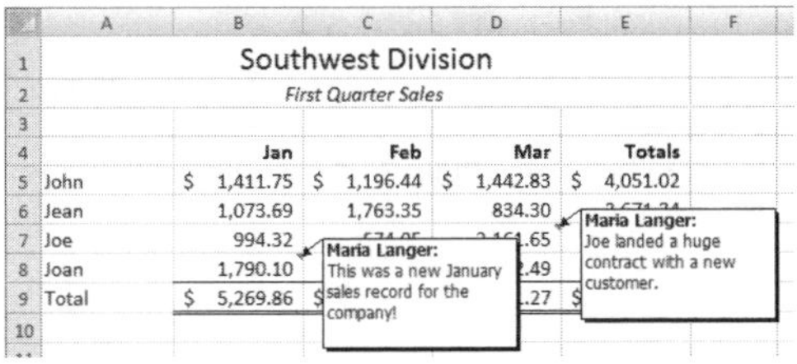

	A	B	C	D	E	F
1		Southwest Division				
2		*First Quarter Sales*				
3						
4		Jan	Feb	Mar	Totals	
5	John	$ 1,411.75	$ 1,196.44	$ 1,442.83	$ 4,051.02	
6	Jean	1,073.69	1,763.35	834.30		
7	Joe	994.32		.65		
8	Joan	1,790.10		.49		
9	Total	$ 5,269.86		.27		
10						

Maria Langer:
This was a new January sales record for the company!

Maria Langer:
Joe landed a huge contract with a new customer.

Figure 9 When you click the Show All Comments button, all comments for visible cells appear.

Edit Comment | Delete | Previous | Next | Show/Hide Comment | Show All Comments | Show Ink

Comments

Figure 10 The Comments group with a cell containing a comment selected.

To view comments

Position the mouse pointer over a cell with a comment marker. A box appears containing the name of the person who wrote the comment and the comment itself (**Figure 8**).

Or

Click Review > Comments > Show All Comments (**Figure 5**). All comments for visible cells appear in yellow boxes (**Figure 9**).

Or

To show or hide a specific comment select the cell containing the comment and click Review > Comments > Show/Hide Comment (**Figure 5**).

✔ Tip

■ If all comments are displayed, you can hide them by clicking Review > Comments > Show All Comments.

To edit a comment

1. Select the cell containing the comment you want to edit.

2. Click Review > Comments > Edit Comment (**Figure 10**).

3. Edit the contents of the comment box (**Figure 7**).

4. When you are finished, click anywhere else in the worksheet window. Your comment is saved and the box disappears.

To delete a comment

1. Select the cell containing the comment you want to remove.

2. Choose Review > Comments > Delete (**Figure 10**). The comment marker and comment are removed.

To print comments

1. Follow the instructions in **Chapter 9** to prepare the sheet for printing and open the Page Setup dialog.

2. Choose an option from the Comments drop-down list in the Sheet tab (**Figure 11**).

3. Click Print.

4. In the Print dialog that appears, click OK to print the sheet and its comments.

✔ Tip

■ I tell you more about the Page Setup dialog and printing in **Chapter 9**.

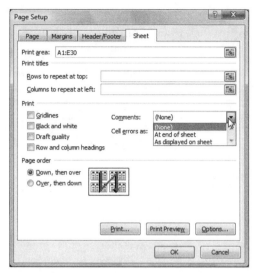

Figure 11 Choose an option from the Comments drop-down list.

Figure 12 Choose Highlight Changes from the Track Changes menu to enable the change tracking feature.

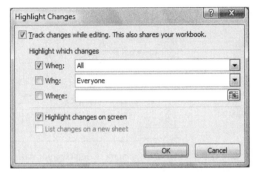

Figure 13 The Highlight Changes dialog lets you enable and configure the revision tracking feature.

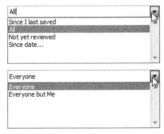

Figures 14 & 15
Use these two drop-down lists to specify which changes to track based on when they were made (top) or who made them (bottom).

Change Tracking

Excel's revision tracking feature enables multiple reviewers to edit a document without actually changing it. Instead, each reviewer's markups are displayed in the document window. At the conclusion of the reviewing process, someone with final say over document content reviews all of the edits and either accepts or rejects each of them. The end result is a final document that incorporates the accepted changes.

To turn change tracking on or off

1. Choose Review > Changes > Track Changes > Highlight Changes (**Figure 12**).

2. In the Highlight Changes dialog that appears (**Figure 13**), toggle check boxes to set up the revision tracking feature:

   ▲ **Track changes while editing** enables the revision tracking feature. Turn on this check box to track changes. Turn off this check box to disable the revision tracking feature.

   ▲ **When** enables you to choose which changes should be tracked based on when the changes were made. If you turn on this check box, choose an option from the drop-down list (**Figure 14**).

   ▲ **Who** enables you to specify which changes should be tracked based on who made them. If you turn on this check box, choose an option from the drop-down list (**Figure 15**).

   ▲ **Where** enables you to specify which changes should be tracked based on which cells the changes were made in. If you turn on this check box, enter a range of cells in the text box beside it.

Continued on next page...

ENABLING CHANGE TRACKING

Continued from previous page.

▲ **Highlight changes on screen** displays revision marks in the document window.

▲ **List changes on a new sheet** records changes in a separate History worksheet. This option is only available after you have saved the workbook file as a shared workbook.

3. Click OK.

4. If prompted, save the workbook file.

✔ Tip

■ Turning on revision tracking also shares the workbook file. I tell you more about workbook sharing later in this chapter.

To track changes

1. Turn on revision tracking as instructed on the previous page.

2. Make changes to the document.

   The cells you changed get a colored border around them and a color-coordinated triangle appears in the upper-left corner (**Figure 16**).

✔ Tip

■ If the document is edited by more than one person, each person's revision marks appear in a different color. This makes it easy to distinguish one editor's changes from another's.

To view revision information

Point to a revision mark. A box with information about the change appears (**Figure 17**).

✔ Tip

■ This is a handy way to see who made a change and when it was made.

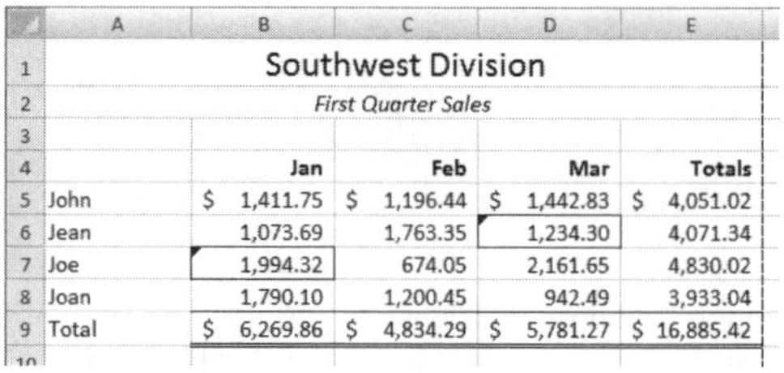

Figure 16 When you edit the document, the cells you change are marked.

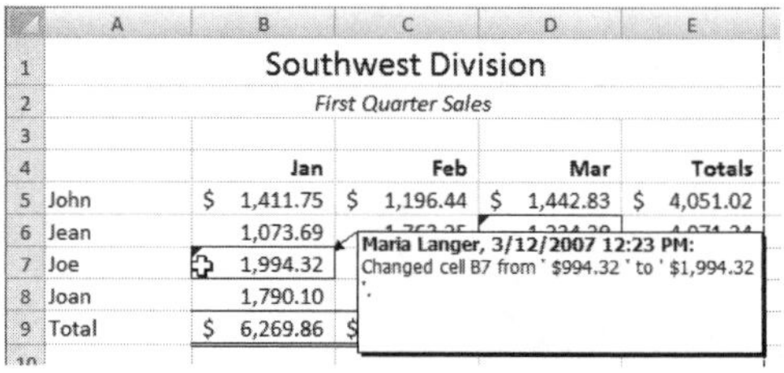

Figure 17 Point to a revision mark to display information about it.

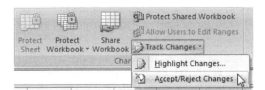

Figure 18 Choose Accept/Reject Changes from the Track Changes menu.

Figure 19 The Select Changes to Accept or Reject dialog.

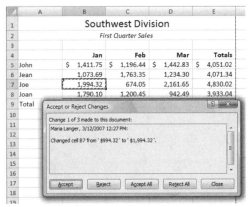

Figure 20 Excel selects the changed cell and displays information about the change in the Accept or Reject Changes dialog.

To accept or reject revisions

1. Choose Review > Changes > Track Changes > Accept/Reject Changes (**Figure 18**).

2. If prompted, save the workbook file.

3. The Select Changes to Accept or Reject dialog appears (**Figure 19**). Set options to select the changes to review. The options work like those in the Highlight Changes dialog (**Figure 13**).

4. Click OK.

5. Excel selects the first change and displays the Accept or Reject Changes dialog (**Figure 20**).

   ▲ To accept the currently selected change, click the Accept button. Excel selects the next change.

   ▲ To reject the currently selected change, click the Reject button. The cell reverts to its original contents and Excel selects the next change.

   ▲ To accept all changes, click the Accept All button. Skip the remaining step.

   ▲ To reject all changes, click the Reject All button. All changed cells in the selection revert to their original contents. Skip the remaining step.

6. Repeat step 5 for each change Excel selects.

   When Excel has reached the end of the document, the Accept or Reject Changes dialog disappears.

✖ Caution!

■ The Undo command will not work after you click the Accept All or Reject All button in step 5. Use these two buttons with care!

ACCEPTING OR REJECTING REVISIONS

To remove revision marks

1. Choose Review > Changes > Track Changes > Highlight Changes (**Figure 12**).

2. In the Highlight Changes dialog (**Figure 13**), turn off the Track changes while editing check box and click OK.

3. A dialog like the one in **Figure 21** may appear. You have two options:

   ▲ **Yes** turns off workbook sharing.

   ▲ **No** keeps the workbook sharing turned on.

   The revision marks disappear.

✔ Tips

■ Removing the revision marks also turns off the change tracking feature.

■ I tell you more about workbook sharing later in this chapter.

Figure 21 This dialog may appear when you turn off the change tracking feature.

Figure 22 The Review tab's Changes group.

Document Protection

Excel's document protection features enable you to limit the types of changes others can make to a document. There are four types of protection:

- **Protect Sheet** protects against certain types of changes to worksheets and locked worksheet cells.

- **Allow Users to Edit Ranges** protects against changes to specific ranges of worksheet cells.

- **Protect Workbook** protects workbook structure and windows.

- **Protect and Share Workbook** enables you to share the workbook but only with change tracking enabled.

You set up all protection options using commands in the Review tab's Changes group (**Figure 22**).

✔ Tips

- ■ I explain how revision tracking works earlier in this chapter.

- ■ I tell you more about sharing workbooks without enabling protection later in this chapter.

- ■ In addition to document protection, you can password protect a document to prevent it from being opened or changed. I explain how later in this chapter.

- ■ If you use the Information Rights Management service offered by Microsoft, you can set other protection options for your Excel workbook files. A discussion of this fee-based service is beyond the scope of this book.

To protect a sheet

1. Click Review > Changes > Protect Sheet (**Figure 22**).

2. In the Protect Sheet dialog that appears (**Figure 23**), turn on check boxes for the types of changes you want to allow.

3. If desired, enter a password in the Password text box.

4. Click OK.

5. If you entered a password, the Confirm Password dialog appears (**Figure 24**). Enter the password again and click OK.

✔ Tips

- Entering a password in the Protect Sheet dialog (**Figure 23**) is optional. If you do not use a password, however, the document can be unprotected by anyone.

- If you enter a password in the Protect Sheet dialog (**Figure 23**), don't forget it! If you can't remember the password, you can't unprotect the document!

- If you try to change a protected item, Excel displays a dialog reminding you that the item is protected (**Figure 25**).

To unprotect a sheet

1. Click Review > Changes > Unprotect Sheet (**Figure 26**).

2. If protection is enforced with a password, enter the password in the Unprotect Sheet dialog that appears and click OK.

Figure 23 Use the Protect Sheet dialog to set protection options for the active worksheet.

Figure 24 If you entered a password in the Protect Sheet dialog, you'll have to enter it again to turn on protection.

Figure 25 Excel tells you when you're trying to edit a protected item.

Figure 26 When a sheet is protected, the Protect Sheet button turns into a Unprotect Sheet button.

PROTECTING & UNPROTECTING SHEETS

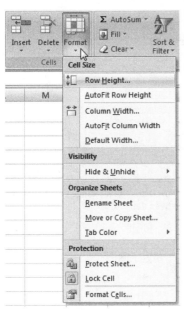

Figure 27 The Cells group's Format menu.

To turn off protection for selected cells

1. If the sheet is already protected, unprotect it.

2. Select the cells you want to allow modification to.

3. Choose Home > Cells > Format > Format Cells (**Figure 27**) to display the Format Cells dialog and click the Protection tab (**Figure 28**).

4. Turn off the Locked check box.

5. Click OK.

   When you protect the sheet's contents, the unlocked cells can be modified.

✔ Tip

- I tell you more about the Format Cells dialog in **Chapter 6**.

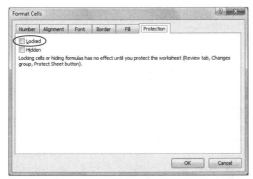

Figure 28 Turn off the Locked check box to allow modification to selected cells in a protected sheet.

To allow users to edit ranges of a protected sheet

1. If the sheet is already protected, unprotect it.

2. Click Review > Changes > Allow Users to Edit Ranges (**Figure 22**). The Allow Users to Edit Ranges dialog appears (**Figure 29**).

3. To add an editable range of cells, click New to display the New Range dialog (**Figure 30**).

4. Enter information into each text box:
   - ▲ **Title** is a name for the range.
   - ▲ **Refers to cells** is the cell reference for the range.
   - ▲ **Range password** is the password that allows you to edit the range of cells.

5. Click OK.

6. If you entered a password in step 4, the Confirm Password dialog appears (**Figure 24**). Enter the password again and click OK.

7. Repeat steps 2 through 6 for each range you want to add. The ranges appear in the Allow Users to Edit Ranges dialog (**Figure 31**).

8. Click OK.

9. Follow the instructions earlier in this section to protect the worksheet.

Figure 29 The Allow Users to Edit Ranges dialog before any ranges have been defined.

Figure 30 The New Range dialog with information for a range already entered.

Figure 31 Ranges you add appear in the Allow Users to Edit Ranges dialog.

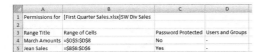

Figure 32 Excel can record permission information in a worksheet.

Figure 33 Enter the password assigned to the range to modify a cell within it.

✔ Tips

- In step 4, an easy way to enter the cell reference is to move the dialog aside and select the range in the worksheet window.

- Not entering a password in step 4 is the same as simply unlocking the cell. I explain how to turn off protection for selected cells earlier in this section.

- You can modify or delete the settings for a range by selecting the range name in the Allow Users to Edit Ranges dialog (**Figure 31**) and clicking either the Modify or the Delete button.

- If you turn on the Paste permissions information into a new workbook check box in the Allow Users to Edit Ranges dialog (**Figure 31**), Excel creates a worksheet with a summary of permissions settings (**Figure 32**).

- If you attempt to edit a cell that is part of a password-protected range in a protected worksheet, the Unlock Range dialog appears (**Figure 33**). Enter the appropriate password and click OK to edit the cell.

- Excel's permissions feature lets you further customize who can modify cell contents. Although this advanced feature is far beyond the scope of this book, you can experiment with it by clicking the Permissions button in the Allow Users to Edit Ranges (**Figure 31**) or New Range (**Figure 30**) dialogs.

To protect a workbook

1. Choose Review > Changes > Protect Workbook > Protect Structure and Windows (**Figure 34**).

2. In the Protect Structure and Windows dialog that appears (**Figure 35**), turn on check boxes for the type of protection you want:

   ▲ **Structure** prevents workbook sheets from being inserted, deleted, moved, hidden, unhidden, or renamed.

   ▲ **Windows** protects workbook windows from being moved, resized, hidden, unhidden, or closed.

3. If desired, enter a password in the Password text box.

4. Click OK.

5. If you entered a password in step 3, enter the password again in the Confirm Password dialog that appears (**Figure 24**) and click OK.

✔ Tip

■ With workbook protection options enabled, Excel disables any menu commands or shortcut keys that you would use to make unallowed changes.

To unprotect a workbook

1. Choose Review > Changes > Protect Workbook > Protect Structure and Windows (**Figure 34**).

2. If protection is enforced with a password, enter the password in the dialog that appears and click OK.

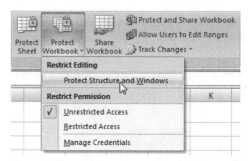

Figure 34 Choose Protect Structure and Windows.

Figure 35 Use the Protect Structure and Windows dialog to protect a workbook's structure or windows.

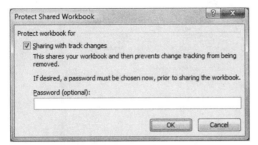

Figure 36 Use the Protect Shared Workbook dialog to allow others to share the workbook, but only with change tracking enabled.

Figure 37 The Unprotect Shared Workbook command in the Changes group.

To protect a workbook for sharing & change tracking

1. Click Review > Changes > Protect and Share Workbook (**Figure 22**).

2. In the Protect Shared Workbook dialog that appears (**Figure 36**), turn on the Sharing with track changes check box.

3. If desired, enter a password in the Password text box.

4. Click OK.

5. If you entered a password in step 3, enter the password again in the Confirm Password dialog that appears (**Figure 24**) and click OK.

6. When prompted to save the workbook, click OK. Excel turns on change tracking and workbook sharing.

✔ Tip

■ I tell you about workbook sharing later in this chapter and about change tracking earlier in this chapter.

To turn off workbook sharing & change tracking protection

1. Click Review > Changes > Unprotect Shared Workbook (**Figure 37**).

2. If protection is enforced with a password, enter the password in the dialog that appears and click OK.

Workbook Sharing

Excel's workbook sharing feature enables multiple people to work on the same workbook at the same time. This feature is designed for work environments with networked computer systems.

To share a workbook

1. Click Review > Changes > Share Workbook (**Figure 22**).

2. In the Share Workbook dialog that appears, click the Editing tab to display its options (**Figure 38**).

3. Turn on the check box beside Allow changes by more than one user at the same time.

4. Click OK.

5. A dialog prompts you to save the workbook. Click OK.

✔ Tip

■ You can identify a workbook that has sharing enabled by the word "Shared" in its title bar (**Figure 39**).

To open a shared workbook

1. Choose Microsoft Office > Open (**Figure 40**).

2. Use the Open dialog that appears to open the network volume on which the workbook resides, then locate, select, and open the file.

Figure 38 Sharing a workbook is as easy as turning on a check box.

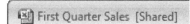

Figure 39 You can identify a shared workbook by the word "Shared" in its title bar.

Figure 40 The Microsoft Office menu.

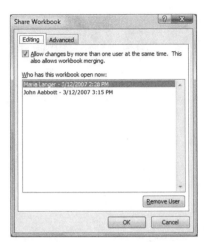

Figure 41 The Share Workbook dialog lists all users who have the workbook file open.

To stop sharing a workbook

1. Click Review > Changes > Share Workbook (**Figure 22**).

2. In the Share Workbook dialog that appears, click the Editing tab to display its options (**Figure 41**).

3. To stop a specific user from sharing the workbook, select the user's name from the user list and click the Remove User button. Then click OK in the warning dialog that appears.

   or

   To stop all users from sharing the workbook, turn off the check box beside Allow changes by more than one user at the same time.

4. Click OK.

5. A dialog may prompt you to save the workbook. Click OK.

✔ Tips

- The Share Workbook dialog for a file lists all of the users who have the file open (**Figure 41**).

- If you remove a user from workbook sharing, when he tries to save the workbook, a dialog appears, telling him that he is no longer sharing the workbook and offering instructions on how to save his changes.

General Save Options & Password Protection

Excel's general save options enable you to set up passwords to prevent a document from being opened or from being modified.

To set save options

1. Click Microsoft Office > Save As (**Figure 40**).

2. In the Save As dialog that appears, choose General Options from the Tools menu (**Figure 42**).

3. Set options in the General Options dialog (**Figure 43**) as desired:

   ▲ **Always create backup** tells Excel to save the previous version of the file as a backup when saving the current version. (The old file is named "Backup of *filename.*")

   ▲ **Password to open** is the password that must be entered in order to open the file.

   ▲ **Password to modify** is the password that must be entered in order to save changes to the file.

   ▲ **Read-only recommended** tells Excel to recommend that the file be opened as a read-only file when the user tries to open it.

4. Click OK.

5. If you entered a password in step 3, a dialog appears, asking you to confirm it (**Figure 24**). Re-enter the password and click OK. (If you entered two passwords, this dialog appears twice.)

✔ Tip

■ I tell you more about saving files in **Chapter 4**.

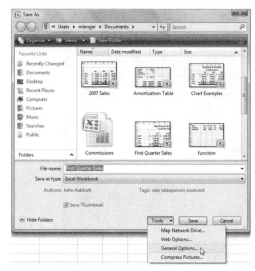

Figure 42 Choose General Options from the Tools menu in the Save As dialog.

Figure 43 Use the General Options dialog to set all kinds of options for protecting a file.

Figure 44 Use a dialog like this to enter a password to open a file.

Figure 45 Use a dialog like this to enter a password to open a file for modification.

Figure 46 If read-only access is recommended for a file, Excel displays a dialog like this one when you open it.

Figure 47 Excel displays a dialog like this if you try to save a file that is opened for read-only access.

Figure 48 Not sure if a document is open as a read-only file? Just look in the title bar.

To open a file that has general save options set

Open the file as usual. Then:

◆ If the file requires a password to open it, a dialog like the one in **Figure 44** appears. Enter the password and click OK.

◆ If the file requires a password for modification, a dialog like the one in **Figure 45** appears. You have two choices:

▲ Enter the password and click OK.

▲ Click Read Only to open the file as a read-only file.

◆ If the file was set up so read-only access is recommended, a dialog like the one in **Figure 46** appears, asking if you want to open the file as a read-only file. You have three choices:

▲ Click Cancel to not open the file at all.

▲ Click No to open the file as a regular file.

▲ Click Yes to open the file as a read-only file.

✔ Tips

■ If a file is opened for read-only access, you cannot save changes to the file—a dialog like the one in **Figure 47** appears if you try.

■ You can identify a file opened as a read-only file by the words "Read-Only" in the document window's title bar (**Figure 48**).

Using Other Programs

Using Excel with Other Programs

Microsoft Excel works well with a number of other programs. These programs can expand Excel's capabilities:

◆ OLE objects created with other Microsoft Office and Windows programs can be inserted into Excel documents.

◆ Excel documents can be inserted into documents created with other Microsoft Office programs.

◆ Excel documents can be e-mailed to others using Microsoft Outlook.

This chapter explains how you can use Excel with some of these other programs.

✔ Tip

■ This chapter provides information about programs other than Microsoft Excel. To follow instructions for a specific program, that program must be installed on your computer.

OLE Objects

An *object* is all or part of a file created with an OLE-aware program. *OLE* or *Object Linking and Embedding* is a Microsoft technology that enables you to insert a file as an object within a document (**Figure 1**)—even if the file was created with a different program. Clicking or double-clicking the inserted object starts the program that created it so you can modify its contents.

Figure 1 A Microsoft Word Document object inserted in a Microsoft Excel document.

Excel's Object command enables you to insert OLE objects in two different ways:

◆ **Create and insert a new OLE object.** This method starts a specific OLE-aware program so you can create an object.

◆ **Insert an existing OLE object.** This method enables you to locate, select, and insert an existing file as an object.

✔ Tips

■ All Microsoft programs are OLE-aware. Many software programs created by other developers are also OLE-aware; check the documentation that came with a specific software package for details.

■ Excel comes with a number of OLE-aware programs that can be used to insert objects. The full Microsoft Office package includes even more of these programs.

■ You can learn more about inserting text and graphic objects in **Chapter 7**.

OLE OBJECTS

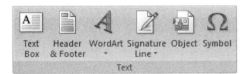

Figure 2 Click Object in the Text group.

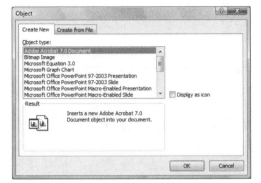

Figure 3 The Object dialog. The options in the Object type list vary depending on the software installed in your computer.

Figure 4 A frame containing a Microsoft Word object inserted into an Excel document. The Ribbon is also for Word.

To insert a new object

1. Select a cell near where you want the object to appear.

2. Click Insert > Text > Object (**Figure 2**) to display the Object dialog.

3. If necessary, click the Create New tab to display its options (**Figure 3**).

4. In the Object type list, select the type of object that you want to insert.

5. Click OK.

   Excel starts the program that you selected. It may take a moment for it to appear. **Figure 4** shows a frame for a Microsoft Word document in the Excel worksheet window. The Word Ribbon appears at the top of the program window.

6. Use the program to create the object that you want.

7. When you are finished creating the object, click outside the object. The object's frame and any toolbars or menus that appeared disappear and you can continue working with Excel.

8. If necessary, resize the object and drag it into position in the Excel document (**Figure 1**).

✔ Tips

■ Some of the programs that come with Excel and appear in the Object dialog may not be fully installed. If that is the case, Excel will prompt you to insert the program CD to install the software.

■ Some OLE-aware programs may display a dialog or similar interface. Use the controls within the dialog to create and insert the object.

To insert an existing object

1. Select a cell near where you want the object to appear.

2. Click Insert > Text > Object (**Figure** 2) to display the Object dialog.

3. Click the Create from File tab to display its options (**Figure 5**).

4. Click the Browse button.

5. Use the Browse dialog that appears (**Figure 6**) to locate and select the file that you want to insert. Then click Insert.

6. The pathname for the file appears in the Object dialog. Click OK. The file is inserted as an object in the document.

✔ Tip

■ To insert a file as an object, the program that created the file must be properly installed on your computer or accessible through a network connection. Excel displays a dialog if the program is missing.

To customize an inserted object

Follow the instructions in the previous two sections to create and insert a new object or insert an existing object. In the Object dialog (**Figure 3** or 5), turn on check boxes as desired:

◆ **Link to File** creates a link to the object's file so that when it changes, the object inserted within the Excel document can change. This option is only available when inserting an existing file as an object.

◆ **Display as icon** (**Figure 7**) displays an icon that represents the object rather than the object itself. Double-clicking the icon opens the object and displays its contents.

Figure 5 The Create from File tab of the Object dialog.

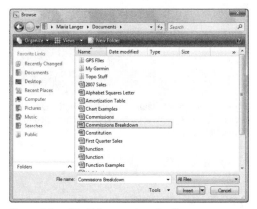

Figure 6 Use this dialog to select the file you want to insert.

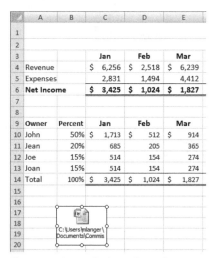

Figure 7 An inserted Microsoft Word 2007 document displayed as an icon.

Using Word with Excel

Word is the word processing component of Microsoft Office. A *word processor* is a program for creating formatted text-based documents (**Figure 8**). Word can also create mailing labels, merge static text with data (a data merge or mail merge), and create documents with pictures and other graphic elements.

You can use Word with Excel to:

◆ Include information from a Word document in an Excel document (**Figure 1**).

◆ Perform a Word data merge with an Excel list as a data source.

✔ Tip

■ Because performing a data merge is primarily a function of Word rather than Excel, it is not covered in detail in this book.

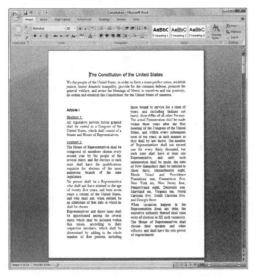

Figure 8 Word processing software like Word is most often used to create formatted documents.

To include Word document content in an Excel document

To insert a Word document as an object in an Excel document, consult the section about OLE objects earlier in this chapter.

Or

1. In the Word document, select the text that you want to include in the Excel document (**Figure 9**).

2. Click Home > Clipboard > Copy (**Figure 10**) or press Ctrl C.

3. Switch to Excel and either:

   ▲ Double-click in the cell where you want the content to appear to position the insertion point there (**Figure 11**).

   ▲ Create a text box to hold the content and position the insertion point inside the text box (**Figure 12**).

4. Click Home > Clipboard > Paste (**Figure 10**) or press Ctrl V. The selection appears in the selected cell (**Figure 13**) or text box (**Figure 14**).

✔ Tips

■ You can also use drag-and-drop editing to drag a Word document selection into an Excel document. I tell you how in **Chapter 3**.

■ I explain how to create a text box in **Chapter 7**.

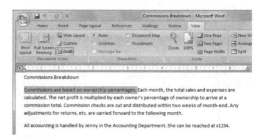

Figure 9 Select the text you want to include.

Figure 10
The Clipboard group is the same in Word as it is in Excel.

	A	B	C	D	E	F	G	H
9	Owner	Percent	Jan	Feb	Mar	Apr	May	Jun
10	John	50%	$ 1,713	$ 512	$ 914	$ 3,901	$ 1,705	$ 5,226
11	Jean	20%	685	205	365	1,560	682	2,090
12	Joe	15%	514	154	274	1,170	512	1,568
13	Joan	15%	514	154	274	1,170	512	1,568
14	Total	100%	$ 3,425	$ 1,024	$ 1,827	$ 7,802	$ 3,410	$ 10,452

Figures 11 & 12 Position the insertion point in a cell (above) or text box (below).

	A	B	C	D	E	F	G	H
9	Owner	Percent	Jan	Feb	Mar	Apr	May	Jun
10	John	50%	$ 1,713	$ 512	$ 914	$ 3,901	$ 1,705	$ 5,226
11	Jean	20%	685	205	365	1,560	682	2,090
12	Joe	15%	514	154	274	1,170	512	1,568
13	Joan	15%	514	154	274	1,170	512	1,568
14	Total	100%	$ 3,425	$ 1,024	$ 1,827	$ 7,802	$ 3,410	$ 10,452

Commissions are based on ownership percentages.

Figures 13 & 14 The text is pasted into the cell (above) or the text box (below).

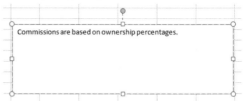

Commissions are based on ownership percentages.

Figure 15 Start with an Excel list, like this one.

Figure 16
Choose a Start
Mail Merge com-
mand for the type
of document you
want to create.

Figure 17
Choose Use Exist-
ing List from the
Select Recipient
List menu.

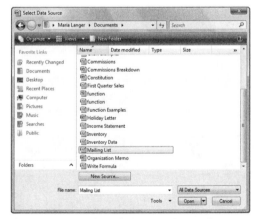

Figure 18 Use this dialog to locate, select, and open
the Excel file you want to use for the merge.

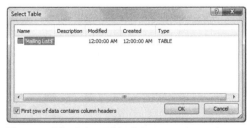

Figure 19 If the Select Table dialog appears, use it to
indicate which worksheet contains the data.

To use an Excel table as a data source for a Word data merge

1. Follow the instructions in **Chapter 10** to create an Excel table and enter data into it (**Figure 15**).

2. Switch to Word and choose an option from the Start Mail Merge menu on the Mailings tab's Start Mail Merge group (**Figure 16**).

3. Choose Mailings > Start Mail Merge > Select Recipients > Use Existing List (**Figure 17**).

4. Use the Select Data Source dialog that appears (**Figure 18**) to locate, select, and open the Excel file containing the table you want to use for the merge.

5. If the Select Table dialog appears (**Figure 19**), select the worksheet containing the data you want to use. If the first row of the Excel worksheet contains column headings, make sure the check box for First row of data contains column headers is turned on. Then click OK.

6. Use the Insert Merge Field menu in the Mailings tab's Write & Insert Fields group (**Figure 20**) to insert fields from the Excel table.

✔ Tip

■ Because performing a data merge is a function of Word rather than Excel, it is not covered in detail in this book.

Figure 20
You can insert
fields into your
Word document
with the Insert
Merge Field menu.

Using Outlook with Excel

Outlook is the e-mail, newsgroup, and personal information management software component of Microsoft Office. *E-mail software* enables you to send and receive electronic mail messages (**Figure 21**). *Personal information management software* enables you to store and organize address book and calendar data.

You can use Outlook with Excel to e-mail an Excel document to a friend, family member, or co-worker.

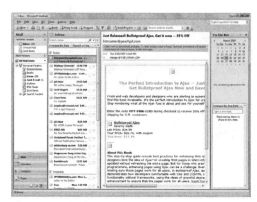

Figure 21 Outlook's e-mail interface.

✔ Tip

- To learn more about using Outlook, consult the documentation that came with the program or its onscreen help feature.

Figure 22 Choose E-mail from the Send sub-menu under the Microsoft Office menu.

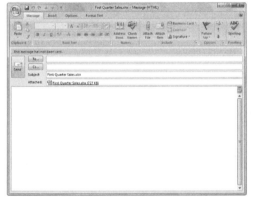

Figure 23 Outlook displays an untitled e-mail form.

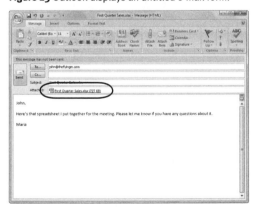

Figure 24 Here's what a finished message might look like. Note that the name of the Excel document being sent appears in the Attachments area.

To send an Excel document via e-mail

1. Display the Excel document you want to send via e-mail.

2. Choose Microsoft Office > Send > E-mail (**Figure 22**).

3. Excel starts Outlook and displays an empty e-mail window with the To field selected (**Figure 23**). Enter the e-mail address for the person you want to send the document to.

4. If desired, edit the contents of the Subject field.

5. In the message body, enter a message to accompany the file. **Figure 24** shows an example.

6. To send the message, click the Send button. Outlook connects to the Internet and sends the message.

7. Switch back to Excel to continue working with the document.

✔ Tips

- These instructions assume that Outlook is the default e-mail program as set in your Windows configuration. If a different program has been set as the default e-mail program, ignore steps 3 through 6 and send the message as you normally would with your e-mail program.

- Outlook (or your default e-mail program) must be properly configured to send and receive e-mail messages. Check the program's documentation or onscreen help if you need assistance with setup.

Advanced Techniques

	A	B	C	D	E
1		Southwest Division			
2		First Quarter Sales			
3					
4		Jan	Feb	Mar	Totals
5	John	$ 1,411.75	$ 1,196.44	$ 1,442.83	$ 4,051.02
6	Jean	1,073.69	1,763.35	834.30	3,671.34
7	Joe	994.32	674.05	2,161.65	3,830.02
8	Joan	1,790.10	1,200.45	942.49	3,933.04
9	Total	$ 5,269.86	$ 4,834.29	$ 5,381.27	$ 15,485.42

Figure 1 The reference to the selected range would be a lot easier to remember if it had a name like *FirstQtrSales* rather than just *A5:D8*.

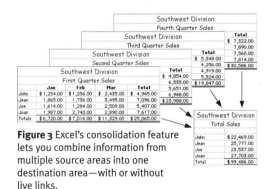

$=SUM('Qtr\ 1:Qtr\ 4'!E4)$

	A	B
1	Southwest Division	
2	Total Sales	
3		
4	John	$ 22,469.00
5	Jean	25,777.00
6	Joe	23,537.00
7	Joan	27,703.00
8	Totals	$ 99,486.00

Figure 2
3-D cell references make it possible to link information between worksheets or workbooks.

Figure 3 Excel's consolidation feature lets you combine information from multiple source areas into one destination area—with or without live links.

Advanced Techniques

Microsoft Excel has many advanced features that you can use to tap into Excel's real power. In this chapter, I tell you about some of the advanced techniques I think you'll find most useful in your day-to-day work with Excel:

◆ **Names** (**Figure 1**) let you assign easy-to-remember names to cell references. You can then use the names in place of cell references in formulas.

◆ **3-D cell references** (**Figure 2**) let you write formulas with links to other worksheets and workbooks.

◆ **Consolidations** (**Figure 3**) let you summarize information from several source areas into one destination area.

◆ **Custom views** enable you to create predefined views of workbook contents that can include a variety of settings.

◆ **Macros** let you automate repetitive tasks and build custom Excel-based applications.

✔ Tip

■ This chapter builds on information in previous chapters. It's a good idea to have a solid understanding of the information covered up to this point in this book before exploring the features in this chapter.

Names

The trouble with using cell references in formulas is that they're difficult to remember. To make matters worse, cell references can change if cells above or to the left of them are inserted or deleted.

Excel's Names feature eliminates both problems by letting you assign easy-to-remember names to individual cells or ranges of cells in your workbooks. The names, which you can use in formulas, don't change, no matter how much worksheet editing you do.

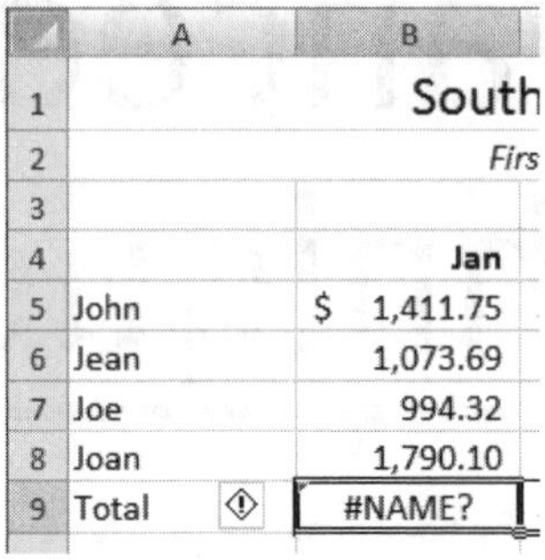

Figure 4 If a name reference in a formula is not correct, a *#NAME?* error appears in the cell.

✔ Tips

- Excel can automatically recognize many column and row labels as cell or range names. I tell you about this feature on the next page.

- Names can be up to 255 characters long and can include letters, numbers, periods, question marks, and underscore characters (_). The first character must be a letter. Names cannot contain spaces or "look" like cell references.

- If you enter an incorrect name reference in a formula, a *#NAME?* error value appears in the cell (**Figure 4**).

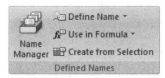

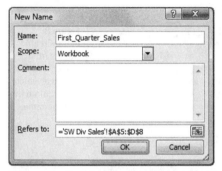

Figure 5 The Defined Names group offers a number of options for working with names.

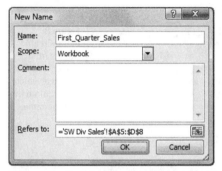

Figure 6 Use the New Name dialog to set a name for one or more cells. As you can see, the name of the worksheet is part of the cell reference.

To define a name

1. Select the cell(s) you want to name (**Figure 1**).

2. Choose Formulas > Defined Names > Define Name (**Figure 5**).

3. In the New Name dialog that appears, Excel may suggest a name in the text box. You can enter a name you prefer (**Figure 6**).

4. Choose an option from the Scope drop-down list to indicate whether the name should be valid in the entire workbook file or just one of its sheets.

5. If desired enter a comment for the name in the Comment box.

6. The cell reference in the Refers to text box should reflect the range you selected in step 1. To enter a different range, delete the range that appears in the text box and either type in a new range or reselect the cell(s) in the worksheet window.

7. Click OK.

✔ Tip

■ Previous versions of Excel enabled you to use column and row headings as labels. That feature is no longer supported in Excel 2007.

DEFINING NAMES

To create names

1. Select the cells containing the ranges you want to name as well as text in adjoining cells that you want to use as names (**Figure 7**).

2. Choose Formulas > Defined Names > Create from Selection (**Figure 5**).

3. In the Create Names from Selection dialog (**Figure 8**), turn on the check box(es) for the cells that contain the text you want to use as names.

4. Click OK.

   Excel uses the text in the cells you indicated as names for the adjoining cells. You can see the results if you open the Name Manager dialog (**Figure 9**).

✔ Tip

■ This is a quick way to create a lot of names all at once.

To modify or delete a name

1. Click Formulas > Defined Names > Name Manager (**Figure 5**).

2. In the Name Manager dialog (**Figure 9**), click to select the name in the scrolling list that you want to modify or delete.

3. To modify the name, click Edit. Then use the Edit Name dialog (**Figure 10**) to modify the name's settings and click OK.

   or

   To delete the name, click Delete. The name disappears.

4. Repeat steps 2 and 3 to modify or delete other names as desired.

5. Click the Close button to dismiss the Name Manager dialog.

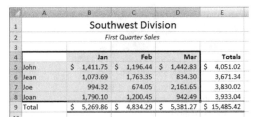

Figure 7 To use the Create Names dialog, you must first select the cells you want to name, as well as adjoining cells with text you want to use as names.

Figure 8 In the Create Names from Selection dialog, tell Excel which cells contain the text for names.

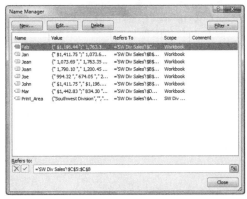

Figure 9 Look in the Name Manager dialog to see how many names were added and to remove names.

Figure 10 Use the Edit name dialog to change settings for a name.

CREATING & DELETING NAMES

	A	B	C	D
1	Southwest Division			
2	First Quarter Sales			
3				
4		Jan	Feb	Mar
5	John	$ 1,411.75	$ 1,196.44	$ 1,442.83
6	Jean	1,073.69	1,763.35	834.30
7	Joe	994.32	674.05	2,161.65
8	Joan	1,790.10	1,200.45	942.49
9	Total	=sum(jan|		
10		SUM(number1, [number2], ...)		
11		Jan		

Figure 11 Once a range has been named, it can be used instead of a cell reference in a formula.

	A	B	C	D
1	Southwest Division			
2	First Quarter Sales			
3				
4		Jan	Feb	Mar
5	John	$ 1,411.75	$ 1,196.44	$ 1,442.83
6	Jean	1,073.69	1,763.35	834.30
7	Joe	994.32	674.05	2,161.65
8	Joan	1,790.10	1,200.45	942.49
9	Total	$ 5,269.86		
10				

Figure 12 When you complete the formula, the result appears in the cell.

Figure 13
You can paste in a name by choosing it from the Use in Formula menu.

To enter a name in a formula

1. Select the cell in which you want to write the formula.

2. Type in the formula, replacing any cell reference with the corresponding name (**Figure 11**).

3. Press Enter or click the Enter button the formula bar.

Excel performs the calculation just as if you'd typed in a cell reference (**Figure 12**).

✔ Tips

- You can use the Use in Formula menu's options to paste a name into a formula for you. Follow the steps above, but when it's time to type in the name, click Formulas > Defined Names > Use in Formula to display a menu of defined names (**Figure 13**). Then choose the name you want to paste in. The Use in Formula menu even works when you use the Function Arguments dialog to write formulas. I tell you about the Function Arguments dialog in **Chapter 5**.

- When you delete a name, Excel responds with a *#NAME?* error in each cell that contains a formula referring to that name (**Figure 4**). These formulas must be rewritten.

To apply names to existing formulas

1. Select the cells containing formulas for which you want to apply names. If you want to apply names throughout the worksheet, click any single cell.

2. Choose Formulas > Defined Names > Define Name > Apply Names (**Figure 14**).

3. In the Apply Names dialog (**Figure 15**), select the names that you want to use in place of the cell reference. To select or deselect a name, click on it.

4. Click OK.

   Excel rewrites the formulas with the appropriate names from those you selected. **Figure 16** shows an example of formulas changed by selecting *Jan*, *Feb*, and *Mar* in **Figure 15**.

✔ Tips

- If only one cell is selected, Excel applies names based on your selection(s) in the Apply Names dialog instead of using the selected cell.

- If you turn off the Ignore Relative/Absolute check box in the Apply Names dialog (**Figure 15**), Excel matches the type of reference. I tell you about relative and absolute references in **Chapter 3**.

Figure 14 Choose Apply Names from the Define Name menu.

Figure 15 Select the names that you want to apply to formulas in your worksheet.

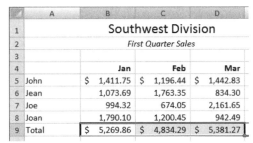

	A	B	C	D
1		Southwest Division		
2		First Quarter Sales		
3				
4		Jan	Feb	Mar
5	John	$ 1,411.75	$ 1,196.44	$ 1,442.83
6	Jean	1,073.69	1,763.35	834.30
7	Joe	994.32	674.05	2,161.65
8	Joan	1,790.10	1,200.45	942.49
9	Total	$ 5,269.86	$ 4,834.29	$ 5,381.27

Figure 16 Excel applies the names you selected to formulas that reference their ranges.

Cell	Before	After
B9	=SUM(B5:B8)	=SUM(Jan)
C9	=SUM(C5:C8)	=SUM(Feb)
D9	=SUM(D5:D8)	=SUM(Mar)

APPLYING NAMES TO EXISTING FORMULAS

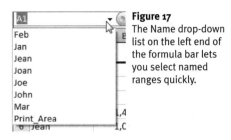

Figure 17
The Name drop-down list on the left end of the formula bar lets you select named ranges quickly.

Figure 18 If you prefer, you can type in a name and press Enter to select it.

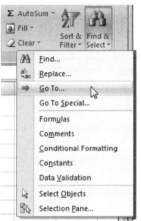

Figure 19
Choose the Go To command on the Find & Select menu.

To select named cells

Choose the name of the cell(s) you want to select from the Name drop-down list on the far-left end of the formula bar (**Figure 17**).

Or

1. Click the Name box at the far-left end of the formula bar to select it.

2. Type in the name of the cells you want to select (**Figure 18**).

3. Press Enter.

Or

1. Choose Home > Editing > Find & Select > Go To (**Figure 19**) or press Ctrl G.

2. In the Go To dialog that appears (**Figure 20**), click the name of the cell(s) you want to select in the Go to scrolling list.

3. Click OK.

✔ Tip

■ When named cells are selected, the name appears in the cell reference area at the far-left end of the formula bar.

Figure 20 Select the name of the cell(s) you want to use from the Go to scrolling list.

SELECTING NAMED CELLS

3-D References

3-D cell references let you write formulas that reference cells in other worksheets or workbooks. The links are live—when a cell's contents change, the results of formulas in cells that reference it change.

Excel offers several ways to write formulas with 3-D cell references:

◆ **Use cell names.** I tell you about cell names in the first part of this chapter. **Figure 21** shows an example.

◆ **Type them in.** When you type in a 3-D cell reference, you must include the name of the sheet (in single quotes, if the name contains a space), followed by an exclamation point (!) and cell reference. If the reference is for a cell in another workbook, you must also include the workbook name, in brackets. **Figures 22**, **23**, and **24** show examples.

◆ **Click on them.** You'll get the same results as if you had typed the references, but Excel does all the typing for you. (This is the method I prefer.)

◆ **Use the Paste Link command.** This command lets you paste a link between cells in different sheets of a workbook or different workbooks.

✔ Tips

■ When you delete a cell, Excel displays a *#REF!* error in any cells that referred to it. The cells containing these errors must be revised to remove the error.

■ Do not make references to an unsaved file. If you do and you close the file with the reference before saving (and naming) the file it refers to, Excel won't be able to update the link.

=SUM(John,Joan,Joe,Jean)

Figure 21 This example uses the SUM function to add the contents of the cells named *John*, *Joan*, *Joe*, and *Jean* in the same workbook.

='Results for Year'!$B$9

Figure 22 This example refers to cell *B9* in a worksheet called *Results for Year* in the same workbook.

=SUM('Qtr 1:Qtr 4'!E9)

Figure 23 This example uses the SUM function to add the contents of cell *E9* in worksheets starting with *Qtr 1* and ending with *Qtr 4* in the same workbook.

=[Sales.xlsx]'Results for Year'!$B$9

Figure 24 This example refers to cell *B9* in a worksheet called *Results for Year* in a workbook called *Sales.xlsx*.

=TotalSales

='Sales Results.xlsx'!TotalSales

Figures 25 & 26 Two examples of 3-D references utilizing names. The first example refers to a name in the same workbook. The second example refers to a name in a different book. In both instances the scope of the named range is set to workbook.

	A	B	C	D	E
1		Southwest Division			
2		First Quarter Sales			
3					
4		Jan	Feb	Mar	Totals
5	John	$ 1,411.75	$ 1,196.44	$ 1,442.83	$ 4,051.02
6	Jean	1,073.69	1,763.35	834.30	3,671.34
7	Joe	994.32	674.05	2,161.65	3,830.02
8	Joan	1,790.10	1,200.45	942.49	3,933.04
9	Total	$ 5,269.86	$ 4,834.29	$ 5,381.27	$ 15,485.42

Figure 27 After typing an equal sign in the cell in which you want the reference to go, you can select the cell(s) you want to reference.

To reference a named cell or range in another worksheet

1. Select the cell in which you want to enter the reference.

2. Type an equal sign (=).

3. If the sheet containing the cells you want to reference is in another workbook, type the name of the workbook (within single quotes, if the name contains a space) followed by an exclamation point (!).

4. Type the name of the cell(s) you want to reference (**Figures 25** and **26**).

5. Press (Enter) or click the Enter button on the formula bar.

✔ Tip

■ If the name you want to reference is in the same workbook, you can paste it in by choosing a name from the Use in Formula menu on the Define Names menu (**Figure 13**). I tell you how to use the Use in Formula menu earlier in this chapter.

To reference a cell or range in another worksheet by clicking

1. Select the cell in which you want to enter the reference.

2. Type an equal sign (=).

3. If the sheet containing the cells you want to reference is in another workbook, switch to that workbook.

4. Click on the sheet tab for the worksheet containing the cell you want to reference.

5. Select the cell(s) you want to reference (**Figure 27**).

6. Press (Enter) or click the Enter button on the formula bar.

REFERENCING CELLS IN OTHER WORKSHEETS

To reference a cell or range in another worksheet by typing

1. Select the cell in which you want to enter the reference.

2. Type an equal sign (=).

3. If the sheet containing the cells you want to reference is in another workbook, type the name of the workbook within brackets ([ ]).

4. Type the name of the sheet followed by an exclamation point (!).

5. Type the cell reference for the cell(s) you want to reference.

6. Press Enter or click the Enter button on the formula bar.

✔ Tip

- If the name of the sheet includes a space character, the sheet name must be enclosed within single quotes in the reference. See **Figures 22, 23,** and **24** for examples.

To reference a cell with the Paste Link command

1. Select the cell you want to reference.

2. Choose Home > Clipboard > Copy (**Figure 28**) or press Ctrl C.

3. Switch to the worksheet in which you want to put the reference.

4. Select the cell in which you want the reference to go.

5. Choose Home > Clipboard > Paste > Paste Link (**Figure 29**).

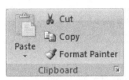

Figure 28
The Clipboard group.

Figure 29
You can use the Paste Link command to paste a link to one cell into another cell.

✔ Tips

- Do not press Enter after using the Paste Link command! Doing so pastes the contents of the Clipboard into the cell, overwriting the link.

- Using the Paste Link command to paste a range of cells creates a special range called an *array*. Each cell in an array shares the same cell reference and cannot be changed unless all cells in the array are changed.

To write a formula with 3-D references

1. Select the cell in which you want to enter the formula.

2. Type an equal sign (=).

3. Use any combination of the following techniques until the formula is complete.

    ▲ To enter a function, use the Function Arguments dialog or type in the function. I tell you how to use the Function Arguments dialog in **Chapter 5**.

    ▲ To enter an operator, type it in. I tell you about using operators in **Chapter 2**.

    ▲ To enter a cell reference, select the cell(s) you want to reference or type the reference in. If typing the reference, be sure to include single quotes, brackets, and exclamation points as discussed on the previous page.

4. Press Enter or click the Enter button on the formula bar.

To write a formula that sums the same cell on multiple, adjacent sheets

1. Select the cell in which you want to enter the formula.

2. Type =SUM((**Figure 30**).

3. If the cells you want to add are in another workbook, switch to that workbook.

4. Click the sheet tab for the first worksheet containing the cell you want to sum.

5. Hold down [Shift] and click on the sheet tab for the last sheet containing the cell you want to sum. All tabs from the first to the last become selected (**Figure 31**). The formula in the formula bar should look something like the one in **Figure 32**.

6. Click the cell you want to sum (**Figure 33**). The cell reference is added to the formula (**Figure 34**).

7. Type).

8. Press [Enter] or click the Enter button on the formula bar.

✔ Tips

- Use this technique to link cells of identically arranged worksheets. This results in a "3-D worksheet" effect.

- Although you can use this technique to consolidate data, the Consolidate command, which I discuss later in this chapter, automates consolidations with or without links.

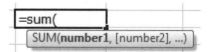

Figure 30 Type the beginning of a formula with the SUM function …

Figure 31 … select all of the tabs for sheets that contain the cells you want to sum …

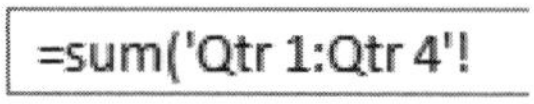

=sum('Qtr 1:Qtr 4'!

Figure 32 … so the sheet names are appended as a range in the formula bar.

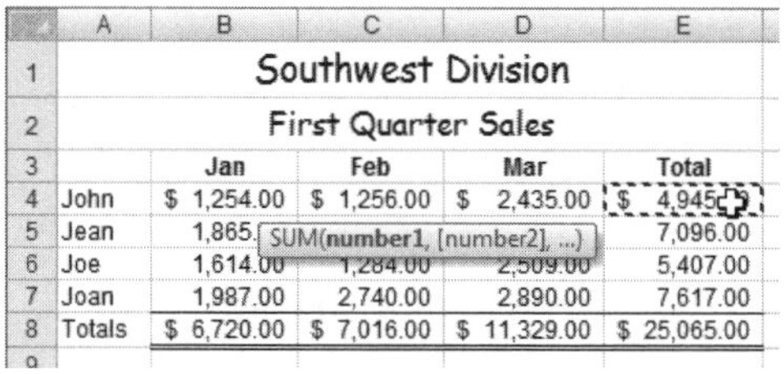

	A	B	C	D	E
1		Southwest Division			
2		First Quarter Sales			
3		Jan	Feb	Mar	Total
4	John	$ 1,254.00	$ 1,256.00	$ 2,435.00	$ 4,945.00
5	Jean	1,865.	SUM(**number1**, [number2], …)		7,096.00
6	Joe	1,614.00	1,284.00	2,509.00	5,407.00
7	Joan	1,987.00	2,740.00	2,890.00	7,617.00
8	Totals	$ 6,720.00	$ 7,016.00	$ 11,329.00	$ 25,065.00
9					

Figure 33 Then click on the cell you want to add …

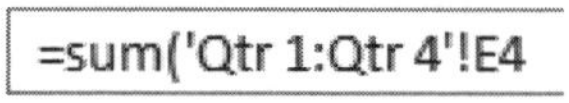

=sum('Qtr 1:Qtr 4'!E4

Figure 34 … so that its reference is appended to the formula in the formula bar.

WRITING FORMULAS WITH 3-D REFERENCES

Figure 35 A security warning appears in the message bar when you open a file that contains a link to another file.

Figure 36 Use this dialog to set link updating options for a specific workbook file.

Opening Workbooks with Links

When you open a workbook that has a link to another workbook file, Excel needs to retrieve the linked information from that file. Whether it does this depends on Excel's Trust Center settings for external content.

By default, Excel is set to prompt you when Excel needs to retrieve content from another file. It does this by displaying a security warning in the Message Bar between the Ribbon and the Formula bar (**Figure 35**).

In this section, I explain how to allow content to be retrieved and how to modify Trust Center settings for all external links.

✔ Tip

■ You can also update a link to another file by simply opening the other file. Excel assumes that if the file is secure enough to open, it's secure enough to retrieve data from.

To allow link updating

1. In the Message Bar's security warning (**Figure 35**), click the Options button.

   The Microsoft Office Security Options dialog appears (**Figure 36**).

2. Select the Enable this content option.

3. Click OK.

   From that point forward, Excel always automatically updates links in the file.

✔ Tip

■ Links can be used to access information on your computer without your permission. You should not update links in a file if you don't trust the source of the file, especially if you weren't expecting the file to include links.

To modify external content settings for links

1. Choose Microsoft Office > Excel Options.

2. In the Excel Options dialog that appears, click the Trust Center item in the list to display Trust Center options (**Figure 37**).

3. Click the Trust Center Settings button.

4. In the Trust Center dialog that appears, click the External Content item in the list to display the External Content options (**Figure 38**).

5. Select one of the Security Settings for Workbook Links options:

   ▲ **Enable automatic update for all Workbook Links** automatically updates links to other files in all workbooks. This disables the security over links.

   ▲ **Prompt user on automatic update for Workbook Links** displays the Security Alert discussed on the previous page when you open a workbook file with links to an unopened workbook file. This is the default setting.

   ▲ **Disable automatic update of Workbook Links** prevents workbook links from being updated automatically. Selecting this option could result in out-of-date information appearing in the workbook.

6. Click OK to save your settings and dismiss the Trust Center dialog.

7. Click OK to dismiss the Excel Options dialog.

✔ Tip

■ If you often open workbook files created by others, it really isn't a good idea to enable automatic update for all workbook links. Doing so can create serious security problems.

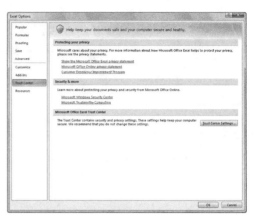

Figure 37 Click Trust Center in the Excel Options dialog to display Trust Center information and options.

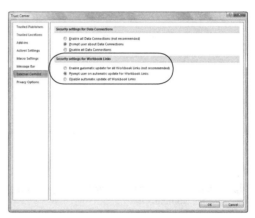

Figure 38 Use the Trust Center dialog to set default options for external content such as links.

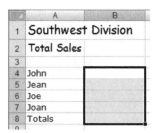

Figure 39
Select the cells in which you want the consolidated data to go.

Figure 40 The Data Tools group on the Ribbon's Data tab.

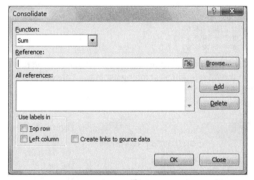

Figure 41 Use the Consolidate dialog to identify the cells you want to combine.

Figure 42
Choose a function for the consolidation from the Function drop-down list.

Consolidations

The Consolidate command lets you combine data from multiple sources. Excel lets you do this in two ways:

◆ **Consolidate based on the arrangement of data.** This is useful when data occupies the same number of cells in the same arrangement in multiple locations (**Figure 3**).

◆ **Consolidate based on identifying labels or categories.** This is useful when the arrangement of data varies from one source to the next.

✔ Tip

■ With either method, Excel can create links to the source information so the consolidation changes automatically when linked data changes.

To consolidate based on the arrangement of data

1. Select the cell(s) where you want the consolidated information to go (**Figure 39**).

2. Click Data > Data Tools > Consolidate (**Figure 40**).

3. In the Consolidate dialog (**Figure 41**), choose a function from the Function drop-down list (**Figure 42**).

4. If necessary, click in the Reference box.

5. Switch to the worksheet containing the first cell(s) to be included in the consolidation. The reference is entered into the Reference box.

6. Select the cell(s) you want to include in the consolidation. The reference is entered into the Reference text box (**Figure 43**).

Continued on next page...

Continued from previous page.

7. Click Add.

8. Repeat steps 5, 6, and 7 for all of the cells that you want to include in the consolidation. When you're finished, the All references scrolling list in the Consolidate dialog might look something like **Figure 44**.

9. To create links between the source data and destination cell(s), turn on the Create links to source data check box.

10. Click OK.

Excel consolidates the information in the originally selected cell(s) (**Figure 45**).

✔ Tips

- For this technique to work, each source range must have the same number of cells with data arranged in the same way.

- If the Consolidate dialog contains references when you open it, you can clear them by selecting each one and clicking the Delete button.

- If you turn on the Create links to source data check box, Excel creates an outline (**Figure 45**) with links to all source cells. You can expand or collapse the outline by clicking the outline buttons (**Figure 46**). A complete discussion of the outlining feature is beyond the scope of this book.

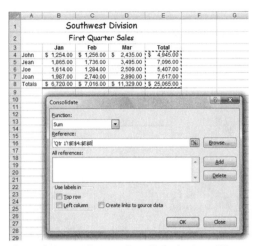

Figure 43 Enter references for cells in the Consolidate dialog by selecting them in the worksheet.

Figure 44 The cells you want to consolidate are listed in the All references scrolling list in the Consolidate dialog.

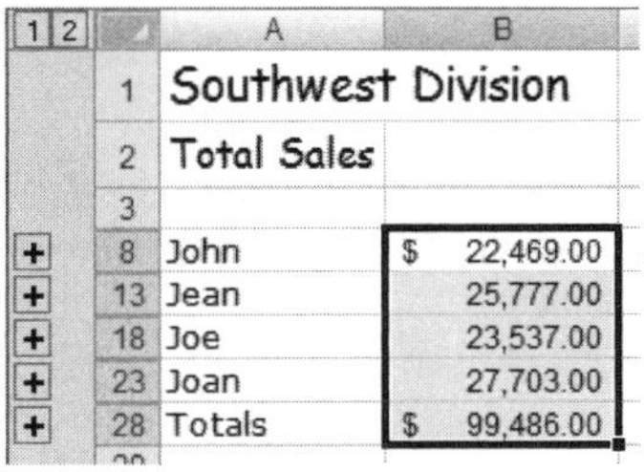

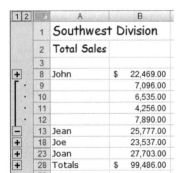

Figure 45 Excel combines the data in the cell(s) you originally selected.

Figure 46 You can click the outline buttons to show or hide individual values that make up a consolidation with links.

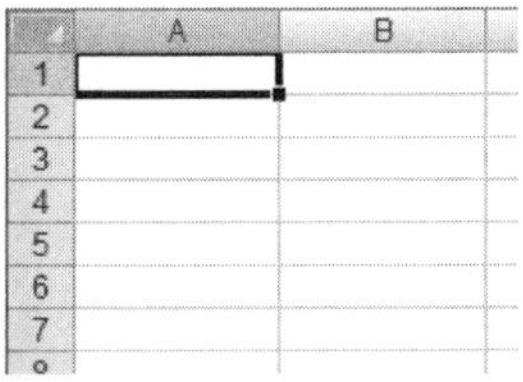

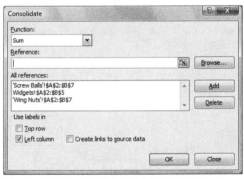

Figure 47
Select the destination cell(s).

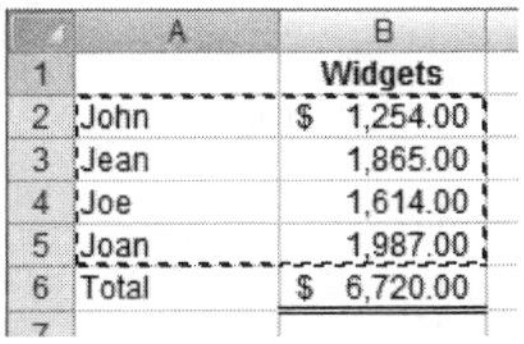

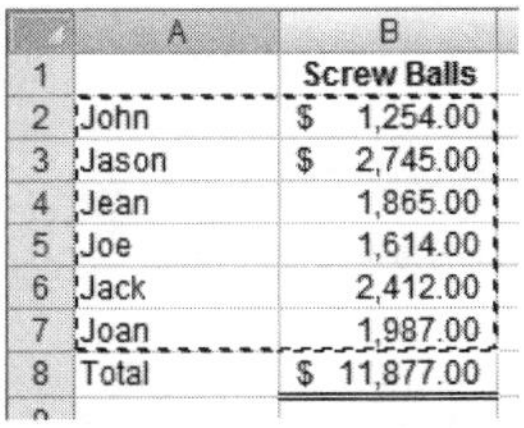

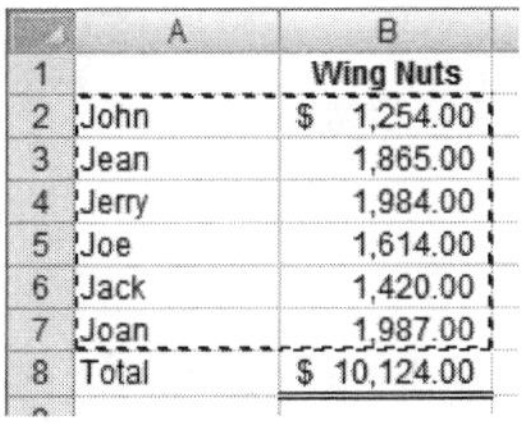

Figures 48, 49, & 50
Select the cell(s) you want to include in the consolidation.

Figure 51 The Consolidate dialog records all selections and enables you to specify where the data labels are.

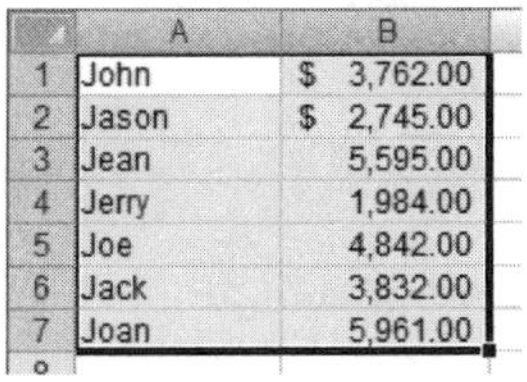

Figure 52
The final consolidation accounts for all data.

To consolidate based on labels

1. Select the cell(s) where you want the consolidated information to go. As shown in **Figure 47**, you can select just a single starting cell.

2. Click Data > Data Tools > Consolidate (**Figure 40**).

3. In the Consolidate dialog (**Figure 41**), choose a function from the Function drop-down list (**Figure 42**).

4. If necessary, click in the Reference box.

5. Switch to the worksheet containing the first cell(s) to be included in the consolidation. The reference is entered into the Reference text box.

6. Select the cell(s) you want to include in the consolidation, including any text that identifies data (**Figure 48**). The text must be in cells adjacent to the data. The reference is entered into the Reference text box.

7. Click Add.

8. Repeat steps 5, 6, and 7 for all cells you want to include in the consolidation. **Figures 49** and **50** show the other two ranges included for the example. When you're finished, the Consolidate dialog might look something like **Figure 51**.

9. Turn on the appropriate check box(es) in the Use labels in area to tell Excel where identifying labels for the data are.

10. Click OK.

Excel consolidates the information in the originally selected cell(s) (**Figure 52**).

Custom Views

Excel's custom views feature lets you create multiple *views* of a workbook file. A view includes the window size and position, the active cell, the zoom percentage, hidden columns and rows, and print settings. Once you set up a view, you can choose it from a dialog to see it quickly.

✔ Tip

- Including print settings in views makes it possible to create and save multiple custom reports for printing.

To add a custom view

1. Create the view you want to save. **Figure 53** shows an example.

2. Click View > Workbook Views > Custom Views (**Figure 54**).

3. In the Custom Views dialog (**Figure 55**), click the Add button.

4. In the Add View dialog (**Figure 56**), enter a name for the view in the Name text box.

5. Turn on the appropriate Include in view check boxes:

   ▲ **Print settings** includes current Page Setup and other printing options in the view.

   ▲ **Hidden rows, columns and filter settings** includes current settings for hidden columns and rows, as well as filter selections.

6. Click OK.

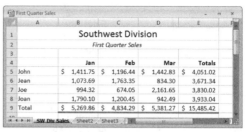

Figure 53 Create a view you'd like to save.

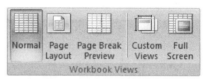

Figure 54 The Workbook Views group on the Ribbon's View tab.

Figure 55 The Custom Views dialog before any views have been added.

Figure 56 Use the Add View dialog to name and set options for a view.

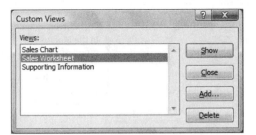

Figure 57 To see or delete a view, select the name of the view in the Custom Views dialog, then click Show or Delete.

Figure 58 When you click the Delete button to delete a view, Excel asks you to confirm that you really do want to delete it.

To switch to a view

1. Switch to the sheet containing the view you want to see.

2. Click View > Workbook Views > Custom Views (**Figure 54**).

3. In the Custom Views dialog (**Figure 57**), select the view you want to see from the Views scrolling list.

4. Click Show.

   Excel changes the window so it looks just like it did when you created the view.

To delete a view

1. Switch to the sheet containing the view you want to delete.

2. Click View > Workbook Views > Custom Views (**Figure 54**).

3. In the Custom Views dialog (**Figure 57**), select the view you want to delete from the Views scrolling list.

4. Click Delete.

5. In the confirmation dialog that appears (**Figure 58**), click Yes.

6. Follow steps 3 through 5 to delete other views if desired.

7. Click Close to dismiss the Custom Views dialog without changing the view.

✔ Tip

■ Deleting a view does not delete the information contained in the view. It merely removes the reference to the information from the Views list in the Custom Views dialog (**Figure 57**).

Macros

A macro is a series of commands that Excel can perform automatically. You can create simple macros to automate repetitive tasks, like entering data or formatting cells.

Although macros are created with Excel's built-in Visual Basic programming language, you don't need to be a programmer to create them. Excel's Macro Recorder will record your keystrokes, menu choices, and dialog settings as you make them and will write the programming code for you. This makes macros useful for all Excel users, even beginners.

✔ Tip

- The macro feature makes it possible to create highly customized workbook files, complete with special dialogs, menus, and commands. A discussion of these capabilities, however, is far beyond the scope of this book.

To record a macro

1. Choose View > Macros > Macros > Record Macro (**Figure 59**) to display the Record Macro dialog (**Figure 60**).

2. Enter a name for the macro in the Macro name text box.

3. If desired, enter a keystroke to use as a shortcut key in the Ctrl+ text box.

4. If desired, edit the description automatically entered in the Description text box.

5. Click OK.

6. Perform all the steps you want to include in your macro. Excel records them all—even the mistakes—so be careful!

7. When you're finished recording macro steps, choose View > Macros > Macros > Stop Recording (**Figure 61**).

Figure 59
The Macros menu in the Macros group offers commands for working with— you guessed it—macros.

Figure 60 Enter a name and set options for a new macro in the Record Macro dialog.

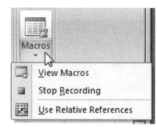

Figure 61
When you're finished recording macro steps, choose the Stop Recording command.

Figure 62 The Macro dialog enables you to run, edit, and delete macros.

Figure 63 Here's the code for a macro that adds formatted column and row headings to a blank worksheet.

To run a macro

Press the keystroke you specified as a shortcut key for the macro when you created it.

Or

1. Choose View > Macros > Macros > View Macros (**Figure 59**).

2. In the scrolling list of the Macro dialog (**Figure 62**), select the macro you want to run.

3. Click Run.

   Excel performs each macro step, just the way you recorded it.

✔ Tips

- Save your workbook *before* running a macro for the first time. You may be surprised by the results and need to revert the file to the way it was before you ran the macro. Excel's Undo command cannot undo the steps of a macro, so reverting to the last saved version of the file is the only way to reverse macro steps.

- Excel stores each macro as a *module* within the workbook. View and edit a macro by selecting it in the Macro dialog and clicking the Edit button. **Figure 63** shows an example. I don't recommend editing macro code unless you have at least a general understanding of Visual Basic!

- More advanced uses of macros include the creation of custom functions and applications that work within Excel.

Web Publishing

Web Publishing

The World Wide Web has had a huge impact on publishing since 1995. Web pages, which can include text, graphics, and hyperlinks, can be published on the Internet or an intranet, making them available to audiences 24 hours a day, 7 days a week. They provide information quickly and inexpensively to anyone who needs it.

Microsoft Excel's Save As command enables you to save worksheets and charts as HTML documents, making it easy to publish Excel data on the Web.

✔ Tips

- This chapter explains how to create Web pages from Excel documents. Modifying the HTML underlying those pages is beyond the scope of this book.

- *HTML* (or *HyperText Markup Language*) is a system of codes for defining Web pages.

- Web pages are normally viewed with *Web browser* software. Microsoft Internet Explorer and Firefox are two examples of Web browsers.

- To access the Internet, you need an Internet connection, either through an organizational network or dial-up connection. Setting up a connection is beyond the scope of this book; consult the documentation that came with your System or Internet access software for more information.

- To publish a Web page, you need access to a Web server. Contact your Network Administrator or Internet Service Provider (ISP) for more information.

- A *hyperlink* (or *link*) is text or a graphic that, when clicked, displays other information from the Web.

- An *intranet* is like the Internet, but it exists only on the internal network of an organization and is usually closed to outsiders.

- If you have access to Excel Services on a Microsoft Office SharePoint Server, you can publish your worksheets to that server for Internet or intranet access. Consult your Network Administrator for details.

Creating Web Pages

Excel has built-in Web publishing features that make it easy to publish Excel documents as standard Web pages (**Figure 1**). This enables you to publish formatted worksheets and charts on the Web so the information can be viewed by others on the Internet or on your company's intranet.

✔ Tips

- **Figure 1** shows what the Web page looks like with Microsoft Internet Explorer 6.0, which is the default Web browser on my system. If your system has a different default Web browser, the page may look different.

- Although previous versions of Excel enabled you to publish workbooks as interactive Web pages, doing so with Excel 2007 requires Excel Services and a Microsoft Office SharePoint Server. A discussion of these server-related features is beyond the scope of this book.

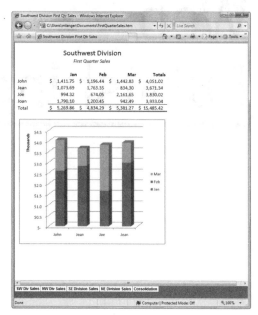

Figure 1 A workbook saved as Web pages. Note the sheet tabs at the bottom of the page; click a tab to view another sheet on a separate Web page.

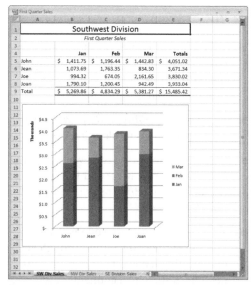

Figure 2 Start by opening the workbook you want to save as a Web page.

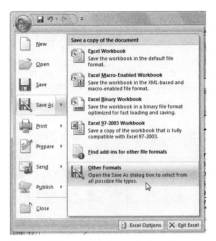

Figure 3 Choose Other Formats from the Save As submenu.

Figure 4 Choose Web Page from the Save as type pop-up menu.

Figure 5 Use this Save As dialog to save the workbook or selection as Web pages.

To save a workbook as Web pages

1. Open or activate the workbook that you want to save as a Web page (**Figure 2**).

2. Choose Microsoft Office > Save As > Other Formats (**Figure 3**) or press F12.

3. The Save As dialog appears. Choose Web Page from the Save as type pop-up menu (**Figure 4**). The dialog changes to offer Web publishing options (**Figure 5**).

4. Use the top portion of the dialog to select a disk location for the Web page and its supporting images.

5. In the File name text box, enter a name for the Web page.

6. Select one of the Save options to specify what you want to save as a Web page:

   ▲ **Entire Workbook** is all the sheets in the workbook.

   ▲ **Selection** is the currently displayed sheet or, if multiple cells were selected when you opened the Save As dialog, the cell reference for the selection.

7. To enter a title for the Web page, click the Change Title button. Then enter a new title in the Set Page Title dialog that appears (**Figure 6**) and click OK.

Continued on next page...

Figure 6 The Set Page Title dialog enables you to enter a custom page title for the Web page.

SAVING WORKBOOKS AS WEB PAGES

Continued from previous page.

8. Click Save.

9. If the workbook, sheet, or selection includes features that cannot be saved as part of a Web page, a dialog like the one in **Figure 7** appears. Click Yes.

Excel creates the HTML, image, and other supporting files required to display the Excel document as Web pages. All supporting files are saved in a folder with the same name as the Web page file (**Figure 8**).

Figure 7 This dialog appears if a worksheet includes features that can't be saved as part of a Web page.

✔ Tips

- You can further customize the appearance of a Web page created by Excel by modifying its HTML code with your favorite Web authoring program or HTML editor.

- Excel can also create single-file Web pages in which all files for a page, including images, are embedded in a single *MIME encapsulated aggregate HTML* (*MHTML*) file. This format, which is supported by Internet Explorer 4.0 and later, is handy for sending Web pages to others via e-mail. To create a single-file Web page, in step 3, choose Single File Web Page from the Save as type pop-up menu.

Figure 8 Excel creates all the HTML, image, and other supporting files necessary to view the workbook, sheet, or selection as Web pages.

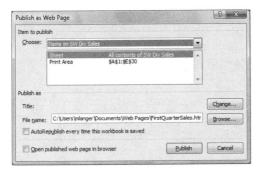

Figure 9 Use this dialog to set additional options for publishing a workbook or worksheet as a Web page.

To automatically save a workbook as Web pages

1. Follow steps 1 through 7 in the previous section to prepare a workbook or worksheet to be saved as a Web page.

2. Click the Publish button in the Save As dialog to display the Publish as Web Page dialog (**Figure 9**).

3. Turn on the check box for AutoRepublish every time this workbook is saved.

4. Click Publish.

✔ Tip

- This feature is especially useful if you can save your Web pages directly to a Web server. This way, the pages are automatically updated—with no additional work on your part—when changed or revised.

Hyperlinks

A *hyperlink* is text or a graphic that, when clicked, displays other information. Excel enables you to create two kinds of hyperlinks:

◆ A link to a *URL* (*Uniform Resource Locator*), which is the Internet address of a document or individual. Excel makes it easy to create links to two types of URLs:

▲ **http://** links to a Web page on a Web server.

▲ **mailto:** links to an e-mail address.

◆ A link to another document on your hard disk or network.

By default, hyperlinks appear as colored, underlined text (**Figure 10**).

✔ Tips

■ Although you can create a link to any document on your hard disk or accessible over a local area network or the Internet, clicking the link will only open the document if you have a program capable of opening it—such as the program that created it.

■ Clicking a cell that contains a hyperlink opens the linked location. To select a cell containing a hyperlink, point to the cell, press the mouse button, and hold the mouse button down until the cell is selected.

	A	B	C	D	E
1		Southwest Division			
2		*First Quarter Sales*			
3					
4		Jan	Feb	Mar	Totals
5	John	$ 1,411.75	$ 1,196.44	$ 1,442.83	$ 4,051.02
6	Jean	1,073.69	1,763.35	834.30	3,671.34
7	Joe	994.32	674.05	2,161.65	3,830.02
8	Joan	1,790.10	1,200.45	942.49	3,933.04
9	Total	$ 5,269.86	$ 4,834.29	$ 5,381.27	$ 15,485.42
10					
11	For questions about this document, contact John Aabbott.				
12	E-Mail John				

Figure 10 A hyperlink appears as colored, underlined text. When you point to it, the mouse pointer turns into a hand with a pointing finger and a box with the link's URL or ScreenTip (as shown here) appears.

	A	B	C	D	E
1			Southwest Division		
2			First Quarter Sales		
3					
4		Jan	Feb	Mar	Totals
5	John	$ 1,411.75	$ 1,196.44	$ 1,442.83	$ 4,051.02
6	Jean	1,073.69	1,763.35	834.30	3,671.34
7	Joe	994.32	674.05	2,161.65	3,830.02
8	Joan	1,790.10	1,200.45	942.49	3,933.04
9	Total	$ 5,269.86	$ 4,834.29	$ 5,381.27	$ 15,485.42
10					
11	For questions about this document, contact John Aabbott.				

Figure 11 Select the cell you want to convert to a hyperlink.

Figure 12
The Insert tab's Links group has only one button.

Figure 13 The Insert Hyperlink dialog for inserting a link to an existing file or Web page.

Address: http://www.marialanger.com/excelquickstart/

Figure 14 Use the Address text box to enter the URL for the link location.

To insert a hyperlink

1. Select the cell or object that you want to convert to a hyperlink (**Figure 11**).

2. Click Insert > Links > Hyperlink (**Figure 12**) or press [Ctrl][K].

   The Insert Hyperlink dialog appears (**Figure 13**).

3. Choose one of the Link to buttons on the left side of the dialog:

   ▲ **Existing File or Web Page** (**Figure 13**) enables you to link to a file on disk or a Web page. If you select this option, you can either select one of the files or locations that appears in the list or type a path or URL in the Address box (**Figure 14**).

   ▲ **Place in This Document** (**Figure 15**) enables you to link to a specific location in the current document. If you select this option, choose a heading or enter a cell reference.

   ▲ **Create New Document** (**Figure 16**) enables you to create and link to a new document. If you select this option, you can either enter a pathname for the document or click the Change button and use the Create New Document dialog that appears to create a new document.

Continued on next page...

Figure 15 The Insert Hyperlink dialog for inserting a link to a place in the current document.

Figure 16 The Insert Hyperlink dialog for inserting a link to a new document.

INSERTING HYPERLINKS

Continued from previous page.

▲ **E-mail Address** (**Figure 17**) enables you to link to an e-mail address. If you select this option, you can either enter the e-mail address in the E-mail address box or select one of the recently used e-mail addresses in the list.

4. Click OK to save your settings and dismiss the Insert Hyperlink dialog.

The selected cell or object turns into a hyperlink (**Figure 10**).

✔ Tips

■ The Text to display box near the top of the Insert Hyperlink dialog (**Figures 13, 15, 16**, and **17**) determines what text appears as the link in the worksheet cell.

■ To specify what should appear in the ScreenTip box when you point to the hyperlink, click the ScreenTip button in the Insert Hyperlink dialog (**Figures 13, 15, 16**, and **17**). Then enter the text you want to appear in the Set Hyperlink ScreenTip dialog (**Figure 18**) and click OK. **Figure 10** shows an example of a custom ScreenTip. Keep in mind that this feature is not compatible with all Web browsers.

Figure 17 The Insert Hyperlink dialog for inserting a link to an e-mail address.

Figure 18 Use this dialog to set up a custom ScreenTip for a hyperlink.

To follow a hyperlink

1. Position the mouse pointer on the hyperlink. The mouse pointer turns into a pointing finger and a ScreenTip appears in a box nearby (**Figure 10**).

2. Click once.

   If the hyperlink points to an Internet URL, Excel starts your default Web browser, connects to the Internet, and displays the URL.

   or

   If the hyperlink points to a location in the current file, that location appears.

   or

   If the hyperlink points to a file on your hard disk or another computer on the network, the file opens.

   or

   If the hyperlink points to an e-mail address, Excel starts your default e-mail program and prepares a preaddressed new message form.

FOLLOWING HYPERLINKS

To modify or remove a hyperlink

1. Select the cell or object containing the hyperlink. (You can select a cell with a hyperlink by pointing to it and then holding down the mouse button until the mouse pointer turns into a fat plus sign.)

2. Click Insert > Links > Hyperlink (**Figure 12**) or press Ctrl K.

   The Edit Hyperlink dialog appears (**Figure 19**).

3. To change the link information, make changes as discussed earlier in this section.

   or

   To remove the link, click the Remove Link button.

4. Click OK.

Figure 19 Use the Edit Hyperlink dialog to modify or remove a hyperlink.

Setting Excel Options 15

The Options Dialog

Microsoft Excel's Excel Options dialog offers five categories of general options that you can set to customize the way Excel works for you:

- ◆ **Popular** options are the most commonly accessed options for display, font settings, and user information.

- ◆ **Formulas** options control formula calculation, performance, and error handling.

- ◆ **Proofing** options control how Excel corrects and formats text.

- ◆ **Save** options control how workbook files are saved.

- ◆ **Advanced** options control other aspects of working with Excel.

✔ Tips

- ■ Excel's default options settings are discussed and illustrated throughout this book.

- ■ Some of the options settings affect only the active sheet or workbook file while others affect all Excel operations. If you want a setting to affect a specific sheet or file, be sure to open and activate it before opening the Options dialog.

- ■ The Options dialog also offers more advanced options for customizing Excel and setting security options. You can explore these options on your own.

To set options

1. Click Microsoft Office > Excel Options (**Figure 1**) to display the Excel Options dialog (**Figure 2**).

2. On the left side of the dialog, click the name of the category of options that you want to set.

3. Set options as desired.

4. Repeat steps 2 and 3 for other categories of options that you want to set.

5. Click OK to save your settings.

✔ Tip

■ I illustrate and discuss most Excel Options dialog settings in this chapter.

Figure 1 To open the Excel Options dialog, click the Excel Options button in the Microsoft Office menu.

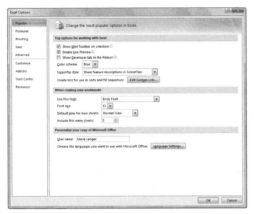

Figure 2 The Popular options in the Excel Options dialog.

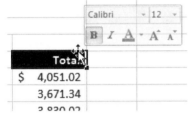

Figure 3 The Mini Toolbar appears as a transparent image when you select text.

Popular Options

The Popular category in the Excel Options dialog includes the options most likely to be modified by users. There are three subcategories of options: Top options for working with Excel, When creating new workbooks, and Personalize your copy of Microsoft Office.

Top options for working with Excel

Top options for working with Excel are the most commonly changed options.

◆ **Show Mini Toolbar on selection** displays the Mini Toolbar, which includes formatting options, when you select cells or text (**Figure 3**).

◆ **Enable Live Preview** displays the affects of an Excel option when you hover over that option. This makes it possible to see how formatting or other commands will affect your work before applying the command.

◆ **Show Developer tab in the Ribbon** displays the Developer tab, which includes commands for macros, form editing, and XML features, in the Ribbon.

◆ **Always use ClearType** (not shown in **Figure 2**) makes the text easier to read onscreen in Windows XP. This option is not available in Windows Vista.

◆ **Color Scheme** enables you to choose Excel's overall color scheme: Blue, Silver, or Black.

◆ **ScreenTip style** determines how ScreenTips appear—or whether they appear at all.

◆ **Create lists for use in sorts and fill sequences** enables you to create or edit custom lists. Click the Edit Custom List

Continued on next page...

POPULAR OPTIONS

Continued from previous page.

button to display the Custom Lists dialog (**Figure 4**), which you can use to define lists. I tell you more about filling a range with a series in **Chapter 3**.

When creating new workbooks

When creating new workbooks are options that apply to all new workbooks you create.

◆ **Use this font** enables you to choose a default font for new worksheets and workbooks.

◆ **Font size** lets you set the default font size for new worksheets and workbooks.

◆ **Default view for new sheets** enables you to choose the default view for new worksheets and workbooks: Normal View, Page Break Preview, or Page Layout View.

◆ **Include this many sheets** lets you set the number of sheets automatically included in all new workbooks you create.

Personalize your copy of Microsoft Office

Personalize your copy of Microsoft Office enables you to set user information and language options. The options you set in this subcategory affect all Microsoft Office applications installed on your computer.

◆ **User name** is the name you want associated with every document you create or edit with your copy of Excel.

◆ **Choose the languages you want to use with Microsoft Office** lets you specify the languages to be used with Excel's proofing tools. Click the Language Settings button to display the Microsoft Office Language Settings 2007 dialog (**Figure 5**), select one or more languages, and click OK.

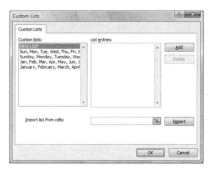

Figure 4 Use the Custom Lists dialog to create and edit custom series and sort lists.

Figure 5 Office supports multiple languages for use with its proofing features.

Figure 6 Formulas settings in the Excel Options dialog.

Formulas Options

Calculation options (**Figure 6**) control the way Excel works with formulas. There are four subcategories of options: Calculation options, Working with formulas, Error Checking, and Error checking rules.

Calculation options

Calculation options control workbook calculation automation and iterative calculations.

◆ **Workbook Calculation** enables you to select one of three options for specifying how formulas should be calculated:

▲ **Automatic** tells Excel to recalculate all dependent formulas whenever you change a value, formula, or name.

▲ **Automatic except for data tables** is the same as Automatic, but does not recalculate data tables. With this option selected, you must click Formulas > Calculation > Calculate Now or press F9 to recalculate data tables.

▲ **Manual** recalculates formulas only when you click Formulas > Calculation > Calculate Now or press F9. With this option selected, you can turn on the **Recalculate workbook before saving** check box to ensure that the worksheet is recalculated each time you save it.

◆ **Enable iterative calculation** sets limits for the number of times Excel tries to resolve circular references or complete goal seeking calculations. Turn on the check box, then enter values below it:

▲ **Maximum iterations** is the maximum number of times Excel should attempt to solve the problem.

▲ **Maximum change** is the maximum amount of result change below which iteration stops.

Working with formulas

Working with formulas controls formula-related features such as references and AutoComplete.

◆ **R1C1 reference style** changes the style of cell references so both rows and columns have numbers (**Figure 7**).

◆ **Formula AutoComplete** displays a list of applicable functions (**Figure 8**) and defined names as you enter a formula into a cell. You can complete the entry by selecting one of the displayed options.

◆ **Use table names in formulas** enables you to reference a table by its name when writing a formula.

◆ **Use GetPivotData functions for Pivot-Table references** instructs Excel to use GETPIVOTTABLE function cell references when working with PivotTables.

Error Checking

Error Checking lets you enable or disable Excel's error-checking feature.

◆ **Enable backround error checking** enables or disables the error checking feature.

◆ **Indicate errors using this color** enables you to set the color of the tiny triangle that appears in each cell in which there might be an error. Choose a color from the menu (**Figure 9**); Automatic is green.

◆ **Reset Ignored Errors** tells Excel to forget about any errors you told it to ignore.

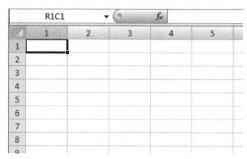

Figure 7 With the R1C1 reference style, both columns and rows have numbers.

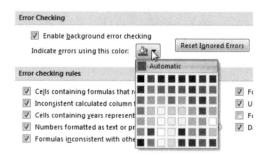

Figure 8 Formula AutoComplete displays possible formula options as you type in a formula.

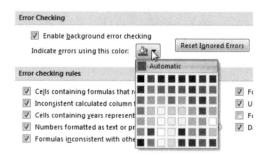

Figure 9 Use a pop-up menu to set the error indicator color.

Error checking rules

Error checking rules enable you to determine the types of errors that should be marked by Excel's error checking feature.

◆ **Cells containing formulas that result in an error** displays an error indicator when the cell's formula results in an error.

◆ **Inconsistent calculated column formula in tables** displays an error indicator for cells in a column that don't contain the same formula as other cells in the column.

◆ **Cells containing years represented as 2 digits** displays an error indicator when a formula contains text formatted cells with years represented as two digits.

◆ **Numbers formatted as text or preceded by an apostrophe** displays an error indicator when numbers are formatted as text or begin with an apostrophe character.

◆ **Formulas inconsistent with other formulas in the region** displays an error indicator when a formula differs from other formulas in the same region of the worksheet.

◆ **Formulas which omits cells in a region** displays an error indicator when a formula omits certain cells.

◆ **Unlocked cells containing formulas** displays an error indicator when a cell containing a formula is formatted as unlocked and the worksheet is locked.

◆ **Formulas referring to empty cells** displays an error indicator if a formula includes any references to empty cells.

◆ **Data entered in a table is invalid** displays an error indicator if data in a table is of a type inconsistent with other data in the same column.

Proofing Options

The Proofing options in the Excel Options dialog (**Figure 10**) control how Excel automatically corrects text in your documents. There are two subcategories: AutoCorrect options and When correcting spelling in Microsoft Office programs.

The options in this category affect how all installed Microsoft Office programs work—not just Excel.

AutoCorrect Options

AutoCorrect options enables you to set a variety of automatic correction options.

Click the AutoCorrect Options button to display the AutoCorrect tab of the AutoCorrect dialog (**Figure 11**). You can then toggle check boxes to set how the Microsoft Office AutoCorrect feature works:

◆ **Show AutoCorrect Options buttons** displays a button beside a cell in which Excel has made an automatic correction. Clicking the button displays a menu of options related to the correction.

◆ **Correct TWo INitial CApitals** sets the second character to lowercase when you type two uppercase characters in a row.

◆ **Capitalize first letter of sentences** automatically capitalizes the first letter of a sentence.

◆ **Capitalize names of days** automatically capitalizes the first letter of day names.

◆ **Correct accidental use of cAPS LOCK key** automatically corrects incorrect capitalization that occurs when you type with (Caps Lock) down.

◆ **Replace text as you type** enables automatic text replacement as defined in the table in the bottom half of the dialog.

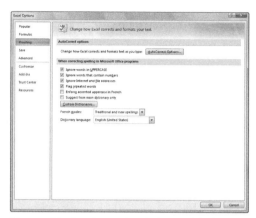

Figure 10 The Proofing options in the Excel Options dialog.

Figure 11 Use this dialog to set how the AutoCorrect feature should work.

When you are finished setting options in the AutoCorrect dialog, click OK to save your settings and return to the Excel Options dialog.

Figure 12 Use this dialog to set up custom dictionaries for working with Microsoft Office programs.

Figure 13
Microsoft Office comes with quite a few dictionaries.

When correcting spelling in Microsoft Office programs

When correcting spelling in Microsoft Office programs enables you to set options for the way the Microsoft Office spelling checker flags a possible misspelled word.

◆ **Ignore words in UPPERCASE** tells Excel not to check words in all uppercase characters, such as acronyms.

◆ **Ignore words that contain numbers** tells Excel not to check words that include numbers, such as *MariaL1*.

◆ **Ignore Internet and file addresses** tells Excel not to check any words that appear to be URLs, e-mail addresses, file names, or file pathnames.

◆ **Flag repeated words** marks the second occurrence of a repeated word.

◆ **Enforce accented uppercase in French** tells Excel that accents should be applied in French text for both uppercase and lowercase characters.

◆ **Suggest from main dictionary only** tells Excel to suggest replacement words from the main dictionary—not from your custom dictionaries.

◆ **Custom Dictionaries** displays a dialog you can use to specify custom dictionary files (**Figure 12**).

◆ **French modes** enables you to select a spelling mode for French text.

◆ **Dictionary language** enables you to select the language of the dictionary that should be used for spelling checks. The drop-down list (**Figure 13**) includes all available dictionaries.

Save Options

Save options (**Figure 14**) control how workbooks are saved. There are four subcategories of options: Save Workbooks, AutoRecover exceptions for, Offline editing options for document management server files, and Preserve visual appearance of the workbook.

Save workbooks

Save Workbooks controls the default workbook file format and AutoRecover settings.

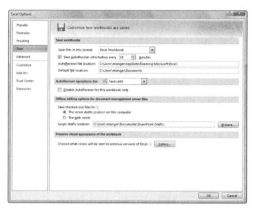

Figure 14 The Save options in the Excel Options dialog.

◆ **Save files in this format** enables you to choose a default Excel format for saving files. Choose an option from the drop-down list (**Figure 15**). Remember, you can use options in the Save As dialog to save a file in a format other than the default format, as discussed in **Chapter 4**.

Figure 15
Choose a default file format from this drop-down list.

◆ **Save AutoRecover information every** *n* **minutes** enables you to set a frequency for automatically saving a special document recovery file.

◆ **AutoRecover file location** enables you to specify a directory for saving document recovery files.

◆ **Default file location** enables you to specify a default directory for saving Excel files.

AutoRecover exceptions for

AutoRecover exceptions for enables you to turn off the AutoRecover feature for a specific workbook file.

◆ **Disable AutoRecover for this workbook only** turns off the AutoRecovery feature for the workbook you select from the drop-down list. The list includes only those workbook files that are currently open, so you must open a workbook before displaying the Excel Options dialog and choosing it from the list.

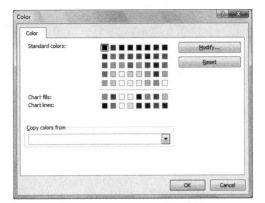

Figure 16 Use the Color dialog to change the default color palette for workbook files opened with previous versions of Excel.

Offline editing options for document management server files

Offline editing options for document management server files control the location of documents shared over a SharePoint server. These options only apply if your network includes a Microsoft Office SharePoint Server.

◆ **Save checked-out files to** enables you to choose one of two possible locations for saving shared files as you edit them.

◆ **Server drafts location** is the directory on your computer in which SharePoint draft files are saved.

Preserve visual appearance of the workbook

Preserve visual appearance of the workbook enables you to set color options for files opened in previous versions of Excel.

◆ **Choose what colors will be seen in previous versions of Excel** enables you to modify the color palette for the current workbook when it is opened in previous versions of Microsoft Excel. Click the Colors button and use the Color dialog that appears (**Figure 16**) to modify selected colors and build a new color palette.

SAVE OPTIONS

Advanced Options

Excel's Advanced options (**Figure 17**) control how most of Excel's features appear or work. There are many subcategories of options:

◆ Editing options

◆ Cut, copy, and paste

◆ Print

◆ Display

◆ Display options for this workbook

◆ Display options for this worksheet

◆ Formulas

◆ When calculating this workbook

◆ General

◆ Lotus compatibility

◆ Lotus compatibility Settings for

In the remaining pages of this chapter, I explain what all of these settings are for.

Editing options

Editing options control the way certain editing tasks work.

◆ **After pressing Enter, move selection** tells Excel to move the cell pointer when you press ⌐Enter⌐. With this option turned on, you can use the **Direction** drop-down list to choose a direction: Down, Right, Up, or Left.

◆ **Automatically insert a decimal point** instructs Excel to automatically place a decimal point when you enter a value. Turn on the check box and enter a value in the **Places** text box. A positive value moves the decimal to the left; a negative value moves the decimal to the right.

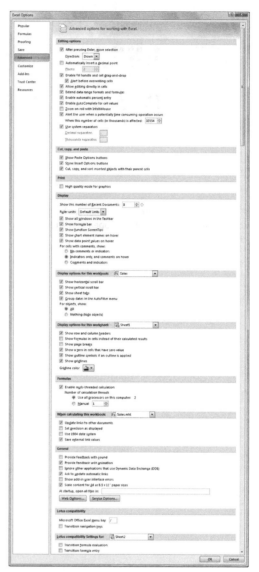

Figure 17 As you can see, there are quite a few Advanced options in the Excel Options dialog.

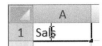

Figure 18 You can edit the contents of a cell, right within the cell.

◆ **Enable fill handle and cell drag and drop** turns on the fill handle and makes it possible to copy or move cells by dragging them to a new location. With this option turned on, you can also turn on the **Alert before overwriting cells** check box to have Excel warn you if a fill or drag-and-drop operation will overwrite the contents of destination cells.

◆ **Allow editing directly in cells** enables you to edit a cell's value or formula by double-clicking the cell (**Figure 18**). With this option turned off, you must edit a cell's contents in the formula bar.

◆ **Extend data range formats and formulas** tells Excel that it should copy the formats and formulas in table cells to new rows added at the bottom of the table.

◆ **Enable automatic percent entry** tells Excel to multiply by 100 all numbers less than 1 that you enter in cells formatted with a Percentage format.

◆ **Enable AutoComplete for cell values** turns on the AutoComplete feature for entering values in cells based on entries in the same column.

◆ **Zoom on roll with IntelliMouse** sets the roll button on a Microsoft IntelliMouse to zoom instead of scroll.

◆ **Alert the user when a potentially time-consuming operation occurs** displays a dialog when an operation could take a long time to process. With this option enabled, you can specify how many cells must be affected to display the warning.

◆ **Use system separators** tells Excel to use the decimal and thousands separator set within Windows. With this option turned off, you can specify your own decimal and thousands separators by entering them in the appropriate boxes.

EDITING OPTIONS

Cut, copy, and paste

Cut, copy, and paste options control how the cut, copy, and paste commands and their related features work.

◆ **Show Paste Options buttons** displays the button for the Paste Options menu (**Figure 19**) after you use a Paste or Fill command.

◆ **Show Insert Options buttons** displays the button for the Insert Options menu (**Figure 20**) after you use an Insert command.

◆ **Cut, copy, and sort objects with their parent cells** keeps objects (such as graphics) with cells that you cut, copy, filter, or sort.

Print

Print options set print quality for graphics.

◆ **High quality mode for graphics** enables high quality printing for graphic objects, including pictures, drawings, and clip art images.

Display

Display options control what appears onscreen as you work with Excel.

◆ **Show this number of recent documents** enables you to specify the number of recently opened files that should appear on the right side of the Microsoft Office menu (**Figure 1**). Enter a value in the text box. This feature is handy for quickly reopening recently accessed files.

◆ **Ruler units** enables you to choose the units for the Layout View ruler: Default Units, Inches, Centimeters, or Millimeters.

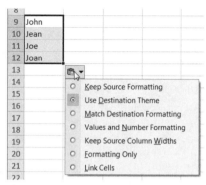

Figure 19 The Paste Options button gives you access to a number of options after you use the Paste command.

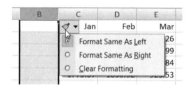

Figure 20 The Insert Options button displays a menu of options after you insert cells.

	A	B	C	D
1		Southwest Division		
2		First Quarter Sales		
3		Jan	Feb	Mar
4	John	1412	1196	1443
5	Jean	1074	1763	834
6	Joe	994	674	2162
7	Joan	1790	1200	942
8	Totals	=sum(		
9		SUM(**number1**, [number2], ...)		

Figure 21 A function ScreenTip can help you enter the correct arguments for a function.

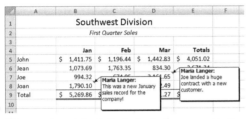

Figure 22 A worksheet displaying both comment indicators and comments.

◆ **Show all windows in the Taskbar** displays a Windows Taskbar icon for each open Excel document window.

◆ **Show formula bar** displays the formula bar above the document window.

◆ **Show function ScreenTips** displays information about function arguments as you enter a function (**Figure 21**).

◆ **Show chart element names on hover** displays the name of a chart element when you point to it.

◆ **Show data point values on hover** displays the value of a chart's data point when you point to it.

◆ **For cells with comments, show** enables you to select one of three options for displaying comments:

▲ **No comments or indicators** does not display comments or comment indicators.

▲ **Indicators only, and comments on hover** displays a small red triangle in the upper-right corner of a cell containing a comment. When you point to the cell, the comment appears in a box.

▲ **Comments and indicators** displays cell comments in boxes as well as a small red triangle in the upper-right corner of each cell containing a comment (**Figure 22**).

Display options for this workbook

Display options for this workbook enables you to set additional display options for the workbook file you select from a drop-down list. Only the workbook files that are currently open appear in the list.

◆ **Show horizontal scroll bar** displays a scroll bar along the bottom of the window.

◆ **Show vertical scroll bar** displays a scroll bar along the right side of the window.

◆ **Show sheet tabs** displays tabs at the bottom of the window for each sheet in the workbook file.

◆ **Group dates in the AutoFilter menu** changes the way dates are listed in the AutoFilter menu for a date filter in a table.

◆ **For objects, show** enables you to specify how objects should appear. Choose an options:

▲ **All** displays all objects.

▲ **Nothing (hide objects)** does not display any objects. Excel will not print objects with this option selected.

	A	B	C	D	E
9	Owner	Percent	Jan	Feb	Mar
10	John	0.5	=C$6*$B10	=D$6*$B10	=E$6*$B10
11	Jean	0.2	=C$6*$B11	=D$6*$B11	=E$6*$B11
12	Joe	0.15	=C$6*$B12	=D$6*$B12	=E$6*$B12
13	Joan	0.15	=C$6*$B13	=D$6*$B13	=E$6*$B13
14	Total	=SUM(B10:B13)	=SUM(C10:C13)	=SUM(D10:D13)	=SUM(E10:E13)

Figure 23 You can display formulas instead of their results in cells.

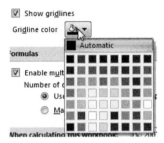

Figure 24 Choose a color for the gridline from the pop-up menu.

Display options for this worksheet

Display options for this worksheet enables you to set additional display options for the worksheet file you select from a drop-down list. Only the sheets in currently open workbook files appear in the list.

◆ **Show row and column headers** displays the row headings and column headings.

◆ **Show formulas in cells instead of their calculated results** displays formulas instead of formula results (**Figure 23**).

◆ **Show page breaks** displays horizontal and vertical page breaks.

◆ **Show a zero in cells that have zero values** displays a 0 (zero) in cells that contain zero values. Turning off this check box instructs Excel to leave a cell blank if it contains a zero value.

◆ **Show outline symbols if an outline is applied** displays outline symbols when the worksheet includes an outline.

◆ **Show gridlines** displays the boundaries of cells as lines.

◆ **Gridlines color** is a pop-up menu (**Figure 24**) for selecting a gridline color. Automatic (the default option) displays gridlines in gray.

WORKSHEET DISPLAY OPTIONS

Formulas

Formulas options enable you to customize how Excel uses your computer's processor(s) to perform calculations.

◆ **Enable multi-threaded calculation** tells Excel to use all the processors on your computer or the number you specify. With this option enabled, you can set the **Number of calculation threads** by selecting an option:

  ▲ **Use all processors on this computer** uses all the processors on your computer, which is indicated by a number after the colon.

  ▲ **Manual** enables you to specify the number of processors Excel should use. This value must be the same as or less than the number of processors your computer has.

When calculating this workbook

When calculating this workbook enables you to set calculation options for the workbook you select from a drop-down list.

◆ **Update links to other documents** calculates formulas with references to documents created with other programs.

◆ **Set precision as displayed** permanently changes values stored in cells from 15-digit precision to the precision of the applied formatting. This may result in rounding.

◆ **1904 date system** changes the starting date from which all dates are calculated to January 2, 1904. This is the date system used on Macintosh computers. Windows computers begin dates at January 1, 1900. Turning on this option enhances compatibility with Excel for Mac OS.

◆ **Save external link values** saves copies of values from linked documents within the workbook file.

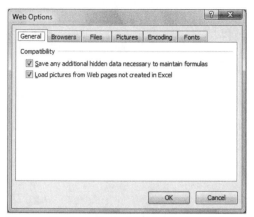

Figure 25 The General tab of the Web Options dialog.

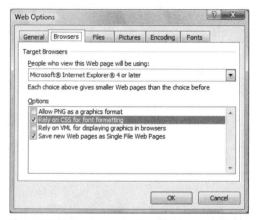

Figure 26 The Browsers tab of the Web Options dialog.

General

General options control a variety of other Excel features.

◆ **Provide feedback with sound** plays sounds at certain events, such as opening, saving, and printing files and displaying error messages.

◆ **Provide feedback with animation** displays worksheet movement when you insert or delete cells.

◆ **Ignore other applications that use Dynamic Data Exchange (DDE)** prevents the exchange of data with other applications that use DDE.

◆ **Ask to update automatic links** prompts you to update links when you open a workbook containing links to other files.

◆ **Show add-in user interface errors** displays error messages in the user interface for Excel add-ins you install and use.

◆ **Scale content for A4 or 8.5 x 11" paper** sizes automatically scales documents so they print properly on A4 or standard U.S. letter sized paper.

◆ **At startup, open all files in** enables you to specify a directory containing files you want automatically opened each time you run Excel.

◆ **Web Options** button displays the Web Options dialog, which you can use to edit the default settings for saving workbooks as Web pages.

  ▲ **General** options (**Figure 25**) control compatibility with other programs and browsers.

  ▲ **Browsers** options (**Figure 26**) control various compatibility and formatting options for Web pages created by Excel.

Continued on next page...

GENERAL OPTIONS

Continued from previous page.

▲ **Files** options (**Figure 27**) control file naming and locations and the default editor for Web pages.

▲ **Pictures** options (**Figure 28**) control the size and resolution of the typical target monitor.

▲ **Encoding** options (**Figure 29**) control how a Web page is coded when saved.

▲ **Fonts** options (**Figure 30**) control the character set and default fonts.

◆ **Service Options** displays the Service Options dialog, which you can use to set workspace or SharePoint server document options.

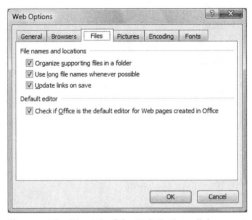

Figure 27 The Files tab of the Web Options dialog.

Figure 28 The Pictures tab of the Web Options dialog.

Figure 29 The Encoding tab of the Web Options dialog.

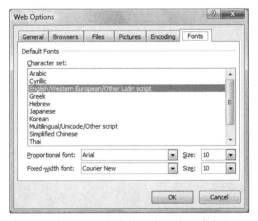

Figure 30 The Fonts tab of the Web Options dialog.

Lotus compatibility

Lotus compatibility options enable you to set up Excel so it works more like Lotus 1-2-3.

◆ **Microsoft Office Excel menu key** enables you to specify a key to invoke mouseless menus. By default, the key is a slash (/) character, which is also used by Lotus.

◆ **Transition navigation keys** activates the Lotus 1-2-3 keystrokes for worksheet navigation, entries, and other actions.

Lotus compatibility Settings for

Lotus compatibility Settings for options enables you to set Lotus-related options for specific workbooks. Choose a workbook from the drop-down list; only the workbooks that are currently open appear in the list.

◆ **Transition formula evaluation** instructs Excel to evaluate Lotus 1-2-3 formulas without changing them. This option may be extremely helpful if you often open files created with Lotus 1-2-3.

◆ **Transition formula entry** converts formulas entered in Lotus 1-2-3 release 2.2 syntax to Excel syntax and changes the behavior of Excel-defined names to Lotus-defined names. This makes it possible for a Lotus 1-2-3 user to use Excel with less retraining.

LOTUS COMPATIBILITY OPTIONS

Index

INDEX

Want More Content?

Visit the companion Web site for this book for:

- ◆ Sample files used throughout the book.

- ◆ Tips and tricks for getting the most out of Excel.

- ◆ Illustrated how-to articles covering topics beyond the scope of the book.

- ◆ Questions and answers about topics covered in the book.

- ◆ Clarifications and corrections for book content.

- ◆ Links of interest to Microsoft Excel users.

- ◆ User polls and comments.

- ◆ Links to companion Web sites for other books by Maria Langer.

What are you waiting for? Come check it out today!

Visit the Site

Point your browser to:

www.marialanger.com/excelquickstart/

Keep Up with RSS

All new site content is also available as a full-text RSS feed. Subscribe to this URL:

feeds.feedburner.com/excelquickstart/

Get New Content by E-Mail

You can also subscribe to the e-mail feed. Your e-mail address won't be sold, shared, or used for spam. Fill out the form at:

www.feedburner.com/fb/a/emailverifySubmit?feedid=599201

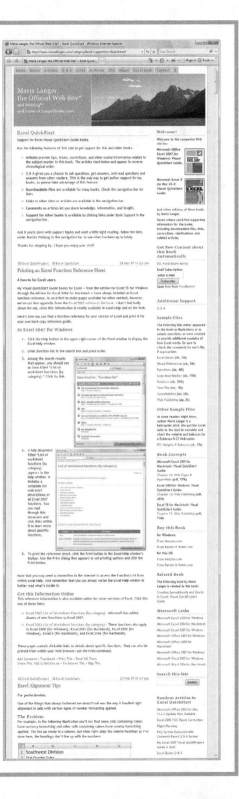

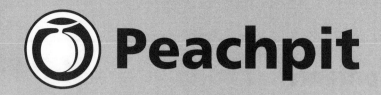

Go Beyond The Ordinary With Your Next Presentation...

...provide a well-designed and rich multimedia experience!

Wouldn't it be great if you could have two of the most sought-after graphic design professionals sitting next to you at your computer as you navigate through the infinite possibilities of your next important presentation? *How to Wow with PowerPoint* is the next best thing. It's the brainchild of Richard Harrington and Scott Rekdal, who have developed an incredible way to help you reach your full creative potential.

A book for non-designers, Richard and Scott guide you step by step through real-world projects with an emphasis on cutting through the clutter and focusing on good design principles as a more effective way to build presentations. You'll receive tips and techniques on everything from selecting and preparing images to integrating sound and motion. The *How to Wow with PowerPoint* companion CD included in the back of the book contains all the templates, photography, audio and other files you'll need to complete the tasks in the book and create a stand-out presentation.

How to Wow with PowerPoint
Richard Harrington and Scott Rekdal
ISBN: 0-321-49573-X
$39.99

Richard Harrington is an expert in motion graphic design and digital video. His skills were recognized by *AV Video & Multimedia Producer* magazine, naming him one of the Top Producers of 2004. A member of the National Association of Photoshop Professionals Instructor Dream Team, Richard is also a popular speaker. His previous books include: *Apple Training Series: iWork '06 with iLife '06*; *Photoshop for Video, 3rd Edition*; and *Understanding Adobe Photoshop*.

Scott Rekdal has worked in the advertising, design, and marketing fields for nearly 15 years. He has directed creative teams for Fortune 500 and government clients from the initial pitch to hands-on strategy and design. He has also produced PowerPoint presentations for advertising pitches, CEO speeches, and annual meetings.

www.peachpitcommons.com

Speak up and join us in conversation!

Peachpit has been publishing books on the latest in graphic design, desktop publishing, video, Web design and development, digital lifestyle, and Macintosh and Windows since 1986, and we love what we do. We thrive at the intersection of publishing and technology and strive to create the best possible books that help us all do the best work we can and have fun doing it.

To share news and happenings in the creative community, we've created Peachpit Commons—a blog where we can converse with each other and discuss:

- **Events that shape what we publish**
- **Product announcements and industry news**
- **Conferences, shows, and author appearances**
- **Tips, insights, and opinions**
- **And more!**

We are passionate about what we do and eager to hear from you about what you find inspiring and exciting in our field. We hope you'll visit **www.peachpitcommons.com** soon and join the conversation!

Peachpit Commons
Giving voice to the creative community

MICROSOFT OFFICE POWERPOINT 2007
Learn PowerPoint the Quick and Easy Way!

GET UP AND RUNNING QUICKLY!

MICROSOFT WINDOWS VISTA
Learn Microsoft Windows Vista the Quick and Easy Way!

CHRIS FEHILY

For more than 15 years, the practical approach to the best-selling *Visual QuickStart Guide* series from Peachpit Press has helped millions of readers—from developers to designers to systems administrators and more—get up to speed on all sorts of computer programs. Now with select titles in full color for the first time, *Visual QuickStart Guide* books provide an even easier and more enjoyable way for readers to learn about new technology through task-based instruction, friendly prose, and visual explanations.

WORDPRESS 2
Learn WordPress the Quick and Easy Way!

MARIA LANGER
MIRAZ JORDAN

Task-Based
Information is broken down into concise, one- and two-page tasks to help you get right to work.

Visual
Hundreds of screen shots illustrate the steps and show you the best way to do them.

Step by Step
Numbered, easy-to-follow instructions guide you through each task.

Tips
Lots of helpful tips are highlighted throughout the book.

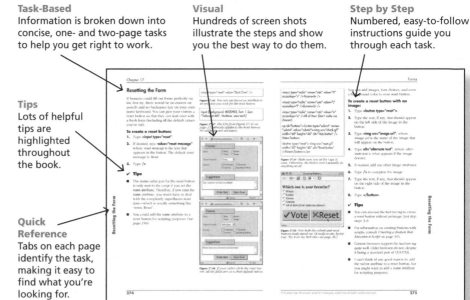

Quick Reference
Tabs on each page identify the task, making it easy to find what you're looking for.

ADOBE ACROBAT 8
Learn Acrobat the Quick and Easy Way!

JOHN DEUBERT

PHOTOSHOP ELEMENTS 5
Learn Photoshop Elements the Quick and Easy Way!

JEFF CARLSON
CRAIG HOESCHEN

WHO IS THIS BUNNY?
Peachpit is proud to announce that a name has been chosen for the well-recognized bunny that has graced the covers of every *Visual QuickStart Guide* since the series began in 1991. Who is this bunny? Visit **www.peachpit.com/vqsbunny** to find out.